The School
Without Walls

The School Without Walls

PHILADELPHIA'S PARKWAY PROGRAM

John Bremer / Michael von Moschzisker

HOLT, RINEHART AND WINSTON, INC.
New York   Chicago   San Francisco   Atlanta
Dallas   Montreal   Toronto   London   Sydney

The authors are indebted to the following copyright holders for permission to reprint previously published photographs: cover, page 195, top page 197, copyright 1969 Delaware River Port Authority; bottom page 197, courtesy of the Pennsylvania Department of Education; page 198, courtesy *Philadelphia Daily News*; page 199, courtesy *Philadelphia Inquirer*.

"The most interesting high school in the U. S. today does not have a classroom it can call its own. But every week, some 30 to 40 school administrators come to Philadelphia to examine the Parkway Program . . ." So wrote *Time* in its March 23, 1970, education section. The visitors still flock to Parkway, but the important development period was completed by the summer of 1970.

The story is worth telling for a number of reasons. First, the renovation of our educational system must have a high priority in our list of national concerns. The Parkway Program suggests a possible direction in which we can move now. Second, the story of Parkway is a case study of what happens when an educator sets out to change the system. Third, this account might provide an antidote to one aspect of contemporary educational theory, namely, that all we need do is to let students do as they like, that education is — or should be — unstructured. Nothing is further from the truth; structure is required and the skill of the educator shows itself primarily in the design of the program. If that is good, nothing else matters; if it is noneducational (as with our existing school systems), innovations are trivial, external embellishments which divert energies away from systemic reform, which act as safety valves, and which pander to administrative vanity.

The prime focus of this book is on the exposition of an actual program which has generated a national — and even international — movement. The principles of Parkway are more important than its history since the former can be duplicated and the latter cannot. For those readers who can accept this point of view, this book should provide easy reading. For those anxious to know, as quickly as possible, what the details of the Program are I would suggest they start with Chapter 19, reprinted from *Philadelphia Magazine*, and written by an experienced, independent reporter, Nancy Love. Another possibility would be to turn to the Appendix which reprints the descriptive brochure, written originally in 1967, describing the Parkway Program. Finally, for those more interested in the how than the what, the political history is set out in Chapters 8 and 9. They can be read as an independent unit.

The accounts of the Parkway experience, which make up Part II of this book, were written by people who have been members of the Program and by a professional reporter. They may seem to show Parkway in opposite or contradictory ways. This may be thought a disadvantage, but in reality it exhibits the fundamental strength of Parkway that, at one and the same time, it can be different things to different people; it can foster and preserve the differences and bring them into harmony so that they can be friendly.

This is a function of the design of the program. To anyone who wants to begin a similar program, I would only say, if you can, adopt the design of Parkway for at least a year. After that, your program will be able to change itself. If you are in doubt, start anyway. You will learn more. Of course, you will make mistakes but they will not be educational mistakes unless you and your colleagues, your fellow-students, refuse to learn from them. Make them your curriculum, boldly and honestly. Nothing else will do. Parkway cannot be destroyed from without, but it can be corrupted from within if we refuse to build our own limitations into the curriculum as learning opportunities for ourselves, if we claim to be wise instead of lovers of wisdom, if we insist on controlling others because we do not know how to control ourselves.

One of the delights of Parkway is the friendship. Joyce Johnson, Tami Williams, Lisa Strick, Tina Craig, Cy Swartz, Anita Hackney, and Ralph Kendricks were the best of fellow-learners. Joel Bloom, Evan Turner, John Bodine, Wynn Shaughnessy, Myles Standish, Paul Abott, J. Reid Thomson, Wilma Stringfellow, Mary Davis, Bill Wilcox, John

Patterson, Athelstan Spilhaus, Gail and Eliot Levinson, Richard de Lone, Graham Finney, Murray Bookbinder, Clifford Brenner, and many more gave help at crucial times. Without them, I would not have survived. Of people outside Philadelphia, the Ford Foundation staff members were always helpful—Ed Meade, Charles Brown, Don Harris and, time after time, without complaint, Mario Fantini, who is now Dean of the College of Education, State University of New York, New Paltz.

Michael von Moschzisker, my co-author, saw the Program from a unique perspective, in fact, from a number of different perspectives. In the first place, he was a long-standing observer of the Philadelphia political scene. In the second place, he had a particular interest in Parkway because one of his daughters was a student in it, graduating in 1971. In the third place, he taught in the Program, offering a course in Journalism in Community Gamma. Michael von Moschzisker still lives in Philadelphia and has continued his interest in Parkway— and he now has a second daughter in the Program. I am particularly indebted to him, not only for his fairness and patient persistence, but because without him this book would never have been written.

My own qualifications for co-authoring this book are relatively simple. I designed and created the Parkway Program and served as its Director until my resignation in August 1970. By that time the essential impact had been made, and from then on Parkway's story is bound up with the misfortunes of the Philadelphia School District under its antiquated system of administration and ineffectual leadership.

But there is hope. During the summer of 1971, Newton College of the Sacred Heart initiated a new graduate program which they had commissioned me to design. One of the students was the mother of an early Parkway student who had graduated in June; naturally, she was visited by her daughter, Claudia, who wrote me afterwards "I'm glad to see you're opening up more minds, the hardest ones to open, 'the elders.' It must be quite a challenge!" It is a challenge, of course, but with the support of students like Claudia it is easier. She wrote: "The whole of Parkway has been concerned about you, especially the old kids. I have cried, laughed, had a mental breakdown, and danced because I loved Parkway and what it stood for. . . ."

Claudia is not alone; we are not short of good students, nor are we short of good teachers. All we lack is a school system worthy of them.

John Bremer
Pugwash, Nova Scotia
August 1971

Contents

[ix]

Contents

America has never had an educational system worthy of itself. After pioneering a continent, developing new forms of social and political organization, absorbing countless immigrants and bringing technology into a close relationship with human life, it is nevertheless true that Americans have adopted principles and practices of education belonging to another age and imported from another society. The Parkway Program tries to provide a mode of education in keeping with the major traditions of American life.

The School
Without Walls

Introduction

William H. Herndon asked Abraham Lincoln's cousin, Dennis Hanks, how he and Lincoln were educated.

"We learned by sight, scent and hearing," Hanks replied. "We heard all that was said, and talked over the questions heard, wore them slick, greasy, and threadbare."

Lincoln spent less than a year of his life "going to school," for attending classes in a special building and learning during prescribed hours were a rarity on the frontier. Life was unified, not divided into compartments of work, study, and play.

Albert H. Beveridge, from whose *Abraham Lincoln* the dialogue with Hanks is drawn, gives this description:

> The amusements of the people were so contrived as to get needed work done, but they were boisterous with rampant jollity. The felling of the splendid forests to make clearings left great quantities of logs that could not be used for cabins or stables; and these logs were burned. So at "log-rollings" everybody helped mightily, ate heavily, and drank much whiskey. . . . Much the same happened when neighbors came to help put up the frames of houses or build cabins, "raisings," as these events were called.

> "Corn shuckings" were the scenes of greatest enjoyment. Men and boys were chosen by two captains and thus divided into equal groups, each strove to husk the most corn. Songs were sung, stories told, jokes cracked; "and pass the bottle around" was the order of the hour. Sugar-boiling, wool-shearing, and hog-killings were scenes of similar festivities.

"Everybody helped mightily." Participation was what was needed, expected, and enjoyed — not necessarily as a skilled expert, but as a social being, as a member of the community, as a cooperator. "Men and boys were chosen by two captains. . . ." And so they learned how to lead, how to follow, how to work with the rest of the group in a variety of ways in order to achieve a common purpose. Boys and men, too, learned not from professional teachers but from and with one another as a part of the natural process of being human. And they kept their eyes and ears open, talking over the events and questions of the day until they were worn threadbare.

Specialization was the exception in such a society — at least in individuals. The logger could butcher, the butcher could entertain, the entertainer sheared wool, men and boys acted together. It was the accepted, the normal — indeed — the obvious, thing to do. How else could the community survive, endure, propagate, and flourish? The young had to learn the ways of their community, but "learn" did not mean to memorize or to describe, for it was intimately connected with the power of the community to do something. The young had to participate in the doing; that is how they learned.

Participation in the communal life made people aware of the high degree of their interdependence, and this made life along the frontier truly democratic. Society was not stratified; men treated each other more as equals — not as if they were the same, but as equals. In the armed forces, for example, militiamen elected their own officers — Abraham Lincoln being one of those so honored.

The historic fact is that a dream of self-government (brought here by the Puritans and reflected when New England property owners assembled in town meetings) merged with the concept of equal rights enunciated in the Declaration of Independence, and together they marked a new, American, way of life. Based on the dignity of the individual, it permitted him freedom of movement. The individual was not tied down to a tract of land, a particular occupation, or a station in life. He was encouraged to push on, to expand the frontier, according to the interests and abilities that he had, and to make the wilderness his own. Such were the needs of the day.

In practice, there were notable exceptions to the principles of this new way of life. The South had slaves; only property owners could vote in the East; women could vote nowhere. But the principles were known and their splendor was recognized; it was only a question of time before what was latent became manifest, before the potential became actual. In time, the demands of a free society won out over slavery. Later, universal suffrage was established. But we are still working out the implications and applications of these principles, and, in time, perhaps we shall achieve a truly democratic society.

The most important factor at work in relation to this goal is, without doubt, formal education. Lincoln and the children of his time and place got along without much schooling, which did not mean, at that time and in that place, that they were not educated. They were of the community, they were educated by the community, and they were educated for the community. But circumstances changed, life altered. Waves of immigrants from abroad and increased industrialization, together with the demands of universal suffrage, brought into being new legislation. Known as compulsory school-attendance laws, these were designed to implant the social qualities suitable for industrial employees, to draw children off the labor market, and to produce a citizenry literate in American English. It was to reach these goals that the unique public education system of the United States was created, and reach them it did, with a large measure of success. There was a price, however.

First, unlike Lincoln and his cousin, the students of the public schools were not of the community; they did not really belong to it, although the expectation was that they would when they had gone through public school. Membership, full membership, was held to be in the future. This quickly turned into an implicit assumption that children were not members of the community—a principle so absurd that it had to remain implicit.

Second, the students of the public schools were not educated by the community; indeed it was thought necessary to remove them totally from the community by placing them in separate facilities called schools. This physical removal increased the control that the professional teachers had over the students and made it difficult for the students to do what Lincoln and his cousin did: "We learned by sight, scent and hearing." This was impossible when the learning environment—the school—was as drab and as all-encompassing as it was. Children "heard all that was said," but only by the teachers, not by members of the community at large. If they "talked over the questions heard," it was only after classes were done. If they wore the questions "slick, greasy, and threadbare," it was not in discussion with their teachers and not with any expectation that action might ensue or be the arbiter of the various opinions.

Third, the students of the public schools were educated for the community in only the most limited, instrumental sense. They were fitted for a particular role and station in the community, but not to be members of it in the ways that true democracy requires. Coming of age, they could be plumbers or doctors or clerks, but they could not really be citizens. They never learned how.

The one-room schoolhouse became the two-room schoolhouse and then grew into the multiclass, professionally staffed and directed school that continues to the present day. But the students are still fitted for a particular role and station in the community. The school is still a sorting mechanism. And still the students are denied the opportunity to learn how to be citizens. They cannot learn as Lincoln learned, "by sight, scent and hearing," any more than they can talk over "the questions heard" and wear them "slick, greasy, and threadbare."

A great deal of educational thinking is still tied to the idea that the school is a kind of factory. Before dealing with the limitations and disadvantages of this view, it must be realized that when it first became prominent it was a radical innovation, devised to cope with the problem of large numbers. Democracy, immigration, and industrialization presented society with the need—and the opportunity—to educate all of its members, at least within certain narrow limits. The magnitude of the task was staggering, and, quite understandably, people turned to the one available model for dealing with large numbers—the factory. The notion was daring, and those who proposed it were the daring innovators, the radicals of their day. But it was a marked departure from the educational tradition of the whole of Western civilization, and, no matter how necessary it was, perhaps the time has come now to give up this aberration of not much more than a hundred years and to return to a far deeper conception of education.

The success of the nineteenth-century factory depended on a number of elements, one of the most important of which was the specialization of labor. Deeply impressed with the success of the factory system, early public educators borrowed the basic elements of that system and built a special building—the school—where (as in a factory or mill) schoolwork could be done. This in itself created a new dichotomy between "work" and "play." Work is serious, important, unpleasant in itself, but done for some external reward such as money, and essentially imposed from without. It is done under duress. Play, on the other hand, is trivial, unimportant, pleasant in itself, perhaps, but one should not expect to "get anything out of it," and since it is generated from within, it can hardly be expected to be socially useful. Clearly, this factory-style analysis depends on one's values.

Just like the factory, the school was a special location, a purpose-made building, equipped with all the machinery to produce learners, if not learning. The machinery was so important that it was hard to see how anyone could learn at home. That would be like supposing that the cottage industries could compete with the factories. However, when certain things had been mastered with the aid of the machinery, it was possible for the student to practice what he had learned; trivial, repetitive exercises were required, and thus homework was invented.

The educational process was broken down into a series of factory-like steps of unvarying sequence (the work of the various grades) through which the raw material (the students) had to pass. Finally, each student was graded and passed or rejected like an industrial product subject to quality control. The crowning, if inevitable, folly of public educators was to reproduce in the school the social and administrative organization of the factory, with manager, overseers, foremen, and operatives masquerading under the titles of superintendent, principals, department chairmen, and teachers.

It is noteworthy that the children to be educated were not conceived structurally as part of the school's social organization. Instead, they were the raw material—transitory, to be molded by the teachers to the extent that their own imperfections would allow. It is true that flesh and blood human beings sometimes established good, friendly relationships that transcended the system which separated student from teacher—but this was exceptional. As often as not, these exceptions were found when a likely candidate for the teaching profession was encountered among the students, and it was assumed that those pupils best able to be molded were those best able to mold others. Perhaps this accounts for the general conservatism of the teaching profession.

The whole model of learning as a product has been taken from the factory and with it the belief that it is by the activity of the teacher that the student comes to learn. If learning were like the production of nuts and bolts, or like weaving, perhaps this would be true, but it is not.

Another consequence of the factory model is the firmly rooted notion that the interests of the owners and managers, on the one hand, are opposed to the interests of the workers, on the other. Management and labor are structurally opposed—an anomaly that education cannot afford—and, in addition, the students are not thought to have any interest at all. There is some possibility that they could be represented by their parents, if they, in turn, were seen to be the owners—but reality does not bear that out.

To be sure, educators and parents alike have ceased to think consciously of the school as a kind of factory, of the students as raw material, and of education as a productive art. The origins of this view lie very deep, however, and many recent developments in education merely cover up root problems that we must face today—particularly the problem of the social organization of the school. Can the social organization of the nineteenth-century factory provide for modern students the social learning that is the prerequisite for and concomitant of "academic" learning?

If there is opposition between the social organization of our schools and the job to be done, either some profound changes must take place in the system or a great deal of energy will continue to be wasted in nonproductive opposition to the schools themselves. And opposition there is, as we all recognize, and hostility.

The British statesman Edmund Burke said that education is the cheap defense of nations. But where is the enemy? From all appearances, the enemy is within—the students are the enemy. That is the role assigned to them in the educational system: to be the enemy. The students themselves realize how they are regarded, and, in turn, come to acknowledge the system as an enemy. There is a situation of armed neutrality at best, open conflict at worst.

There will be no improvement in this hostile atmosphere, no reduction of its tensions, until it is seen that education or learning must be a cooperative venture, based on friendship and mutuality of interest. Education is not something done to children by teachers, it is something that teachers and children do together. But this "doing together" requires a social organization of a kind altogether different from what we now have in our schools. Consider the present organization, the present role of the students, and the behavior expected of them; what must a student be and do in order to learn in an "approved" fashion?

First, children must "go" to school. If learning does not take place in school, it is not really learning. School is a place, not a process; a location, not an activity.

Conceivably, a school can embrace an entire community, with all of its institutions being used for learning, for educational purposes. Yet we persist in regarding the school as a building (just like the mill or the factory) and, in our want of common sense, the community is divorced from the education of its children, while the latter, in turn, are cut off from the riches of their community.

It is an irretrievable loss, for the community cannot come to the school. The impact of the occasional visiting speaker, like the effect of current affairs bulletins, is lost, since the children know little of the "outside" world of the speakers and the bulletins except that nothing in it relates to the artificial "inside" world of the school building.

All this is no reflection on teachers and administrators. Handicapped by a specialized role that limits their participation in the other affairs of the community, teachers and administrators can do little or nothing to bring the outside and inside worlds together. The outside world is changing so fast that one has to be where the action is in order to keep abreast of it. Any attempt to capture the latest events, the current thinking, and the most recent discoveries in textbooks for children is almost fruitless—so soon are the texts out of date.

Under these circumstances, can school buildings, staffed only by full-time teachers, continue to give young people what they need?

The element of time is another important consideration, we misuse it so. There are school days and nonschool days; school hours and nonschool hours. We are made to invest very large sums in buildings which we then use for less than half the days of the year—and for only six hours a day at that! The economics make no sense at all—and the education makes even less! Whoever thought that education begins when the student enters the school building and that it terminates when he leaves?

There is homework, of course. Instead of drawing upon life outside school, however, it intrudes on it. Instead of enriching life, it diminishes it.

Not only do we remove schoolchildren from the community and cut them off from present affairs, but also we separate them from each other, usually grouping them in classrooms according to the arbitrary standard of age. This is not because we reasoned it out and concluded that children learn little from being with older and younger students—for all the evidence is that children learn a great deal in such circumstances, as any parent of a large family knows.

It is time for a change.

But what change? What is the minimum change that would enable an educational program to help children become happy and, in their own terms, successful and law-abiding citizens?

The fundamental contention of this book is that no changes will be of any significance unless the social organization of education is totally changed. By changing the social organization of total educational systems, the social organization of schools is changed, and the roles and relations that students and faculty learn can become human, and hence educational, once again.

The miserable state of human relations in most schools and school systems is well known. Force and coercion are everywhere. The system cannot operate without them—and we are now realizing that education cannot operate with them. The usual view of teachers is that, first, you must control students and then, second, you teach them. They need to realize, however, that when you control a student, you cannot ever help him learn. You may force him to repeat what he hears or reads, and thereby pass examinations. You may succeed in modifying his outward behavior—although not necessarily its significance; you may corrupt him by bribery; you may even make him obedient. But help him learn? Never. Learning is something he must do for himself.

This is why the factory model must go. So long as the student is regarded as something to be kept under control, as raw material to be processed, he will not learn. He cannot learn, he can only be taught. His role is essentially passive, not active. He has no contribution to make to his own education. The greatest harm is done by the fact that in no way are students ever given a clear, human, and responsible role in the organization of the school. They are not really a part of the educational system at all. They are just the material upon which it feeds. The students know it, and they respond negatively to their position of indignity. This is what must be changed.

The Parkway Program

1
The Social and Administrative Organization

The fundamental contention of this book and of the Parkway Program is that no changes in an educational system will be of any significance unless the social organization of education is totally changed, that is, unless the system itself is changed. Nothing less will do, for it is the whole system that defines the nature and function of the parts. As a consequence, imaginative and fruitful ways of helping students to learn become, ultimately, only new ways of subordinating the student to the present system, only another way of keeping the student under control. New methods, new materials, and new machinery are used as new means of continuing the old pattern of fitting students into a pre-ordained social structure.

If you ask a school or college administrator to describe the curriculum of his institution, he will probably give you a list of subjects offered together with the administrative department responsible for each one. At the college level, the catalog will list academic departments and the courses offered in them. At the school level, there is usually a detailed syllabus for each of the well-known subjects — English, mathematics, history, biology, Spanish, and so on. Schools and colleges are administratively organized in terms of these traditional subjects. In our present educational system, it is the conventional — and now outmoded — divisions of knowledge, and not the students' needs, that determine the organization of a learning institution. There is no secret about this, and, indeed, many administrators would take pride in affirming it. There is no intent to deceive when the curriculum is stated to be English, mathematics, and so on, but the motive is quite beside the point and it may well be that educational administrators do not know what they are doing. The fact is that every educational organization has one fundamental curriculum, which is never stated explicitly but which is the essential precondition of everything else. The fundamental curriculum is the social and administrative organization of the institution and the student's role in it. If the student does not learn this, then he learns nothing else that the school claims to offer.

This is particularly true of educational organizations, but it is true of every human group. The newcomer—no matter where he is to be introduced into the group, no matter what his status—has to learn the organization of the group and, especially, the role assigned to him. If he does not do this, the group will exert pressure upon him until he behaves properly; if he does not fall into line, he will be rejected and ejected. In educational systems this is true not only of the student but also of the superintendent. The superintendent is not expected to change the system, only to join it, and so far that is what every superintendent has done. This judgment may seem harsh, but in reality it is a tribute to the power of a group to form and mold its members. The only alternative to succumbing to this power is to educate the group so that it changes itself. For this reason the superintendent must be a master teacher.

For his part, the student must first of all learn his role in the school and the educational organization and through his proper behavior come into contact with the knowledge available in the school, particularly through its teachers. If the student cannot behave properly, that is, perform his defined role, then he is denied access to the knowledge available. It cannot be emphasized enough that behavior precedes understanding in any human group—that is, that moral education precedes intellectual education. Our major difficulty in schools is that the morality required belongs to an earlier time, a more limited view of society. It is as if schools were saying, "Adopt our life style and in exchange we will give you access to our wisdom." The hardships that this demand inflicts on all students, particularly those from minority groups, are real but easily overlooked, largely because educators take their own life style for granted.

It is easy to see how this works in practice. A student must sit at a desk, answer questions, read a book, complete an assignment, not talk to a neighbor, and so on. If he does not, he is reprimanded and his relation with the teacher becomes the focus of his attention, the problem in which he invests his energy. What happens to the subject he is supposed to be learning? It is forgotten in the face of a personal confrontation. Worse, it becomes another weapon with which the teacher attacks the student. The student responds by refusing to learn (even in the school's limited use of the word), because if he learned it would mean that he had surrendered, that he was beaten.

The moral education of the student begins, however, long before he actually enters a school or college. It begins when he applies to the institution. If he wishes to attend a college or a high school with limited enrollment, he has first to satisfy the admissions requirements; from the moment he starts to fill in the questionnaires he is programmed to think about the kind of person he is supposed to be if he is to be acceptable to the institution. Whether he is accepted or rejected, the school or college has done its work, for the student is either grateful or regretful. In either case, his role is cast as an inferior.

Most high school students, however, are simply assigned to their local school. There is no consultation, no conference, no consideration of alternatives. The morality of such a practice is totally unacceptable, and students learn more from it than educators can afford to admit. Students come to see themselves as pawns in a game of chess, to be moved at the administrator's will—the only free choice for them is to leave school altogether when the law permits. If they value their freedom and independence, this is what they often do.

It is worth considering the process by which a student enters a school simply because it structures the student's feeling about himself as a member of that school. The only way such an indelible effect can be eradicated is through a different structuring process, and that is where the Parkway Program began.

The admissions procedure for the Parkway Program was simple. First, it was open to any student in the city who was in grades nine through twelve, or who would be in those grades if he were in school. Second, the student had to apply, that is, he had to choose to come. He was self-selected. Third, he required the permission of at least one parent. Nothing else was required—no letters of recommendation, no tests, no records of behavior, no statement of aspirations or of reasons for wanting to join Parkway. All Parkway wanted was the student's signature on the completed four-line application form.

The letter describing the program, with the application, was supposed to have been distributed through the schools to all eligible students in the public school system. With more than fifty thousand students in the high schools and more than twenty thousand in the junior high schools, it is hard to know exactly how many students actually received the information. It was certainly true that most schools were less than efficient in distributing the letters. Some were excellent, but many were unable to handle the task, with reasons varying from loss of the letters to disapproval of the program. More than one school managed the compromise of giving out the letters on the same day that applications were due. Naturally, the deadline was extended.

When the Parkway Program began in February 1969, the plan was to admit about one hundred and twenty students, but it soon became clear that there was going to be a much larger number of applicants. In fact, there were nearly two thousand applications from city students in public schools and, in addition, about two hundred from suburban students and an additional hundred from private and parochial school students. Many people wrote or phoned for applications, and it was policy to mail them on request. The problem was how to select the planned number of students when there were nearly twenty applicants for each place.

It would have been easy at this point to have selected students who seemed able and amenable enough to learn in the program. But this approach would have been a betrayal of Parkway's mission to provide an educational program suitable for and available to anyone who wanted it. Clearly, the student body could be so selected as to ensure "success," but the victory would have been a hollow one. Rather, it was decided to have a lottery in which all applicants would have an equal chance. The absence of judgment meant that the students who did enter Parkway did not do so on the basis of being "better" or "more worthy." Institutionally, Parkway said that all students were created equal—none had preference. Under the circumstances of limited enrollment, the students themselves accepted that some were lucky and others were not. But it was only luck and not merit.

The lottery was held in public and was reported on television, radio, and in the Philadelphia newspapers. The whole city knew about it and to some extent became involved. Prospective students and their parents came and the whole affair had an exciting, dramatic quality about it, which together with its swiftness made it a marked contrast to the usual dreary school procedures.

Although students were admitted by lottery, it would be more accurate to say that they were admitted through one of eight lotteries. The school district of Philadelphia was divided into eight separate school districts, each with its own district superintendent. By historical accident, presumably, these geographical districts tended to follow housing patterns and a number of them seemed to be ethnically or economically segregated. Since the media—particularly radio and television news and the newspapers—were primarily geared to the white, middle class population, it seemed probable that there would be considerably more white students applying than black. If this were so, there would be a good chance that the outcome of a general, common lottery would be a predominantly white student body.

John Bremer, the director of the Parkway Program, felt very strongly that this would be a violation of a fundamental educational principle, namely, that the learning community should be perceived by its members as a reasonable representation of the larger community in which they expected to live. If this were not so, the first thing the students would learn would be separatism, elitism, and racism. In addition, a considerable amount of energy would be diverted from learning into dealing with feelings of guilt and, more fundamentally, of fear. This is the major difficulty facing suburban school systems, and there was no need to duplicate it in the city.

As a way of reconciling the two principles of lottery and representative community, the director arranged a lottery for students from each of the eight school districts, with an equal number of places allocated to each district. By this means, the racial ratio among the city students was approximately the same as for the public school population, namely, 60 percent black and 40 percent white.

There was certainly an inequality in the distribution of the applications received. District Six, including the Germantown and Chestnut Hill areas of Philadelphia, provided more than twice as many applicants as any other district. Dissatisfactions with the provisions for public education in the district were heightened by the fact that the city's two selective high schools—one for boys and one for girls—are located there, and these two schools alone provided more applicants than any other district, and this although students reported that they had to demand application blanks. It is perhaps noteworthy that some of the girls sent in several applications—after all they were part of the intellectual elite and understood probability and the laws of chance. It seems that if you attend a competitively selective school you learn how to be competitive. Compete and win is the ethic.

The following June, the Parkway Program received nearly ten thousand applications for admission and again the lottery by district system was followed. But there were only four hundred and fifty places available in the foreseeable future, with the result that there were a lot of disappointed students and parents.

Apart from students in the public school system, there was considerable interest from students in suburban systems and also from the superintendent of the Roman Catholic archdiocesan system.

Some people saw the Parkway Program as a way of cooperation between the public school system and the Catholic parochial schools. It should be remembered that the mayor of Philadelphia and other members of the city hierarchy were products of the latter system, and their understanding of and sympathy for the problems of public education were not notorious for their profundity. Some people felt that if the public and parochial schools cooperated on Parkway and other ventures, the city administration would be more helpful to public education and less inclined to play politics with it. As long as the budget of the school district for operating and capital expenses was close to four hundred million dollars, this feeling was more remarkable for its simple piety than for its grasp of political reality.

There was no doubt that the parochial school system was powerful, and it reportedly had two students enrolled for every three students in the public schools. But it also had problems—financial, behavioral, and theological—and it suffered from all opposition to change experienced by the public schools, backed up by a vague, superstitious feeling that to change parochial education was to tamper with the divine plan. There is no doubt that the mayor and the city council were easier to deal with.

The superintendent of the archdiocesan schools apparently saw Parkway as a possible way of injecting life into a moribund system and favored letting students from the two centrally located Catholic high schools (sexually separate but equal) participate in Parkway for one year, after which time they would return to their original schools, presumably to be the leaven that leavens the lump. This idea was modeled on the junior year abroad plan of some colleges. John Bremer, the Parkway director, did not view this plan with much enthusiasm, since he felt it was unfair to the students and not likely to loosen up the rigidities of the parochial schools, which was not his business anyway. After many discussions, the representative of the archdiocesan superintendent and priests from the two Catholic high schools raised the question as to whether there could be such a thing as a secular education. At this point, Parkway's director, not wishing to interfere in a religious matter that has plagued Christianity for nearly two thousand years, declared that he would assume that secular education was impossible for them unless he heard to the contrary. The representatives of the parochial schools said they would notify their schools and counsel any students interested in applying to the Parkway Program. In the final analysis, four parochial school students enrolled in Parkway as regular members at its inception and three of them were black.

The case of the suburban students was very different. In the first place, they applied to Parkway directly without going through their local school district. The students initiated the process. In the second place, they themselves had to persuade their local school board to meet one of the two conditions laid down by Parkway—either pay the tuition or take a city student in exchange. There was no shortage of interest among the students, and in one suburban district the local superintendent is reported to have confiscated a list of between one and two hundred names of interested applicants and to have forbidden the students to have anything to do with Parkway. As might be expected, this was in a Republican stronghold where most people were dedicated to free enterprise.

[16]

When about twenty students from the suburbs, representing seven or eight districts, finally entered the program, it was demonstrated that the city-suburb boundary could be crossed. Later, city students began to attend the suburban high schools as the exchange condition was met by districts which opted for it.

The total student body had equal numbers of blacks and whites, since all the suburban students were white. This educationally acceptable ratio was maintained at the second lottery when more students entered the Parkway Program.

The original Parkway student body was made up of one hundred and twenty students from the city public schools, twenty from the suburbs, and four from the parochial schools. This made a grand total of one hundred and forty four. Although John Bremer had originally expected only ten students from suburban and parochial schools, it seemed more than worthwhile to exploit the obvious interest of suburban students, and the total of one hundred and forty-four students was not unwieldy. It soon became apparent, however, that the size of the learning community was an important factor in the minds of the students. Time and again they expressed their dissatisfaction with their former schools in terms of the large numbers which denied them their own individuality. One student wrote:

> There is a common trust between people, a common friendship which you don't and can't find at a public school. I think that this is largely a result of the freedom, but most so because of the faculty. They make you feel human again; and that's something. At least in comparison to my old school. There, I was nothing but a computer card—my number was 75815—my roster was made by a computer, my tests were for the most part marked by a computer and made into a report card by a computer and who knows what else was done. It knew me better than my mother, and my mother knows me pretty well. . . .

How the Parkway faculty treated the students was partially—indeed, largely—determined by the way they were treated by the director and the way they treated each other. This, in turn, was largely influenced by the size of the community. In a large group, close friendly relations are difficult to achieve; in a small group, they are hard to avoid. Of course, the relations could have been close and hostile, but in relation to learning, even this would have been better than the mechanical, nonrelationship of the large high school, for hostile feelings are a manifestation of humanity and, in a sense, acknowledge the importance of the other person. To see yourself as "known by a computer" is to see yourself simply as data, as a given, of no more significance than any other piece of data, and capable of being placed in relation to other data without any personal contribution on your part. You are converted into a readily manipulable form, and then, of course, you are manipulated. Always for your own good, it is to be understood, but the idea of the student's good has been radically transformed as well—it is now conformity to the computer's cosmos. "It knew me better than my mother. . . ."

This perception of students in regular high schools is a major cause of anxiety. The other major cause is over-crowding. Together these conditions raise the anxiety level of students, and therefore of faculty and administrators, beyond all reasonable bounds. The responses to anxiety are obvious and well known—hostility, destructiveness, drugs—and yet few educators seem to understand them for what they are.

One major purpose of the Parkway Program's social and administrative structure was to minimize anxiety by placing the responsibility for organizing his learning on the student, thus abolishing the computer; by making it possible for the student to get away from group situations that he could not handle, thus respecting individual privacy; and by keeping the learning community small, thus preserving the interdependence of its members.

After some experimentation, it seemed quite easy to work within a community of about one hundred and sixty students. This figure is not absolute, for it depends upon the structure of relations inside the community and the anxiety level of the students. But as the Parkway Program expanded, it did so simply by duplicating the original unit, slightly expanded, but with the same internal organization. Each unit was self-governing and responsible for its own day-to-day operation. More will be said of this in the next chapter, but it has been a cardinal principle of Parkway that each community should be responsible for its own management. One important by-product of this educational principle is the lack of any large centralized administration. This both saves money and preserves flexibility, since decisions affecting the learning community can be made quickly and on the spot.

By September 1969, there were three units of the Parkway Program, each named after a letter in the Greek alphabet. Community Alpha, the original unit, began in February 1969; Community Beta began in July 1969; and Community Gamma began in September 1969. These three units were expanded slightly at the end of January 1970 at which time close to five hundred students were enrolled.

When students enter the Parkway Program, they do not enter a particular building but rather join in an activity, the activity of learning.

Essentially, the Parkway Program is an activity, planned and carried out by a group, with the purpose of improving the learning of the members of that group. There are no particular commitments to times and places which always seem to be the determining factors in schools; the commitment is primarily to learning and then to the means of achieving that end.

Since it had no building, at least in the conventional sense, the Parkway Program came to be known as the school without walls. In reality, this was not quite accurate, and it would have been truer to have said that it was a school without its own walls. Its motto may well have been "mortgages are for others," for it utilized the buildings within Philadelphia as it needed them and could negotiate them. Even this was not completely true, since each community, or unit, had its own permanent headquarters which served at least as an administrative headquarters.

The original unit of Parkway, later known as Community Alpha, had its headquarters at 1801 Market Street, four blocks from City Hall. It was photographed for *Life* magazine (May 16, 1969), which described it as follows: "Parkway has no classrooms or school building and its only facility is a rented loft where 150 students — half black, half white — have their lockers and hold a weekly meeting with the faculty."

The facility was certainly rented, although not originally by Parkway. It was on the second floor of an old and cheaply constructed building which had been rented by the school district. The ground floor was already occupied and an isolated part of the second floor was also used, but the main second floor space nobody would use. It was certainly not pleasant, and perhaps for that reason it was an embarrassment to the school district, since it was in center city and the president of the home and school council was asking questions about the cost of rented space. There was some relief felt when the director of Parkway took it over. One floor-to-ceiling partition and two smaller ones were put up and it went into service. The heat didn't work very well when it worked at all, and occasionally rain came through the roof, but it was Parkway's space.

When the second unit, Community Beta, began, it had palatial quarters at 125 N. 23d Street, on the corner of 23d and Cherry streets, so that it came to be called Cherry House. Once the headquarters of an interior decorating firm, its walls were elegantly papered and the floors were carpeted. At the first parents' meeting held at Cherry House, one mother confided to the director that she thought it had been a bordello. Denying all knowledge of the subject (even academic knowledge), the director began to regret the possibilities that the name Cherry House afforded.

The building contained about 6000 square feet of space and the rental was $1.50 a square foot a year. Compared with the cost of a school building, this was infinitesimal. For reasons of safety the second floor was eventually closed off, but it had always been assumed that an area of 3000 square feet was sufficent to house a Parkway unit and there was no hardship. As the unit became more experienced, there was a strong move to give up the building altogether and locate Beta's headquarters in a small storefront. There was little doubt that such a place could be made to work, and Beta was the community to do it. When a learning community is prepared for it, it can do without space of its own.

Community Gamma, the third of the Parkway units, had a stormy career to begin with and its trials and tribulations will be reported later. Even its baptism was by fire. The director wanted to provide a facility which would not only be a headquarters for a regular-sized Parkway unit but also provide adequate space for about a hundred and fifty elementary school children. In late spring of 1969, by a series of accidental circumstances, an appropriate building became available, at least for some time. The school district wanted to build a new complex at a site about ten blocks north of City Hall and very close to Broad Street, the main north-south thoroughfare through Philadelphia. As a preliminary step, they had purchased a number of buildings which were to be vacated and torn down. However, after the land was purchased, the bond issue supposed to provide money for the demolition and the new construction was defeated in May 1969, while the last occupiers were transferring themselves elsewhere. One of these empty buildings had housed the venerable Spring Garden Institute, a private, nonprofit school with a strong science and technology program, which had provided itself with fine new facilities in Chestnut Hill. When the Institute vacated its old building, Parkway's director looked with hungry eyes at what was available, at least until another bond issue could be promoted and passed.

The old Institute had three separate buildings, connected rather inadequately with makeshift openings. It seemed natural to use the two floors of the north building for the elementary school program, the southeast building on the ground floor only for the high school program, and to block off the southwest building altogether. The place did not seem to require a lot of building work, and the facilities division of the school district promised to discuss the situation with the fire marshal's office and to provide an estimate.

Toward the end of July, the bombshell came. The former Spring Garden Institute could be made legal and fit for occupancy by Philadelphia schoolchildren only at a cost of $35,000. The director protested in vain that this was absurd, that the building had been occupied by a school the previous month, that the Parkway Program could use it for only a year, and that this amount of money was simply not available. Presumably, the work allegedly required was yet another element in the continuing and unwarranted interference by the city administration in school district affairs. Why had the alleged infractions never been remedied under the previous tenant?

The facilities division promised to attempt another way of using the buildings, which might cost less; in fact, some time in August, the cost was reduced to about $20,000, but by this time the director had looked elsewhere. With some misgivings, but little choice, he decided to open an old school building which had been handed over to the Redevelopment Authority of Philadelphia, reportedly for tearing down to make room for an expressway. The Redevelopment Authority agreed to give it back to the school district for one year. The term was subsequently extended for another year.

The Parkway Program had been trying to get away from notions of school and the like, and it seemed rather dangerous to open a unit inside an old school, the Paxson School, as it was called (as a result Community Gamma was also known as the Paxson Parkway). Time was short, however, and the decision was made. The proposed elementary school program would occupy the basement and first floor levels, while the high school program used the second floor. The only other difficulty was location, for the Paxson School, now the Paxson Parkway, was in the eastern part of the city, close to the Delaware River, at 6th and Buttonwood streets. This was just one block south of Spring Garden Street, a major east-west thoroughfare, but it was nearly twenty blocks from City Hall and more than that from Community Alpha. Community Beta was eight blocks beyond Alpha. It emerged much later that Paxson was near the turf boundary of one of Philadelphia's gangs.

The director, optimistic to the last, reckoned that if Parkway would work at Paxson, it would work anywhere. And under its unit head, Cy Swartz, it worked beautifully. In any case, it was rent free and later on other organizations came to share the building. They were promptly exploited — not unwillingly — and Community Gamma was strengthened by an alliance with the Media Center, sharing the facility.

Affected no doubt by the type of building it occupied, its location, and the date of its founding, each Parkway unit developed its own style, and, as a result of its leadership, its own problems and complaints. But each had its own beauty and its own strength, unique but equal in worth.

When students entered Parkway, they entered a program, not a school; a process, not a place; an activity, not a location. What was absolutely essential was that each unit form a cohesive group, held together by the common task of promoting their own learning.

The students themselves, selected by lottery, were not prestructured by the admissions procedure into any kind of caste or graded system. There was no hierarchy, since nobody had a pedigree or a set of test scores or political influence by which he could claim precedence. They were in Parkway by chance, by fortune and not by merit or power. This meant that quite early on students began to see each other directly for what they were, and particularly they realized that certain of their fellow-students were more companionable or more able to help them to learn. They were not bits of data brought together by a computer, only to be kept separated by the rules of a school classroom until the computer's instructions dispersed them. They could choose certain people and certain kinds of relations. They could also evaluate themselves, their fellows, and their relations in terms of common goals and common interests instead of using the usual stereotypes and the question, "Is he like me?" The questions became more, "Did we do something together?" "Could we do something together?" and "We did do something together: how did it happen?"

The students were not the only members of a Parkway unit. Each unit had nine or ten full-time, certified teachers, one of whom was appointed unit head by the director, in consultation with other members of the community. In addition, at least an equal number of university students, graduate and undergraduate, designated as interns, worked with each unit. They came from Antioch College, the University of Massachusetts, Penn State, the University of Pennsylvania, Oberlin College and several others. The intern's role was, perhaps, the most difficult and stressful one in the program, except possibly the director's. Young, inexperienced, and serving without pay, they were expected to share the same responsibilities and face the same problems as the regular faculty.

Finally, each unit employed someone who was skilled in office procedures and secretarial matters. Alpha had Tami Williams, an administrative officer who also did typing, Beta had Priscilla Witherspoon (later Wilmore) as secretary, and Gamma had Betty Barth as administrative officer. It was sometimes easy to forget that these people were essential members of the Parkway units. But, for example, Tami taught a course in typing and Joyce Johnson, the director's secretary, taught shorthand; they were all members of a learning community.

These were the full-time members of a Parkway unit, numbering about one hundred and eighty at its maximum. There were many other people involved with each unit but on a part-time basis, and their contributions will be discussed in connection with the curriculum.

It could almost be said that a principle of Parkway's group composition is heterogeneity. In conventional schools, where homogeneity is at least desired, the closer the group comes to this desired state, the less likely it is that the group has a dynamic to sustain its own learning. Change is generated out of difference, and learning arises out of discontinuities, discrepancies, separations, and gaps. The Parkway Program takes it for granted that homogeneity is not possible in reality, that schools create a semblance of it only by studiously avoiding all but the most trivial factors (such as age). Since a student-faculty group is bound to be made up of different kinds of people, the Parkway Program accepts this heterogeneity, tries to maximize it, and then puts it to educational use.

The internal structuring of a Parkway unit is never determined by age. The program is nongraded. While it is true that students are eligible only if they are in grades nine through twelve of a conventional school, once they enter the program this factor is ignored, since it does not have any established, demonstrable connection with learning. Parkway tries to keep its priorities clear. It is a learning community, and the problem is how to provide internal structuring or grouping in such a way as to promote learning, not hamper it or simply be irrelevant to it.

The mode of admission to a Parkway Program unit and its size are of fundamental importance. Once inside the program, however, every member of the unit, student and teacher alike, belongs to a basic social group called a tutorial. Each tutorial is made up of about sixteen students, one of the full-time, certified teachers, and one of the university interns. People are assigned to a tutorial by lottery. The selection is random but compulsory. Everyone belongs, for the tutorial is the one required part of the program. In the beginning, the tutorial was scheduled to meet four times a week for two hours at a time. Later, this schedule was adapted in different ways by each of the three communities; the times and the purposes were changed, but not in any fundamental way. Since the tutorial groups are small, there is at least one place where a student or faculty member can be sure of friendly support and advice and can be certain of some interest and concern on the part of others. A visitor once remarked that the tutorial was an extended homeroom; the connotations are perhaps unfortunate, but the comment suggests one aspect of the tutorial's function.

The tutorial, since it has a small, permanent membership and meets frequently, is an ideal unit for communication and administration purposes. It is particularly valuable, as will be seen later, for evaluation purposes.

Finally, the tutorial has, as its academic function, the development of the so-called basic skills. Originally the tutorials were to focus on

[23]

language and mathematics, but some units found that much time had to be spent on personal and group problems, and so while language was continued, social studies replaced mathematics. This trend was helped by the fact that many of the faculty were afraid of mathematics, or at least unskilled in it. The learning experiences within the tutorial and other groups will be fully explored in the next chapter. All that needs to be noted now is that the tutorials are randomly selected groups to which everybody belongs. It is the only compulsory group and every other group and activity is chosen by the students and faculty in the light of their own purposes.

The major part of every student's time is spent in regularly scheduled courses taught by the faculty, interns, businessmen, parents, students, librarians, curators, and individual volunteers. Each instructor brings to the course whatever interests him in his field of expertise. The students choose their own courses in consultation with their parents, so that the number of students in each course is highly variable. It did not matter if, in the past, some courses had only one student; if the instructor was willing, the course went on. Students' reasons for choosing their particular courses vary considerably. Sometimes the motive is interest in the subject itself, sometimes the character of the instructor, sometimes the fulfillment of a state requirement, sometimes parental insistence, sometimes to be with a friend, or a combination of any of these or other motives. Whatever the motives, they themselves become objects of inquiry, something to be understood by the students, and this is possible only because the motives are able to move the student. The administrative structure permits it—or, more correctly, requires it. After a brief settling down period, during which changes can be made, the student commits himself to a particular series of courses, and this is regarded as a kind of contract to which he and the Parkway Program are held.

In addition to taking some of the courses offered by the Parkway unit, a student can elect to spend part of his time on independent study.

Since each Parkway unit is responsible for its own day-to-day operations, special groups are set up within each unit to help members learn the necessary managerial skills and to assume responsibility for carrying out particular assignments—the most obvious one being the creation of the community's catalog of courses. These are called management groups and they are open to anyone—students, faculty and parents. They can be continuing groups—standing committees—or temporary groups set up to solve a particular problem. Time is set aside for management groups as a way of encouraging participation.

Periodically, each Parkway unit brings together all of its members in a town meeting. At the beginning of a unit's life, town meetings are held once a week (or even more frequently), but as the community develops, the business to be transacted becomes less in quantity and less urgent. Every other week seems to be the common rhythm. Although unit heads usually call town meetings, anybody can call one, and at the beginning of Parkway, Bremer, faculty members, and a small group of students all called town meetings to deal with problems that were on their minds.

Finally, groups are often set up on an *ad hoc* basis to undertake a specific task or to accomplish a particular purpose.

To summarize, a student in the Parkway Program must belong to a unit, or community, of about one hundred and sixty people, and within that community he must belong to a tutorial group. Beyond that, he may belong to a number of courses of study, to one or more management groups, to *ad hoc* groups for this or that purpose, and he may attend town meetings. In addition, he can elect to work independently.

It is important to state again that this social organization is not determined by accidental, geographical factors nor by the physical design of a particular building. As will be seen in the next chapter, each element in the social and administrative organization is included because of its educational function. The organizational structure is not without its problems—no organization that is alive is without problems —but it is arranged so that the problems generated are helpful to the students' learning. The problems of conventional schools cannot be solved within the context of the schools; the problems become a way of life. What is called discipline is an obvious enough example. Since schools are set up so that the interests of the students are in opposition to the interests of the teachers and administrators, it will never be possible to eliminate the mutual antagonism and distrust. The Parkway Program is constructed upon the principle of identity of interest, so that even when opposition and hostility arise, they are not structurally determined but personally created. Therefore, these problems can be personally dealt with; that is, people can learn from them. Discipline problems at Parkway have been so minor and so few that for all intents and purposes they can be disregarded. This is not because Parkway admits only angels—indeed, many students were serious behavioral problems in the schools from which they came—but because the social structure is humanizing and respectful of the individual while at the same time recognizing group or social obligations.

It would have been possible in the design of Parkway for students to have been admitted to the program as a whole—rather like being admitted to a school of four thousand students, but then would have arisen the difficulty of separating out into smaller groups. If you cannot separate yourself, you cannot belong either. In the director's view, it was more beneficial educationally to set up the separate Parkway units and then face the problem of how to come together, if that was a real problem. It appears that this might not be a problem, since there are very few purposes that can be usefully served by physically coming together. On occasions, all Parkway units supported a particular principle, but they decided to do so separately. The director felt no need to see everyone all at once, although on one occasion some students did. As a consequence, a joint total town meeting was held on the screened-in roof of Paxson. It was never tried again.

The only other topic of concern at this time is the location of authority in the Parkway Program. In John Bremer's view, authority in the Parkway Program is vested in the group as a whole and can be legitimately exercised by any individual member if it promotes the common task. Authority is, as it were, available to be used by anyone in the program if it furthers the ends of the program. Leadership roles are available, but they are not occupied permanently by certain individuals; they are rotated, not in any systematic way but as the needs of the moment and the skills and willingness of people change.

It is hard for people to accept the fact that authority for getting the job done is vested, for example, in the tutorial group as a whole. It is so easy to fall back into the position of letting the faculty do it—they have the authority, let them be responsible for the tutorial's learning progress. There is little doubt that one of the causes of difficulty with mathematics in the tutorial is a feeling on the part of some teachers that they are responsible for performing the task; that is, that they must *teach* mathematics. But the work task of the tutorial is to ensure that its members *learn* English and mathematics; for the teacher to assume total responsibility is to deny the leadership role that a student must play with respect to his own learning. Those who see the profession of educator as a means of establishing, maintaining, and promoting themselves find it almost impossible to accept this view. It denies them the security of status and the permanence of position which it has been their aim to achieve. Such an aim has a place only within a world of static roles; the students are the means by which professional people move from one role to another—and even if they are not intended to be instrumentalities (and usually they are not), that is the actual result for the students. Most people would agree that students should be held responsible, but by that they usually mean that students should do as they are told, that they should be obedient. The paradox of this situation is that to do what someone else legitimately tells you to do is to turn yourself into an instrument (into a slave, Aristotle would say) which cannot be held accountable for the consequences. Whoever gives the command is accountable.

To put this another way, you are only responsible when you have a choice and the power to carry out what you have chosen. There is no other way to learn how to be responsible. It is for this reason that authority is vested in groups in Parkway, and, as a result, choosing, or freedom, is the basic curriculum of the Parkway Program.

2
The Curriculum

The curriculum of the Parkway Program can be looked at in a number of ways, if by the word "curriculum" we mean what it is that the students can learn. Contrary to the conventional way of thinking and speaking, the curriculum is not a simple, straightforward collection of subject-matters—not even in a conventional school, and certainly not in Parkway. If only educators would recognize the complexity of their curriculum, the way would be opened for a much-needed reform in education that would be of assistance to everyone, but particularly to students. Parkway's curriculum can be seen, by and large, as having five different aspects.

The first aspect of Parkway's curriculum is freedom. That is, students are supported as they learn to be free, they are encouraged to be free, and, in a way, they are forced to be free.

They are forced to be free simply because they must take the initiative: they must choose to enter the Parkway Program and to share in its communal life. With only one exception, the tutorial, the student must choose everything he does within the program, and if he does not, cannot, make a choice, then nothing happens until he does.

Students are encouraged to be free—that is, courage is aroused in them so that they choose, and it is aroused in them by companions, other students and faculty alike, also engaged in having to choose.

Students are supported as they learn to be free by the structure surrounding them and by their fellow-participants. It is frankly recognized and explicitly stated that the curriculum is freedom, so that it has the sanction of the learning community, and there are no punishments or penalties for choosing "badly" or "wrongly." What would this mean? A punishment is extrinsic—it is outside the choice and its consequences; it is imposed from without when a choice is disapproved by somebody with power, in authority. What can a student learn from that? Certainly he cannot learn anything but submission or rebellion. He can learn to be dominated by others or to impose his will upon others when he gets the chance. In either case, he learns that might makes right, that force need not be justified. That is what schools teach.

There is another way, a way that used to be well known among us, that used to be called the democratic way before the words were corrupted. This way requires the student to learn from the intrinsic consequences of his choice, from what naturally happens because of what he does, and not from some arbitrary imposition from without. This way requires of all of us great courage and strength of purpose, great faith in the student, but it works and it is the only way that works. It is easy to imagine the cries of "License! Permissiveness!" but such cries only come from people in the final stages of intellectual demoralization. As a nation we are committed to freedom as an end, but such people have contempt for and reject the only means to that end. They cannot bear the thought that the student might do as *he* likes, and therefore insist that he do as *they* like. What is distressing is that there are only two possibilities in their scheme of things—do as you like or do as somebody else likes. Such a restricted view is clearly irrational (it is a form of neurosis common among politicians, police and superintendents) and it assumes that the world is fixed, that our likes and dislikes are immutable, and that we cannot learn. But the business of Parkway is to show that we can all learn.

It should not be thought that the life of a Parkway student is easy. On the contrary, it is probably more demanding than most other ways of life. First, it is difficult to choose; it is much easier, even though we complain, to be told what to do. We are not only excused the trouble of weighing alternatives, assessing evidence, and estimating consequences, but we are also blameless (since we are doing only what we were told to do) and not responsible. And on top of that, we can complain bitterly about our lack of freedom. Second, to choose requires us to accept the fact that we never have all the data, we are never in possession of complete justification; we must choose without certainty, without total assurance that our choice is the best way. In short, we learn how to deal with probabilities and possibilities—which is uncomfortable but inevitable. Third, when we choose we assume responsibility for the consequences; we accept our accountability to ourselves and to our friends. No one else is to blame: we chose. This is to subject ourselves to a harder, sterner taskmaster than students and schoolmen have ever known. It is to submit ourselves to ourselves;

the consequences of our chosen act belong to us, they are ours. And we are theirs. We learn because the questions arise (not intellectually, but practically), "Is that what I intended?" "Is that who I am?"

Can students in the Parkway Program do as they like? No. They can learn as they like, but commitment to learning is required. How they learn, what they learn, when they learn, and with whom they learn is left open. The only commandment is *Thou shalt learn*. And even that commandment is interpreted generously and with humility. It's possible to learn when outwardly nothing seems to be happening; after traumatic experiences in school, recovery time is required and healing is learning. Rather than chasing and harassing students, Parkway prefers to help them where they have chosen to learn—and, if nowhere else, in the tutorial to which everybody belongs. The results are very surprising but very real if we are prepared to wait with faith, hope, and charity. If, however, we are committed to all the paraphernalia of the school—to the nonsense about grade levels and learning by increments, month by month—then there is no doubt all this must be hard to understand.

The following anecdote can be related only because of the importance of freedom as the curriculum.

In Community Gamma (also known as the Paxson Parkway), there was a joint elementary and secondary educational program. The elementary program was so successful that the superintendent of schools had to close it, a story which will be related hereafter. While it was running, each student at the high school level could elect to work with one or more elementary-level students. One high school student, who had been in much trouble and who was on parole when he joined Parkway, formed a close attachment to a seven-year-old boy, and they shared many things together. One day, the small boy was to go to a local store with the parolee (whom we shall call Peter) to buy some things for a group to which he belonged in the morning. Peter arrived that afternoon and the two of them set out for the store. A block away from Paxson, they met some of Peter's former friends, who persuaded him to go with them, so he sent the seven-year-old back to the school, one block away, and went off to do what young men will do. The next day, Peter was very concerned about what he had done and went to find his seven-year-old to describe the exciting adventure he had in store for that day. The seven-year-old looked at him for a moment and then said, "Yesterday you sent me back. I don't want to be with you." And then he walked away.

Parents, relatives, teachers, counselors, principals, lawyers, policemen, and judges had all tried to teach Peter something about social responsibility and they had failed. A seven-year-old boy succeeded.

The lesson was powerfully learned, but only because Peter was able to choose something, some activity, some circumstance, that gave him the opportunity. *He* chose it and, quite unconsciously but inevitably, exposed himself to learning a very difficult thing. If a school had been assigning high school students to work with young children, Peter would have been passed over as "unsuitable." It is almost as if a student can participate in an educational activity only when he can show that he does not need to learn anything from it.

This leads naturally to the question, "But don't students make mistakes? They don't know enough, do they?" Of course students make mistakes — they are, after all, only human — but they make their own mistakes and not somebody else's. What is a mistake, an educational mistake? It is simply an experience from which the student did not learn. That is all. One does not need to be omniscient in order to learn: in fact, it is reported to be a handicap. To commit ourselves to a course of action, or to an answer to a question, even if the act produces unexpected and undesirable consequences, even if the answer is inexact, inappropriate, or just plain wrong, is to expose ourselves to the possibility of learning, provided we see why we were right or wrong. Nothing is more deadly to learning than being in the possession of the right answer without knowing *why* it is the right answer. In fact, in this case, we don't possess the answer, the answer possesses us.

It is possible that the law-and-order boys will find this view unsympathetic to their needs. It is easy to suppose, since they are people who have great difficulty in controlling themselves. The aftermath of a convention for people dedicated to law and order has been likened to the carnage after the fall of Troy, and this suggests a psychological disposition needing rigidity and authoritarianism. But there is little point in elevating their neurosis into an educational principle. Indeed, they are very much like the population of a school, which, to borrow a phrase from John Ruskin, is "anarchy plus a constable." If the constable — all those exercising control or police functions in a school — were to be taken away, all that would be left would be anarchy and chaos. It is precisely to avoid this situation that Parkway insists that students learn how to be self-controlled, to be responsible for themselves. There is no responsibility without freedom, and there is no freedom without responsibility. What students learn in a conventional school is to be obedient when "authority" is around, and when it is not. . . .

It would be a lot tidier if there were another way to learn how to be free, but there is not. We learn how to be free by being free, we learn how to choose by choosing, and we learn how to be responsible by being responsible — that is, by experiencing the consequences, expected or unexpected, good or bad. That is the Parkway curriculum, in one aspect.

The second aspect of Parkway's curriculum is the social and administrative organization of the program itself and, more particularly, the role of the student. What is the role of the student? What are the virtues, the attitudes, and the skills a student requires to participate fully in Parkway?

This aspect of Parkway's curriculum can be conveniently organized under three separate headings: the student as cooperator, the student as manager, the student as artist or poet.

The student as cooperator, as someone learning the skills of cooperation, can be seen very clearly in the life of the tutorial group.

Chosen by lot from applicants of high school age, regardless of marks, aptitudes, and disciplinary records, girls and boys come to the Parkway Program from every neighborhood and all social, economic, and ethnic groups. Each day they scatter over the city, students of like interests taking elective courses together and working in management groups of their own choosing.

Without careful structuring, such a program might mean that a youngster from the inner city would go one way and one from an affluent neighborhood another: whites with whites, blacks with blacks, fifteen-year-olds with those of the same age, young people who are enriched by the world of books scarcely knowing others who have reading difficulties, and so forth.

Under these circumstances, the Parkway Program would not be a learning community but a list of courses. Few of its students would learn to understand each other, although this is essential to good citizenship—and unless its students learn citizenship, Parkway is nothing.

None of these dangers was overlooked. The Parkway Program is indeed structured; at the center of the structure are tutorial groups, and they bring the students together.

A tutorial group consists of approximately sixteen young people chosen at random who meet for four hours a week with a faculty member and a university intern—one a man, the other a woman, and, if possible, one black and one white. The meetings may be for one hour four times a week or for two hours twice a week.

It is here that personal encouragement, support, and counseling are given, and here special attention can be paid to basic skills of language and mathematics (in addition to the regular courses in those subjects). Here, too, there is continuous evaluation of Parkway by all who are in it, and here much personal attention is paid to the progress each student is making. If a child is in trouble and parents must be consulted, it is from the tutorial leader or the unit head that they hear.

Tutorial groups have produced plays, engaged in poetry writing and calligraphy, painted and decorated their rooms, functioned as encounter groups, and organized parties, outings, and athletic events. Members of tutorial groups have read together, reasoned together, learned mathematics together, played together, and visited each others' neighborhoods and homes. Participation in such a group is the one activity required of every person at Parkway, student and teacher alike.

Cy Swartz, who taught at unit Alpha from the first day of the Parkway Program and then at Beta before becoming director of Gamma, calls tutorial groups the most vital part of the Parkway Program, the ingredient that transforms what might be a list of courses into a unified process of learning with a sense of community.

A tutorial group's meetings need not be like regular classroom sessions, Swartz declares. But the group and its leader should see that every student sets appropriate learning goals, chooses a reasonable schedule of classes, and then puts his best foot forward. This is accomplished by members of the group working and counseling together.

It is not always easy. The group leader must walk a narrow path between disorder and oversolicitude as he seeks to generate activities that appeal to all, whatever their backgrounds.

Attendance sometimes suffers in the first excitement of new-found freedom at Parkway. Facing this, one tutorial leader at Alpha helped his group set up a "buddy system" for contacting absentees. In time, this led to visits by students to each others' homes, and students began to show concern when someone missed a meeting. The visits were welcomed, attendance at school and at tutorials picked up, and both the visitors and those visited learned in the process.

The same teacher encouraged his group to tour points of interest in the city, after which teacher, intern, and students wrote about what they had seen and published the reports in a pamphlet.

It was a short step from this activity to creative writing, including poetry writing. Then someone suggested that the group build a scale model of the room at the Insurance Company of North America where the tutorial met. Everyone was able to contribute something to this work, which involved mathematics. At this point, students had learned some English and math and had gained a knowledge of their city as well as of each other.

The following account is from a journal kept by Dan Shapiro, an adult student from Goddard College and one of the first interns:

> A vignette: Today I went to a tutorial that usually meets in the art museum located in Fairmount Park along the Schuylkill River. The park is beautifully landscaped and it was the first day of spring. The museum itself is a replica of a Greek temple

and has Greek pavilions along the river. We decided to have class outside, went down to the river, and in one of the pavilions found three men playing congo drums and a woman doing African dances. It wasn't long before George, the head of the tutorial and head of our dance class, joined the African dancing with the woman, and a crowd soon gathered. A black policeman came over, saw what was going on, and walked away. Five minutes later he was back with his friend. Two men working with wheelbarrows stopped, and in about ten minutes, a crowd of about fifty people had gathered, standing around laughing and singing and talking. Some of the Parkway students joined in the dancing. It was a thoroughly exciting experience. I looked up toward the museum and saw another tutorial meeting outside. Some kids were throwing stones into the river, a record player was going, and they were discussing poetry. All this made me feel that this is what education should be "about." But at the same time, I feel guilty; "it's too much fun." After about an hour of singing and dancing, we decided to finish up the day's meeting inside and discuss a few things. This was the group that had been filmed for a TV documentary, and they decided that they would like to contact the lady who had made the documentary, and interview her, to find out her observations and reactions to the Parkway Program.

As time goes on, the initiative in tutorial groups passes more and more to the students. Establishing a library of their favorite paperbacks, members of one group read each others' selections, wrote reports, and then read them aloud. Some students' need for special help in reading became apparent. Assistance from their buddies was forthcoming; so was the willingness to accept it.

Elaine, age 16, came from a family that enjoyed games. She described some of them, and the group made its own, constructing scrabble sets and cribbage boards—no mean aids for reading and mathematics. At the urging of a boy who came to Parkway from an inner-city junior high school, the group soon invented its own game, "Parkway," inspired by Monopoly. Doing this, the students gained practice in writing and considered mathematical probabilities as well.

Keeping constant watch, the tutorial leader decided with which students he might discuss the need for basic mathematics or English. The tutorial group had become a helpful and popular institution for students and leader. It created new forms of learning. It permitted constant evaluation. Well attended, it was marked by a family feeling. Its discussions led to suggestions at a town meeting for the improvement of Parkway itself.

When unit Gamma opened in September 1969, Bernie Ivens—an eight-year teaching veteran from West Philadelphia High School— was placed in charge of a tutorial group. To his chagrin, the students appeared apathetic. They didn't know what to do. Then Ivens, groping, handed the young people a list of ten books, asking them to vote on four that might be purchased with school funds. *Catcher in the Rye* by J. D. Salinger, *Soul on Ice* by Eldridge Cleaver, *I Never Promised You a Rose Garden* by Hannah Green, and *Nigger* by Dick Gregory were chosen. Then copies were bought, everybody took turns reading them, and discussion ensued. Later, the group purchased more books before selecting movies to attend together, two students making arrangements for reduced-price tickets.

Now there was group feeling in Bernie's tutorial. Boys and girls identified themselves as belonging to it: "Who are you?" "Jim Brown, I'm in tutorial six." When one girl thought she might drop out of Parkway to travel across the country, she came to the group for advice, and the students persuaded her to stay with them, at least until summer.

Ivens felt that some meetings of his tutorial were disorderly, even wild. But the young people learned from each other as they never had at West Philadelphia High. They were able to work together because they were free to communicate. Ivens decided that he could put up with the noise.

It is in the tutorial that cooperation is most needed—and where it is most difficult to achieve. The need is obvious, since the students have a common task, to help themselves and their fellow-students learn, and they cannot do the one without the other. The difficulty is also obvious, for although the group has a common task, it does not select the task nor choose the people with whom to share it.

The common task is, basically, assigned by the Commonwealth of Pennsylvania in the form of the English and mathematics requirements it sets for graduation. Since the group is determined by chance, students have the task of learning how to learn with a group of people arbitrarily selected—not your friends, not people you would auto- matically choose, not people with an expressed common problem or with a shared inquiry. Just a group at random. The Parkway student must learn how to get along with anybody and everybody.

A further function of the tutorial is that, since it is the only as- signed, mandatory part of the Parkway Program, it is the focus of the learning that students must carry out with respect to authority. High school students tend to rebel against authority—or else to accept it complacently. Either way, they are controlled by it and have not understood and accepted its possibilities and limitations. Through the tutorial, students come to terms with authority in the sense that they see it for what it is, as a given with advantages and disadvantages, to be used, manipulated, and obeyed. If students cannot consider a proposal without first considering its source, there is little hope that they will ever be free in the sense of being able to make free, creative contributions to the society in which they live. The casual visitor to Parkway has undoubtedly heard complaints about the tutorials—that they are not working, that they are a waste of time—but unless he ceases to be a casual visitor and becomes a member of the community, he will not understand that the criticisms are necessary, healthy, and a sign of strength.

Coming to terms with authority is not only a problem for the students. It is an even more severe problem for the faculty, who constantly focus all of their complaints on the tutorial. They, too, must learn. However, for faculty and students alike, the learning with respect to authority is clearly located in one element of the program instead of being diffused through everything as in a conventional school. The concentration intensifies the problem, which must, therefore, be dealt with. It cannot be ignored; learning is required.

The student as manager, the second of the three headings in this topic of the curriculum as the social and administrative organization, does not exist in conventional schools. How could it, since there is nothing for students to manage beyond the yearbook, the selection of the class ring, and the annual dance? In the Parkway Program, the learning of managerial skills, of administrative arts, is concentrated in management groups and town meetings, although not exclusively in these activities.

Enroll children in a school without walls after they have been at the beck and call of elementary school teachers for eight years and one can expect a certain amount of commotion. Years in which initiative was subordinated to obedience are bound to turn some of the students off instead of preparing them for responsibility. At Parkway, this was apparent when the matter of school government came up.

Parkway seeks to eliminate the form of student government in which authority descends on young people from above. Because such traditional "sandbox government" denies students a role in important school decisions while raising a façade of self-determination, it inspires apathy in some students and rebellion in others.

The problem is how to let the students run their own show as much as possible. Administrators of the Parkway Program, therefore, found that they faced a dilemma. Leave school government to students, whose entire school lives have deadened them for assuming such responsibility, and most of them will fail to pick up the reins. On the other hand, to draw too many guidelines for the students is to decide things from on high, in the old-fashioned way. Finding these alternatives unacceptable, Parkway sought a golden mean, through what it calls management groups and town meetings—starting points for self-government, created by the staff, but on which the students are free to build.

When Alpha, the first unit, opened in February 1969, each student was advised that there would be certain management groups and that he was expected to join at least one. These groups had to do with Parkway office matters, athletics, school facilities, fund-raising, social activities, public relations, publishing a school newspaper, and conducting a study of the Parkway Program in action.

An additional group, again open to any student who cared to join, was formed to consider what further steps Parkway might take for its own government. Meanwhile, weekly town meetings were held, attended by students, teachers, and the director. These town meetings will be discussed later.

Teachers were not assigned to the management groups, lest their presence as faculty advisers lead to their dominating the work. Individual teachers helped the groups, however, joining wherever the assigned activity interested them most.

If the faculty members had taken the lead, it is probable that most management groups would have survived only as teacher-dominated student organizations do in traditional schools. Instead, Parkway's faculty let the students make what they would of the groups, and many of the groups foundered—perhaps because they were born out of what the administration conceived to be the needs of the students rather than out of the young people's own conception of what would make the school community thrive.

The office management group addressed envelopes and did some work in the school office. The facilities group combined with the fund-raising group. Cakes were sold outside Alpha's headquarters and the proceeds were used to buy paint for the stairwell. For the most part, students showed little interest in the management groups, although for a time the group charged with considering further forms of self-government was active.

Mark Lyons, a young Californian on Alpha's staff, worked with the latter group and found that it was concerned both with the making of decisions for Parkway's governance and with how the decisions should be enforced, once made.

Lyons recalled later that the students showed little interest in formal machinery for rule enforcement. If smoking and gambling on Alpha's premises were to be prevented, for example (and they were), it suited the young people to have this done informally, by social pressure.

Students could call on someone who was misbehaving to stop. They felt there was time enough to consider formal controls, if their original plan failed.

Apart from enforcement, how was Alpha to adopt rules? The students showed little enthusiasm for representative government. What is more, the black students (as Dan Shapiro noted in his journal) were reluctant to submit to majority rule, a concept under which minority rights had not always flourished.

After many meetings and much discussion, the group recommended policy-making procedures which the Alpha community failed to approve but which are worth reporting as an interesting variation upon democracy in action.

The group suggested that any person, be he the director, a teacher, or a student, acting alone or with others, might decide any matter of school policy on a tentative basis, put it in writing, and post it on the bulletin board, where everyone would see it. Unless twenty persons asked that the tentative decision be taken up at town meeting, it was to become law.

This was an original and imaginative proposal. However, it failed to be adopted, and no formal method for making school policy came in its stead. Town meetings decide some matters, by consensus. Others are resolved by the unit head. With time, this situation may change. If Parkway needs a clearly defined self-government, nothing stands in the way.

Meanwhile, the students formed two additional management groups that the faculty had never envisioned, and these prospered.

First, a senior activities group was founded by students, most of them black, who felt a social vacuum at Parkway. Collecting money, they sponsored a prom and arranged for class rings.

Second, students formed an altogether remarkable curriculum group. Credit for the extensive list of elective courses in the catalogs largely belongs to this group.

In the view of the students who started the curriculum group, Parkway was not doing enough to help young people learn the basic skills of reading and mathematics, and it was not offering electives of sufficient scope and variety.

The students saw that whoever printed the school catalog could affect the curriculum. To this extent, the medium was a means for control of the message. The young people decided to reform the curriculum by what they put in the catalog.

Suggesting courses to individual faculty members, the students secured commitments that they would be taught and then listed those courses in the catalog.

Next, the students sought graduate students at the University of Pennsylvania who might be interested in teaching at Parkway. Several courses resulted, notably one on consumer education and another dealing with major crises in U.S. history.

The curriculum group saw the need for more remedial work in English and mathematics, and into the catalog went courses on basic writing, grammar, spelling, vocabulary, reading workshops, at three levels, and basic mathematics.

Transforming the curriculum in this fashion was a learning experience in itself. Study of the program had become an important part of the program itself, and Alpha was the better for it.

Beta, the second unit, opened in July 1969, and unit head Tina Craig soon decided that it served no purpose to force anyone into a management group. Instead, group activity was entirely voluntary, although staff members suggested that the Beta students consider forming groups to deal with some of the following subjects:

Places to hold classes

Public relations

Newspaper

Social affairs

Lunch sales

Parkway credit union

Finances

Interior decoration at Cherry House

Short-term projects

Communication with parents

Library

Athletics

Health services

Part-time employment placement

In this case too, the teachers left it to the students to get the groups going, and again most of the groups simply went under, exceptions being the newspaper group and the one for communication with parents, which handles correspondence before and after parent-teacher meetings.

Once again, the students themselves formed management groups, doing so according to their conception of what was needed, however.

And again groups flourished, notably a college admission information agency and a curriculum-planning and catalog group, which sent out the following communication early in 1970:

IT'S SPRING

Catalog & course offerings time!

If you have ever been unhappy

	because a course you
	wanted wasn't offered
Or	because you didn't like
	something about a course
	that was offered,

NOW'S THE TIME TO DO SOMETHING ABOUT IT

If the next catalog is to be full of courses you really want and need, we've got to start getting it together now. That means YOU, Beta person, have got to figure out what you want to learn and where to find it.

HOW?

Begin by reading over the Catalog Survey Sheet and discussing it in tutorial. Each person should add: (1) Any types of courses not on the list (2) Any suggestions for people or institutions to contact for any of the courses suggested— people you, your friends, or family know about. Each tutorial should find at least one person who wants to work on getting courses lined up during the next few weeks. People who volunteer for this job will be making phone calls, writing letters, and going to visit prospective institutions & people.

Catalog people will get together at Cherry House next Thursday at 3:00 to interpret requests for courses and pull resources together.

TUTORIAL LEADERS

Please return Catalog Survey Sheets for each student, and the name of AT LEAST ONE STUDENT from your tutorial who wants to work on this venture to Linda by next Monday. merci.

CATALOG SURVEY SHEETS—SPRING! 1970

We would like to find institutions to offer the following kinds of courses for this spring. Please check the kinds of courses you are interested in, write in names of people or institutions who might be contacted about courses, and add the names of courses you would like which are not listed here. merci.

Architecture, Engineering, Drafting
Computers, Data Processing (for training and jobs)
Insurance, Banks, Consumer Economics (for math & economics)
Radio, TV, film & photography
Art, Textiles, Crafts
Hospitals, Laboratories (for bio & chemistry)
Library Science
Office Skills (training and jobs)
Retailing & Marketing (training and jobs)
Wood, metal & electrical shops (technical skills)
Auto mechanics
Hospitals, Day Care Centers, Neighborhood projects (volunteer work)
Dressmaking
Food & Nutrition
Publishing
Universities—grad students to teach courses, esp. Math, Reading, Sciences, etc.
Art Schools
Encounter & other T-group things, black-white & others
Counseling—Draft, psychiatric, medical, academic

As at Alpha, the pupils were playing a significant role in creating the curriculum.

When unit Gamma opened in North Philadelphia in September 1969, its management groups paralleled those at Alpha and Beta. During Gamma's second semester, a girl student who transferred to Parkway from a suburban school described the unit's newspaper management group:

> Cy [Cy Swartz, the unit head] suggested that we get something out, even if we had to print it by hand with potato blocks. He said the newspaper groups at Alpha and Beta had not done much, because they tried to be too perfect. Even so, I think we only published about four issues the first semester. The students didn't seem to know what was going on, and the teacher and the intern whom we thought were going to help us didn't take over.
>
> There were 15 students in the group, but in the second semester most of them quit to go to other groups, and kids from other groups joined us, because they decided by this time that putting out a newspaper interested them. Now

[41]

things are humming. We have had two issues already. We type on stencils, and use the mimeographing machine.

We had a long discussion about what to print, and decided that anything submitted by anybody at Gamma would go in. One boy said we should only use what he called good quality writing, but we decided that would be unfair. It's everybody's school, and if some kids didn't learn much in the schools they went to before, how can we say that's their fault?

We decided a teacher could talk over mistakes in grammar with a kid, but we're interested in what a student has to say — not his grammar — and we will print a piece, mistakes and all, if that's how the student wants it.

When we met as a group in the first semester, attendance was terrible. Now it is almost perfect. Attendance in class is much better too. I think this is because kids at Parkway take a semester or so to find out what really interests them.

In summary, what can be said about Parkway's experience with management groups?

First, the achievement of faculty-created groups has been spotty. Where teachers' notions of what the school needs vary widely from what students think, not much is accomplished.

On the other hand, where a management group — such as the curriculum group — emerges because of the concern of students for their education, there is no holding it back and no need for a prestructured student government to help it function responsibly.

Only time will tell the ultimate role of the management groups. Meanwhile, the best of them are as unique as Parkway itself — and as different from student organizations in the traditional high schools as Parkway's town meetings are from the orderly "assemblies" conducted in such institutions.

At 11:30 A.M. on Friday, March 13, 1970, the students and teachers of unit Beta — or about half of them, for attendance was not compulsory — met in town meeting in a lecture hall in Philadelphia's Free Library.

A visitor noted little similarity between this meeting and a school assembly. In the first place, the students did not file in, led by teachers. They arrived singly and by twos and threes, coming from their classes here and there in the city. Students sat where they pleased, not divided by class or by age. Here there was a cluster of boys, there a group of girls, elsewhere students were mixed. For the most part, blacks sat with blacks and whites with whites.

What is more, no one presided. Boys and girls from one of Beta's tutorial groups were on the stage, and their tutorial leader — a young teacher—led part of the discussion, but students on the stage led parts of it too, the role of discussion leader passing from one person to another with an utter absence of formality.

Teachers were scattered through the hall, and in the middle of the room, unit head Tina Craig sat silently.

The tutorial leader spoke first. In fact, the visitor had to be told he was a tutorial leader and faculty member, for nothing in his appearance distinguished him from the older students. Clad in slacks and a GI shirt, the tutorial leader was no father figure.

It had been previously agreed, the tutorial leader declared, that a two-thirds vote of those present was needed in order to decide anything. Then he posed the first question before town meeting: whether decisions for the governance of Beta should be made at town meetings or by tallying votes taken, after discussion, at meetings of the several tutorial groups.

Discussions then ensued, conducted in a fashion that would make a parliamentarian spin in his grave. Students interrupted each other; students interrupted teachers; if there was a chair, no one addressed it. When a standing vote was taken, three-fourths of those present chose the town meeting rather than the tutorials to be their decision-making body.

Routine announcements concerning social engagements, and so forth, followed. Then the meeting took up the question of whether teachers' evaluations of students at the end of the semester should be mailed to the young people's homes, as was current practice, or whether they should be handed out in tutorial meetings. Teachers were invited to respond to this point, but none did. It was apparent that the question had been amply discussed before the day's meeting. When a vote was taken, the practice of mailing evaluations was reaffirmed by a wide margin.

At that point, a girl near the back of the hall rose to complain that young people from another school were appropriating the student lounge at Cherry House—so much so that Betas felt like outsiders on their own premises.

The discussion this time was boisterous. When the visitor remarked to a young teacher that the meetings might go better if students were recognized and then addressed the chair instead of talking directly to each other, and sometimes interrupting to do so, he was assured that the young people would probably find this out for themselves in time. (*Moral:* there is no spoon-feeding at Parkway!)

The visitor had to admit that the discussion was productive. As it progressed, he learned that more than appeared at first blush was involved in the matter of the outsiders frequenting the lounge at

Cherry House. The interlopers were young ladies, it was disclosed, and every one of them came to the lounge at the invitation of a Beta boy.

There will be violence one of these days, a Beta girl predicted, perhaps a stabbing. No one denied this. Finally, a Beta youth—black, and known as Woody—rose to say that he would speak to his friends, they would speak to the girls from outside, and courtesy would be restored to the lounge. Before adjourning, the meeting solicited, and received, Woody's assurance that he would report back the next week.

Later, the visitor reflected how differently such a meeting would have been handled at the high school he attended. The matters decided that day would have been unilaterally determined by staff or by the school principal without a word from the students. Perhaps the principal would have asked members of the student government to help keep visitors out of the lounge. It is certain, however, that the decision would not have been left to the students. Nothing would have been done to make them feel that they were responsible for their school and that it was up to them to see that it functioned harmoniously.

Clearly, differences surface at Parkway town meetings. There have been disputes, and every species of the growing pains that accompany learning, especially when it is learning by doing, and most especially when it is learning to live with other people by doing precisely that.

At Alpha, for example, students rose in town meeting and protested a faculty decision that prohibited gambling at unit headquarters. The teachers had no right to make such a decision without consulting the students, they protested. The young people won this point too: faculty agreed that the issue of gambling should be resolved by teachers and students together. This was done, and gambling was again prohibited.

Unit Beta had growing pains too. The rule that no decision should be made without the concurrence of two-thirds of the students, for example, was adopted as a result of stormy town meetings that saw the unit almost equally divided, along racial lines, as to whether student groups should have their own club rooms at Cherry House.

Black students wanted the club rooms while white students protested that such a practice would represent the private use of what they considered to be everyone's territory. The issue remained unresolved until it was rendered obsolete by the fire marshal's padlocking that part of Cherry House where the rooms in question were located. Meanwhile, the students had faced a real issue about their education and had learned something about life, about each other, and about themselves. The social organization of Parkway not only permits such experience, it mandates it. This is what the program is for.

All of this is not to suggest that Parkway students devote a great deal of time to school politics. Quite to the contrary, problems are faced when they arise, and few arise in a relatively happy learning environment.

It must be emphasized that the learning of administrative arts, of managerial skills, can be accomplished only by doing, which means that a program such as Parkway will not look very tidy as people practice these skills. Administrators must learn to keep their hands off problems that they can solve easily lest learning opportunities are denied the student. This is a difficult rule for an administrator to learn, but he can do a great deal of harm if he makes an administrative decision too early; he should hold back for as long as possible. Of course, he then may discover that he was not needed at all—which may be a blow to administrative vanity and presumption, but this can be mollified by the thought that his saving presence made possible the student's learning attempt.

The student as artist, the third heading in this section, cannot be located primarily in any one part of the Parkway Program. It may be the role the student has available to him when he is free, cooperative, and able to manage his own life, but it is a role that all students should play.

The Parkway Program sets out to create an environment in which students are likely to be constructive. Consider the potter and his pot as an analogy. There are three basic elements in the potter's activity; they are the shape in the potter's mind, the material to be shaped (the clay), and the skills by which these two are brought together. This is not necessarily the order of these elements in the potter's actual activity, but they are all required.

Consider the shape in the potter's mind. It is an idea, an ideal, a shape, a form, a structure, a dream, a vision, and even, on occasions, an hallucination; in short, it is a good to be realized. Similarly, in our minds and in the student's mind there is a good to be realized. It may be vast, cosmic, and ambitious or it may be small, local, and modest, but it is there. We all see, students see, the possibilities of the world, how good can be molded into it, how it can be made better. Youth especially is a time of idealism; young people see more clearly than their parents certain kinds of injustice, ugliness, and dishonesty, and they want to improve the world. It is, of course, true that their visions are sometimes very simple (even simplistic) and sometimes unrealistic or mere fantasies, but this cannot mean that they are to be disparaged or ignored. On the contrary, what the young have, what students possess, is priceless, and for too long our society has refused to heed and to encourage them. That is why the quality of life has declined—the young have been shut off from it. It is no disgrace to admit that we, of older generations, have had our visions and are now committed, for the most part, to realizing them, to living them, and to acting them out, so that our originality, our creativity, our idealism has all but vanished. It is no disgrace because it is the way of life for all men; it cannot be avoided. What is disgraceful is the forcing of the young to act out *our* ideals instead of their own. The young must set out to reform the world — in whole or in part — and in accordance with their own ideal, their own idea, and they see the shape of things to come, as the potter sees, in his mind's eye, the shape of his pot.

The potter, to realize his vision, to embody his shape, needs skills. It is by his activity that the ideal is made actual, and this activity constitutes the main part of his art. What is the counterpart in the student? It is to be found in the managerial and communication skills he develops, in the skills of using the city, of forming, shaping, and manipulating the city so that it is better than it was, so that it embodies the ideal. This reshaping, this restructuring, is what urban renewal is really about. And students need to learn the social and political arts by which this is done.

It is now obvious that just as the potter has clay, the student needs a material to work upon and that this material is nothing other than the city itself. By this is not meant the city as a conglomeration of streets separated by buildings, not the city as a giant factory or shopping mart, but the city as the life and livelihood of its citizens. The city *is* the living, the city is process.

This brings us to another aspect of Parkway's curriculum. The first aspect, we have seen, is freedom and responsibility. The second aspect is the social and administrative organization and more particularly the student's role, which in Parkway is seen to be as cooperator, as manager, and as artist (the third aspect). But the student as artist needs to know his material; just as the potter must know, understand, and respect his clay to see its possibilities, so the student must know, understand, and respect his material — the city. It is the city, therefore, that constitutes the fourth aspect of Parkway's curriculum. Every student must come to know the city, the complex of places, processes, and people with which he lives. He must know it for what it is, understand it in terms of what it can do, and respect it for what it could be. He must know it, respect it, and revere it simply because he is about to change it — not do it violence, not destroy it, but change it — that is, transform it in terms of the principles of its being into what, potentially, it already is. Since the Parkway Program has the city as its curriculum, it must have the city as its campus. This is the educational reason for the school without walls. To learn about the city, to let it become familiar, to see it as the earthly counterpart of the City of God, can be accomplished only in the city; only academics suppose that this is learned in a course called Urban Dwelling 1 followed by Urban Dwelling 2.

Parkway students, perhaps, seem to start a long way behind us, sophisticates that we are, but there is no advantage to be gained by complaining. Before the program began, John Bremer visited a school to talk with students about it. As he was leaving, a faculty member stopped him and said, "What you don't understand is that most of these students have never been more than a few blocks from their home, let alone into center city." Replied Bremer, "What you don't understand is that precisely *that* is the starting point of their education."

Simple city skills come hard at first, but students rapidly catch on and also acquire the courage to attempt more imaginative projects. What is public space? Who can reasonably be expected to help us? How do we ask? when? where? What organizations of men are there in the city? What do they do? why? What is a telephone for? How does a telephone directory help us? The answers to such questions may seem simple, but they are not simple, and certainly not to students — particularly to students from minority groups. They all need to acquire the skills of dealing with the city, to gain a small measure of power over it, for without this they cannot make a contribution. It would be foolish to imagine a potter with no knowledge of his clay and with his hands tied behind his back, but that is effectively the situation of students in most schools, and then there are complaints that they are idle, destructive, and takers of hallucinatory drugs. They are pressured toward the psychedelic by the impossibility of achieving anything in the real world. "Mind expansion" is encouraged if there is no way of realizing ideas in the actual world. In Parkway, the taking of drugs declined markedly as the students' capacity for action increased. Instead of pressuring the student to live an inner, fantasy life, Parkway exerts pressure in the other direction by having no space of its own and by using the expertise of the citizens for educational purposes. If anything happens, it is because members of Parkway take the initiative, go out into the city, and make the city their curriculum by making it their campus.

The fifth and final aspect of Parkway's curriculum is contained in its catalogs, some pages of which are reproduced here. In it are listed conventional subjects, not so conventional subjects, and completely unconventional ones. The catalogs indicate that courses are taught by certified teachers, university interns, students, parents, individual volunteers, cultural institutions, businesses, social service agencies, and city employees. These courses are held in any part of the city, wherever is convenient, appropriate, helpful, or possible. Although

CAN WE LEARN TO HELP EACH OTHER?

BY HELPING EACH OTHER?

Sign Up

Conferences

1 TO 1

One-to-one conferences between members of the community.

To be held in the Resource Center.

Open the Eye of the Mind

Sign Up to teach and learn your favorite skills, hobbies, and subjects. Both participants will receive credit.

Helpers: Marlene Kravitz, Steve Wahrhaftig, Bobby Siefert, Marge Zabor, Jack, Don, Mary Jo, Beth, Julie, Lena, Paul, Ed, Stokes, Bob London, You...

SIGN UP WITH BOBBY SIEFERT

[48]

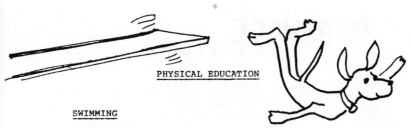

PHYSICAL EDUCATION

SWIMMING

A chance for free swim with instruction
if desired. We will use the Spring
Garden Community Center pool located
at 1812 Green Street.

Limited to ten students.

Wednesdays
9:45-10:45

Julie and Beth

SWIMMING

You may arrange to take swimming lessons
any afternoon at the Spring Garden Community
Center - 1812 Green Street. 3:00 in the
afternoon.

Swimming
1812 Greene Street
Any day at 3:00

KARATE

Theory class and practice.
Japanese karate.

Karate
Paxson Gym
Wednesday - 3:00

PHYSICAL EDUCATION FOR BOYS

This is a general course in phys. ed.
Calisthetntics and games

Phys Ed. for Boys
Paxson
Monday- 1:00-2:45

Julius Bennett

RESOURCE CENTER

The Resource Center is a lot like what Bobby's room was last quarter... only bigger, and, we hope, even better. It will include MATH and SOCIAL STUDIES as well as **ENGLISH**. You can wander in at any time between

        9 - 11 on M T W Th F
        1 - 4:30 M T   Th .

There are lots of things going on; join in or do your own thing.

write a painting
make a tape
work in the library
PROBE
talk, read, write
rehearse a play
SCRIBBAGE share information
GAMES
Battleships
MAPS
share information
You can Help Others
FRITZ
fieldtrips
compose songs
do an underground newspaper
you can learn
Poems
sense relaxation
try your latest idea

ALSO there are people available at any time if you'd like help with something...

- if you're having trouble with a book for another class
- if someone assigned a research paper, and you don't know how to write one
- if you can't find a good poem on love
- if you're having trouble reading your own handwriting
- if you're tired of those jive words like "supercilious" and not knowing what they mean...

Resource Center staff: Mary Jo, Jack, Don, Stokes, Bobby, Nancy, Julie, Marge, Lena, Judy, Beth, Bob London, and a cast of thousands.

CREDIT MAY BE ASSIGNED FOR ANY WORK IN THE RESOURCE CENTER, IF YOU'RE INTERESTED IN THAT....

THIS NEED NOT BE A COURSE & YOU NEED NOT REGISTER FOR IT.

SOCIAL STUDIES

THE UNITED STATES AND WORLD AFFAIRS

A course in world cultures and modern history for
people who are not well versed in this field and
want to understand what's happening. What tensions
are developing in the Middle-East, in Southeast
Asia, in the underdeveloped lands newly freed from
colonialism, and in the confrontations between new
empires like Russia, China and America. We'll try
to make sense out of the muddle of history by setting up a skeleton outline of what has and what is
taking place. We all need to know what the great
powers may do as history moves from crisis to crisis. Where are we going? What has the past taught
us? One way in which we will approach other cultures
is through the leading figures in other lands: temper-
aments like Freud or Sartre, Strauss or Huxley; per-
sonalities like Churchill, Charles de Gaulle, and Hitler;
revolutionaries like Marx, Lenin, Stalin, Castro, Che
Guevera, Mao, and Ho; economists like Adam Smith, Keynes,
and Galbraith, etc.

U.S. & World
Affairs

Wed. 3:15 – 5:00
(or anytime)

William L. Smyser,
U.S. Diplomat,
Lecturer on Inter-
national Relations
at U. of Pa.,
Columnist, Critic

(ME 5-2018)

MUNICIPAL AFFAIRS

INSTRUCTOR: Committee of Seventy
TIME: 9 - 10:45
PLACE: 1420 Walnut Street
             Suite 910
             KI5-7017

Mun. Affairs

Wed. 9-10:45
1420 Walnut Street
Suite 910

DESCRIPTION: History and structure of Philadelphia
government- Political party history and structure -
municipal finances - legislative process - court
system - election procedures - campaigning -
regional transportation - housing and redevelopment -
city planning- (This is a continuation of last
quarter's course, however, new students are welcome.)

WEDNESDAY

WHEN ARE WE GOING TO GET IT TOGETHER
AND RUN THE SCHOOL DEMOCRATICALLY??

WE HAVE A GREAT BUNCH OF PEOPLE WHY
DON'T WE HAVE A
COMMUNITY?
WE HAVE TIME ON
WEDNESDAY AFTER-
NOONS - WE CAN
WATCH MOVIES OR
PLAY GAMES - you
mean we can do
WHAT WE WANT TO
DO? we can sing
songs or dance or
talk or read or
build a house or?
WE CAN DO WHAT WE
WANT TO DO WE CAN
DO WHAT WE WANT TO
DO WE CAN DO WHAT
WE WANT TO DO IF WE
GET TOGETHER AND
DECIDE PEOPLE ARE
LISTENING -- ITS OUR
SCHOOL HOW DO WE RUN
IT? WHAT DOYOU WANT
TO DO? we can have
speakers and learn
about the panthers,
WELFARE RIGHTS, SHAPP

HOW ABOUT SOME MORE
IDEAS   HOW ABOUT SOME
STUDENT IDEAS?????????

HOW ABOUT STUDENT GOVT?
I WANT TO MEET MORE OF
THE PEOPLE
AND
GET   NOW
TO
KNOW THEM BETTER

WE CAN WATCH MOVIES
OR HAVE A TOWN MEETING
LETS HAVE A TOGETHER
COMMUNITY?? YOUMEAN
WHERE EVERYBODY GETS
A SAY ?? YES YES YES
AND EVERYBODY HAS TO
GIVE THEIR OPINION???
YESYESYES we candance
ortalk or play games we
can just have fun and be together YEA
YEAYEATOGETHERYEAWEDNESDAYAFTERNOONYEA

SOCIAL SCIENCES

THE REBIRTH OF WONDER (1)

Getting into clouds, shadows, unrises, lemons, and anything else you haven't noticed for a while.

(Limited to five students.)

WONDER
Julie
Thursday
1-3:00
Paxson

AFTER KIDS WITH LITTLE NOONS

Students wishing to tutor or just "be with" elementary students are welcome. In order to receive credit, high school students will be asked to attend a minimum of one session per week on a regular basis. The elementary kids are fun and full of love. They need your help. Sign up for two (2) possible days, please.

KIDS
3:30-4:30
Julie and
Beth
Paxson

_____Monday

_____Tuesday

_____Wednesday

_____Thursday

_____Friday

THE DEVELOPMENT AND WORKINGS OF LAW

Development from Sumer on. How it grew, how it developed, and how it works now.

Mrs. Polen teaches "Legal Memoranda" at the University of Pennsylvania Law School, and also has a private law practice of her own.

Devel. & Work. of Law
Tues. & Thurs.
9 - 11
Esther Polen
(Lo 8-5700)

[53]

ENGLISH

COLLEGE BOARD PREPARATION

Tips on test-taking, practice in taking
sample tests, gimmicks, and games for
vocabularly building, beginning speed
reading.
WE ESPECIALLY URGE 9th and 10th graders
who intend going to college to start
EARLY, and not wait until 11th grade

C.B. PREP.

Th,Fri. 9-11
4th and Arch
Bobby Seifert
Marge Zabor
Bob Stokes

TRIPS

A trip means many things to many people.
To me it means learning to see things
you could not see before.
Classes will meet twice a week, once for
an excursion; once for planning, thinking,
language arts session.
We can go to: the zoo, arsenal, Acme back-
stage, hermit's cave, Italian Market, YGS,
movie studio, Greek restaurant, court trial,
etc.
An opportunity to develop a meaningful relationship between teacher and students.

TRIPS

Mon,Fri.
3-5:00
(app.)
Marge Zabor

WIP RADIO II

A continuation of last quarter's course for
the production of our half-hour documentary
on Parkway. We need 10 people altogether and
people from last quarter will have priority-
There will probably be 3 new openings. Do not
take this course unless you are prepared to
WORK.

WIP RADIO II

Wed. 9-11
Wellington Bldg
19th and Walnut

FRITZ*FRITZ*FRITZ*FRITZ
FRITZ*FRITZ*FRITZ*FRITZ

FRITZ, THE DYNAMIC (?) PAPER OF PAXSON,

IS BEING OFFERED FOR ENGLISH CREDIT. I

WOULD LIKE TO SEE A REGULAR NEWSPAPER STAFF

FORMED WITH ITS OWN STUDENT EDITORS,

    REPORTERS

                              TU. & TH. 9-11

       ARTISTS

    WRITERS

       ETC,

THE "COURSE" WORK WILL CONSIST ENTIRELY

OF OPERATING THE PAPER. THERE SHOULD

BE 150 PEOPLE IN THIS COURSE.

        WHY?

BECAUSE EVERYONE IN PAXSON HAS

     SOMETHING TO SAY....

(YOU CAN SAY THAT AGAIN AGAIN AGAIN
AGAIN AGAIN AGAIN
AGAIN AGAIN AGAIN

THIS IS THE
BASIC QUESTION:
WHERE ARE YOU?

	MON	TUES	WED	THURS	FRI	SAT
9-11:00						
11:15-12:15	TUTORIAL		MANAGE-MENT GROUPS	TUTORIAL		
LUNCH 12:15-1:00		LUNCH	LUNCH	LUNCH	LUNCH	LUNCH
1:00-2:45			Keep this open!			
3:00-4:30						
after-noon + evening						

this list of courses resembles, in form, the curriculum of an ordinary school, it should never be forgotten that the preparation of the catalog (that is, the creation of the curriculum) is part of the curriculum.

In reflecting on the Gamma catalog, it should be remembered that it provides the curriculum, in the conventional sense, for one hundred and fifty students. The other units in Parkway have similar catalogs. Catalog in hand, the Parkway student, during the vacation, chooses with his parents what he will study the next term. Which brings the curriculum back to freedom.

3
The Faculty

In the past, the teacher was defined and respected in terms of his mastery of subject matter. This mastery was reflected in the state requirements for certification, at least at the secondary school level, and was further buttressed by the learning requirements necessary for a student's graduation. A student was and is compelled to study so many years of science, let us say, under the tutelage of a fully qualified, that is, a certified, teacher of that subject. The elementary school teacher, on the other hand, was often considered to be a mere baby-sitter, not requiring any subject-matter mastery, only a smattering of knowledge derived from "education" courses. This was often reflected in a lower pay scale.

Times are changing and some improvements have been made, but subject-matter mastery is still in the forefront of many people's minds, and learning is still thought of in terms of the conventional — and now antiquated — subjects. "*What* are you teaching?" "*What* are students learning?" These questions continue to be raised, and for some strange reason, the most satisfactory answers to them always turn out to be "Trigonometry" or "Synonyms and antonyms," for example. On hearing these replies, people think they have substantive and precise answers. To try to answer in terms of ability to be effective in a process, in terms of managerial ability, in terms of skills, only produces disbelief and amazement. Some teachers, particularly in social studies, have tried to emphasize the acquisition of skills over the memorization of subject matter, simply because they understand that the skills are the content of their teaching. Final examinations are still framed in terms of subject matter and not in terms of skills, however. It seems that courses such as typing, pottery, and woodworking have a tremendous advantage because they are kept honest by the frank acknowledgment that they are how-to-do-it courses and not "academic" courses, or courses in "appreciation."

There is much confusion about the qualifications for teaching, and although the old ways of teacher training are unsatisfactory, the universities are still trying to catch up with the invention of printing. In the selection of faculty for the Parkway Program, a number of principles were laid down:

1. State-certified teachers were assumed to be fully competent in their subject areas.

2. Only self-selected teachers would be accepted; that is, they would all be volunteers.

3. The particular virtues sought in potential Parkway teachers were not dealt with by state certification procedures but were general human qualities, managerial skills, emotional stability, and, above all, the capacity to learn.

Since the Parkway Program represents a marked departure from traditional school organization, curriculum, and teaching methods, one might have expected public high school teachers to avoid it. This did not turn out to be the case, however. Instead, there were many applications from men and women already certified to teach in the Philadelphia school system, so that the original faculty was recruited entirely from that source. This was a matter of principle with John Bremer, who believed that if the program was to be successful, it had to work with teachers and students already in the system. He did not feel that success required the presence of an elite from Harvard, Chicago, or Stanford but simply the liberated energy of ordinary humans freed from the corruption of a system the universities help to perpetuate. It had also been the practice of elitist superintendents to import people from outside to work in special programs, thus denying teachers with many years of devoted service the opportunity to benefit from improved educational programs. This, too, the director felt was wrong. Finally, to take experienced teachers from the system improved the chances of helping the system as a whole improve itself; it had nowhere else to look for help.

If Parkway teachers resembled their counterparts in other schools, the manner of selecting them was notably different, especially in the fact that high school students were involved in the selection process.

The program was to open in February 1969, but interested teachers contacted John Bremer throughout the preceding summer. The names of these individuals were kept, and in December Bremer wrote to each of them. Eight full-time faculty members were to be selected for a student body of 120. Were the teachers still interested? If so, applications, with resumes and brief statements of the contribution each teacher believed he could make, would be welcome by January 3d. Eighty teachers applied.

Meanwhile, Bremer met with civic groups, describing the forthcoming Parkway Program to Philadelphians of all ages, some connected with the public schools and some not. With the help of persons whom he met in this way, Bremer formed a number of voluntary, unpaid committees to screen teacher applicants.

Each committee included (1) a high school student, (2) a professional educator not then teaching in the public schools, (3) either a parent of a high school student or an active member of a community organization, and (4) a college student. (These were drawn from a number of Antioch [Ohio] College students who were in Philadelphia as part of a program in which they spent time away from campus working for government, industry, and cooperating institutions, of which the Parkway Program was one.)

Dan Shapiro has described the first screening of the eighty teacher applicants:

> It was a beautiful scene. Broken into four subcommittees, each committee's job was to screen teacher applicants. The committees were allowed to spend twenty minutes in the interview and ten minutes to evaluate the teachers. The evaluation was to be done on a sheet handed to each member of the subcommittee for each teacher interviewed. The teachers were given an over-all grade from one to five in various areas and there was space for the comments of the individual screeners.
>
> Each screening committee consisted of at least one high school student, one co-op student, one member of the community (either a parent or an active member of a community organization) and a person from the field of education. Some committees were larger.
>
> In the screening committee, there were no prescribed criteria for what a teacher had to be. Each person asked questions and started discussions with the teacher on things that he felt relevant to help him find whether or not this would be someone well suited to the Parkway Program.
>
> The teacher was allowed time to ask questions, was usually introduced to the members of the screening committee, and

was told who they were. After the screening, they then went to see John [Bremer] and George Crowell [an Antioch co-op student] as a second stage to this first screening and they could then ask any questions about either the procedure or the Parkway project. John and George also made an evaluation and handed in sheets. There was little or no adverse reaction to this type of screening on the part of teachers or the screeners. The sessions were generally very intelligently handled, the high school and college students especially had pertinent questions to ask. As a personal comment, it was certainly a beautiful learning experience for everyone involved. The teachers were exposed to members of the community in an open discussion, along with high school and college students and got an insight into a different way of screening teachers, and also an introduction to the kind of style that Parkway Program would be using. I'm sure the students, members of the community, and members of the board of education learned a great deal by this fairly large exposure to the teachers in the school system. We would assume that the ones that would apply to be teachers at the Parkway Program would be the cream of the Philadelphia school system. Wow!

Out of the eighty teachers that applied, twenty (later twenty-three) of them were to be selected for further screening.

The panel members asked the applicants a variety of questions, and what one panel asked another did not. But nobody talked as though a faculty member should teach *at* a student.

Mrs. Dan Shapiro, who served on a panel, recalls that members asked why the teachers wanted to join the program; how they felt about experimental education; whether they thought black children required special help; and how they liked being screened by students.

Cy Swartz, an applicant who was to direct Parkway's third unit in 1969–1970, remembers being asked about his teaching methods and whether he thought children should have a voice in constructing their own curriculum. A Puerto Rican mother on the panel also questioned Swartz's evaluation of his own ability to listen to children and to communicate with them.

Anita Hackney, who became a teacher in the Parkway Program and later was unit head at Alpha, recalls that one panel member asked what black authors she was familiar with; another wanted to know whether she thought black teachers were better for black children; and a third sought her opinion as to the desirability of teaching from a prepared lesson plan, drawn up a week in advance in accordance with material furnished by the school district.

[61]

Anita Hackney, Natalie Shapiro, and Cy Swartz all remember that the panel put hypothetical questions to the applicants. For example: a student asks advice on what college to apply for. You recommend a technical institute. The student replies that he assumed you would name any one of several small liberal arts colleges. What do you do next? If what you do depends upon additional factors not mentioned in the hypothetical question, what are they?

In this informal way, with questions and answers and a great deal of talk, community influence and a measure of student participation were brought to the process of selecting a faculty.

The applicants for the second part of the screening process were selected by averaging the scores given in the first evaluation, adding one point for any significant experience outside the traditional teaching field (such as Peace Corps work), dividing the applicants into groups according to whether they had taught English, mathematics, social studies, science, foreign languages, or business education, and then inviting applicants to the number of twenty-three, selected from the top members of each subject-matter group, to return for further screening. The use of subject matters as a factor was a concession to traditional expectations and the need to meet state requirements.

At the second screening, the twenty-three men and women formed new groups and were told: "As you know, there are eight faculty places to be filled and there are twenty-three in this group. Please discuss this problem." Members of the original citizen screening panels observed while the applicants took part in this exercise. Then the panel members sat down with John Bremer and considered which of the applicants should be offered positions.

This was not an easy task. The following is an instructive example. The director had known no one in Philadelphia before his arrival, although he had met and talked with a small number of people in the school district on one or two occasions. He believed that one man he had met was a sound, knowledgeable administrator who would be of great service to the Parkway Program. He had a fine record, was clearly very concerned about students, knew Philadelphia and its system, and was interested in joining the program. This individual went through the screening process and to Bremer's disappointment did not score high enough to be invited back. After discussing the matter with some of the Antioch interns, and aware of the danger, Bremer invited him back anyway. The second screening process eliminated him again, quite unmistakably. This put the director in a quandary—he wanted the man, but believed in his process. The process won. But having reaffirmed the process he himself had quite freely invented, he learned that he wanted this fine administrator because of his own doubts and misgivings. A small part of the director had not matured. He still wanted to be respectable and safe, and his commitment to the man signified a remaining commitment to the establishment.

The decision not to appoint the man was right as it turned out; the process was correct and Bremer was not. However, the rightness of the decision had nothing to do with the qualities of the candidate (which were excellent), but rather with Bremer's reasons for wanting him.

From the second screening process, nine candidates were appointed instead of the anticipated eight. The reasons had to do with subject-matter coverage and the distribution of personal qualities. It was held that a certain range was desirable, and the range could not be covered with eight teachers. The pioneers, in addition to the director, were Penny Bach, Tina Craig, Anita Hackney, Dorice Wright, Matt Hickey, Ralph Kendricks, Mark Lyons, Cy Swartz, and one other man who, in his own words, "found it hard to communicate with the students" in Parkway's setting and left after about six weeks. Bremer, at forty-two, was older than any of the faculty, the youngest of whom was twenty-three. There were four women and five men, four blacks and five whites, one with eleven years experience and one with less than one.

The screening process was designed to help people see what might be called general human qualities (in themselves as well as in others) and to experience some of the uncertainty and anxiety that would be unavoidable in Parkway once it began. Thus, it gave prospective teachers an opportunity to feel what it would be like to be in the program, plus a chance to interview Bremer.

The second time faculty were appointed there were about three hundred applicants from all over the country, not just Philadelphia. There had been no advertising for faculty; interested teachers simply wrote and expressed their interest in joining Parkway. The first screening reduced the number to about fifty, and the second produced the required eighteen (for two new units).

Although some faculty have left for personal reasons, during the first two years only the teacher mentioned earlier left Parkway because of dissatisfaction and inability to help students learn in the program's structure.

Before considering the faculty function, it is as well to remember one of the principles of Parkway: that the city is full of experts—people who utilize specialized knowledge as part of their daily lives—and Parkway taps these individuals to teach their special subject matter. Apart from certified teachers (who are invited to offer whatever courses they wish and as many as they wish), university students or interns offer courses of study, as do administrators, secretaries in the program, students, parents, outside volunteers, institutional and business representatives, city, state, and federal employees, and workers in various social agencies. No offer of help is refused; it becomes an item in some unit's catalog. Of course, this means that Parkway is guilty of the heresy that it is possible to learn from unlicensed personnel. One doesn't have to be certified in order to teach, and nobody ever thought otherwise. Parkway merely accepts the reality. However, Parkway does not think that teachers are unimportant or dispensable. On the contrary, they are vital and essential and in approximately the same proportion to students as in traditional schools—about nine faculty to one hundred and sixty students at this time. It is simply that their job is different, and it does not depend mainly on mastery of conventional subject matter.

In the first place, the faculty are treated like responsible professionals. Their task is to help the students learn; they are simply asked to get on with it. The only requirement, as with the students, is that they belong to a tutorial. Apart from that, they decide how to use their time—whether to teach formal courses and, if so, how many and in what subjects. If they wish to spend more of their time with individual students —talking, counseling, socializing, and sharing—that is their own decision. As a consequence, the teachers feel differently about themselves, about their task, and therefore about the students. These quotations from the *American Teacher*, the official publication of the American Federation of Teachers (Vol. 54, No. 5, January 1970), make the point admirably:

> For example, Beta unit teacher Sheldon Berman, like most of the Parkway faculty a member of the Philadelphia Federation of Teachers, says one of his classrooms is in the basement of a Y some blocks from the old warehouse on Cherry Street where Beta sits. "It's a little psychedelic," he notes, adding, "I also use the executive boardroom of Pomerantz," a business firm still farther away, "and it is really interesting to see the kids tramp through. They get a chance to see what's happening, and the people there get used to the kids."
>
> Berman teaches math courses ranging from a class for kids who are "uptight" about math to advanced functions and logic. "If the idea of the Parkway School was institutionalized from K up, children would blossom as is undreamed of now," he says. In describing his vision, Berman's round 23-year-old face, rimmed by shoulder-length hair, beams as if the blossoming children were standing before him. "Teaching here is unbelievable," he adds. "It's like a way of life. In regular schools, teachers are condescending; kids are taught not to think but to regurgitate. Some kids will never get over

these hangups. By the time we get them they've been fed the whole story for nine years, and the patterns are already well established. But some are really educating themselves in the Parkway way."

More explicitly:

HE'S "HEAD TEACHER"

Cy Swartz, Paxson's administrator, is actually "head teacher." He is 32, and was membership chairman of Local 3 from 1959 to 1962, when it was building up to win a collective-bargaining agent election. "Belonging to the union in those days was unpopular," he remembers. "We were the left-wingers. But things have changed. For example," he said, "we've gotten salaries up to levels we never even dreamed possible, but most teachers are still moonlighting. We have pay for extra-curricular activities, but what are they spending the money on? I remember when we had our first picket line in 1959, around the board of education on a Saturday, because we weren't brave enough to leave school. We got 500 people out, and Al Shanker, who was membership chairman of the UFT, came down and picketed with us.

"You realize," Swartz continued, "that I'm not an administrator. I'm a teacher. Our perception is that this is a rotating job; you spend two years helping the teachers in this kind of community. Our work here cuts through all the administrative lines, a structural difference that allows us to behave toward our children in a different way.

"I think," Swartz went on, "we're really on to something. First, we use the community resources. We couldn't have our class size what it is unless we had the institutional offerings. Second, we use teachers' energies in a totally different way. We've removed the conflicts. Teachers usually say, 'Well, I can't do such and such because of the principal. If he'd only do this or this,' and the principal says that about the people above him, and everyone passes the buck. It's the same with the kids.

"We're very much in consonance with the spirit of unions in the past. Our union should be in the forefront of working for new kinds of elementary structure. Here, we accept each others' differences. We enhance our individuality and our kids' individuality. Our staff meetings in the high school are open to the kids. We don't let them talk, because it's the one

[65]

time we have to get together, but they do talk, and the parents and community talk, at our "town meetings."

And finally:

> Bernie Ivens, like Swartz a Local 3 stalwart (building representative at West Philadelphia High School for the last five years, and a nine-year veteran of the Philadelphia system), says, "Here, you're treated like a professional, and you act like one. For example, in the Philadelphia system, they don't give you your paycheck until 2 P.M. on the last day of school. They do that to keep you there until 2 P.M. Well, teachers say to themselves, 'Okay, you play your stupid little game, I'll play mine.' Here, it's like a partnership between staff, parents, and students. It is an integrated, community-controlled school.
>
> "Kids' hangups and problems are not really that obvious in a regular school," Ivens continued. "Here things are in the open and obvious.
>
> "We had this about a month ago in one of our town meetings. A lot of talking was being done by white kids and that's when decisions are made, the government of the school—we've had some loud, screaming meetings—well, 80 or 90 persons showed up, and a large group walked out. It's something we will have to work out ourselves."
>
> Ivens, who is 35, said that "when you teach in a regular school, you become an SOB. 'I'm sorry, I can't get around to you; there are 34 other people,' 'Sit down because I told you to sit down.'
>
> "My daughter Debbie is here at Paxson with me. Last year she brought home a paper from school with the word 'Philadelphia' marked out; her teacher told her she had spelled it wrong. She took the paper up to him and pointed out she had spelled it right. He pushed her away from his desk."

One may well ask, "But don't teachers goof off?" In the first place, everyone "goofs off," that is, needs time for *not* doing something. Students goof off, teachers goof off, the superintendent goofs off (only it is called attending conferences). It is human. In the second place, the intimate structure of Parkway, and the size of its units, keep people accountable to one another in a sustained but informal way. If you let people down, you have to live with their opinion of you. Most Parkway faculty do not need to do this, for their reputations among the students are, for the most part, good, and their reputations are the outcome of their behavior.

If teachers are structurally defined as lazy, careless, and irresponsible, they tend to behave as if they were. In Parkway teachers are structurally defined as hard working, energetic, and responsible, and they tend to conform to the role definition provided for them. Teachers in conventional schools are often unfairly criticized because they have conformed to the role that the system has defined for them, and it is for this reason that the system has to be changed. It is the system that has corrupted many of the teachers, and it is the system that has endorsed the labor-management dichotomy in education, and then has embittered that relation. If superintendents were more imaginative administrators, they would seek to change this structure, but they are as much controlled by the system as the teachers.

All of this points to new skills that teachers — indeed, all educators — must have. They must be masters of new subject matters, but the subject matters are not inert bodies of knowledge, not academics but *activities*, not products but processes. They are the skills that Parkway students learn: the social skills of cooperation, the political skills of management, and the interactional skills of communication. Parkway faculty have begun to acquire these skills, and this is what justifies them as teachers, since it is through them that students are helped to learn. It is possible to help somebody learn something that you yourself do not know. If this were not so, knowledge could not increase at all. But it is the knowing *how* that now must take precedence over knowing *what*. The *knowing how* is what characterizes the Parkway faculty.

4

A Student's Day

For Colette, the road to Parkway had many turnings. Born in October 1953, she attended country day and convent schools in the United States and in Ireland until the spring of 1969, when she heard about the Parkway Program. At this time, Colette's family was living in Philadelphia's Chestnut Hill community and she was a student at the Shipley School, a private girls' school on the Main Line.

Numbering the wives and daughters of leaders in this country's Protestant establishment among its alumnae, Shipley is one of the foremost boarding and day schools for young ladies. At a glance, its alumnae directory yields the names of a Cabot, four Rockefellers, a Firestone, eight Pews, and a solitary Pillsbury. Colette liked the school and appreciated its high academic standards. Shipley is conventional but top drawer. Headmistress Isota Tucker Epes brooked no nonsense and saw to it that the students studied, although she was open to new ideas and invited John Bremer of Parkway to meet with the students and faculty of her school. When Colette learned about Parkway and saw how involved with the community it was, she applied for admission and was selected in the June 1969 drawing. Then she left Shipley, to return one morning in the following spring—as a guest, invited to address her former fellow-students on the subject of her education. On this occasion, Colette described a day at Parkway. Let us join her for such a day.

Rising at seven, Colette made her breakfast, tidied her room, and then walked a block to a Penn Central Railroad station to catch the 8:04 train for the twenty-eight minute run to downtown Philadelphia.

The end of the line is Penn Center Station, at 16th Street and John F.

Kennedy Boulevard, not far from the Benjamin Franklin Parkway. But today Colette's first class took her south and east, away from the Parkway, to the Hall Mercer Hospital, at 8th and Locust streets, some twelve blocks from the railroad station. This was for a meeting of her tutorial group.

In the fall, Colette's tutorial had met at 4th and Poplar streets in the inner city, using space provided by the Dolly Madison Ice Cream Company. Then the tutorial leader had advised the students on which streets to walk the few blocks from Gamma headquarters, minimizing the chance that the presence of strange young people would antagonize neighborhood gangs. On this spring morning, however, Colette passed City Hall, then office buildings and banks, as she walked down Broad Street by the Union League Club, paused to inspect the window of Shapp for Governor Headquarters, and passed the Academy of Music. She then turned left and walked along Locust Street, with its supper clubs and honky-tonk bars, until she reached Hall Mercer Hospital, an affiliate of the Pennsylvania Hospital, where members of her tutorial were already gathering.

Seven boys and eight girls were there, with faculty members Julius Bennett and Nancy Donovan, he a veteran history teacher who came to the Parkway Program from the city's regular public schools, she, young, pretty, and an English major recently graduated from the University of Massachusetts. It was Bennett who had been so solicitous of the students' safety when the group met at the ice cream company. This spring he had accomplished something for their comfort as well: arranging for tutorials at Hall Mercer when he learned that the meeting room there opened onto a small garden which the class could use in nice weather.

Now the sun was shining, the day was warm. The girls repaired to the garden with Nancy to discuss a subject some of them had brought up the week before—a local campaign, much publicized, in which feminists were seeking the legalization of abortions. Nancy suggested that they divide into sides for this discussion, and this they did, some advocating abortions for any women who wanted them, others taking the opposite view, all of them bringing into the debate things they had heard and read, then talking them over, back and forth. This was instruction in science, social studies, and law, with a bit of theology thrown in. When it ended, indecisively, Nancy Donovan suggested that the girls take turns reading aloud from Shirley Jackson's short story "The Lottery." Then the class adjourned, arranging to meet with Bennett, Nancy, and the boys for tutorial in Fairmount Park the next day.

Since the boys needed special work in mathematics, they sometimes met separately from the girls. Today Bennett helped some with their math workbooks, showed others how to use number ladders with plus and negative factors, and then encouraged them to play with number cards, flashing each other problems for instant answers. When two of the boys ceased this activity, it was to read and write, one of them immersing himself in *The Time Machine* by H. G. Wells while the other busied himself with a letter. Intimately acquainted with each youngster's progress in the basic skills of language and mathematics, Bennett saw that all of them used their time wisely before they too left for other classes, to meet with him, with Nancy, and with the girls in the park the next day.

For Colette, the next stop was three blocks away at 1001 Chestnut Street, headquarters of the Vietnam Moratorium Committee. There she worked for an hour, answering the telephone and filling orders for buttons and literature. Then she met a friend for lunch at Martindale's, a health food bar on 11th Street, south of Market Street, just two blocks from the Vietnam committee's offices and across from Philadelphia's Community College.

Lunch completed, Colette window shopped for a few minutes, then took a bus across town to the headquarters of Gamma unit in an old school building at 6th and Buttonwood streets in the inner city. There Colette had a class of almost two hours in geometry taught by Bernie Ivens. In Ivens' class, a standard text was used, there was assigned homework, and the atmosphere in some ways resembled that of a traditional school. The students gave their teacher rapt attention, however, bringing their chairs to the front of the room so that they might do so. A visitor noted that when a boy or girl had to leave, this was done quietly, but without seeking permission. In each case, the departing student returned in a few minutes.

Bernie Ivens' class ended shortly before 3 P.M. Using public transportation again, Colette then traveled south and west into a quiet residential area of row houses where, at 705 North 25th Street, she joined students from Alpha unit who were working in the offices of James Reid Thomson, an architect. Here the students gathered to design houses and school buildings (some using drafting equipment, others cutting them out of cardboard), to talk with Thomson, and to explore his library of books on architecture and city planning. Class went on for a minimum of two hours, but a number of the young people came early, again and again, spending all afternoon in the office. On occasion, Mrs. Thomson served them cookies and ice cream. Then the conversation ran to every aspect of the city's life, the young people attending avidly to Thomson, who had lectured in this country and in Germany, and he listening to their views with equal respect. To Colette, this was the best time of a fascinating day, one which had taken her through the city's financial district, into the administrative area of a hospital, to the offices of a citizens' committee interested in foreign affairs, out for lunch, and then to geometry class before spending a glorious two hours in the architect's office. Upon leaving Thomson's office, she went a few blocks out of her way to see the Van Gogh exhibit at the Philadelphia Museum of Art. On her way to the train that would take her home, she strolled down the Benjamin Franklin Parkway, past the Rodin Museum, the Youth Study Center, the Franklin Institute, Moore College of Art, the Academy of Natural Sciences, and the Insurance Company of North America building.

Colette's complete schedule for the spring semester of 1970 is included here.

	Monday	Tuesday	Wednesday	Thursday	Friday
9:00 A.M.	Leather Workshop	Tutorial		Vietnam Moratorium Committee	Philosophy
10:00 A.M.		Vietnam Moratorium Committee			
11:15 A.M.	Tutorial		Management Group	Tutorial	Tutorial
1:00 P.M.		Geometry			
1:45 P.M.	Spanish		Town Meeting		
3:00 P.M.		Architecture	Foreign Policy	Issues in Science	Issues in Science
5:00 P.M.					
8:00 P.M.			Oriental Religions		
10:00 P.M.					

Miles from Colette's home, at 2240 West Susquehanna Avenue in the heart of the inner city, Emmanuel Havens rose at seven to start his day in the Parkway Program.

For Manny, Parkway came as a deliverance. A talented, sensitive boy with a bent for drawing apparent since the age of five, he had found himself at sixteen one of 4000 students attending Olney High School, as destructive an experience as one could have in the Philadelphia school system. Olney has had a troubled history, marked by violence between Jewish youths and self-styled Fascists in the 1950s and between blacks and whites a decade later.

Robert Rafsky, a perceptive observer, described the situation at Olney for the *Philadelphia Evening Bulletin:*

> Many lavatories in the school are locked all day because there isn't enough staff to patrol them. Keeping order in the lunchroom is a daily struggle. Towards the end of the day, when nonteaching assistants and other security personnel eat lunch, the halls become chaotic.

Apart from racial tension, it is clear that the young people hate the school. And the teachers know it.

"If the kids hate us because they hate all institutions," a veteran faculty member observed, "There's nothing we can do about it, as teachers. But if they hate us because of our courses, or the way we teach, that's something else."

The same teacher described the school curriculum as "basically the same as it was thirty-five years ago." It is up to teachers to become more involved in changing the school curriculum, he remarked. Little was done about this, however. Instead, it was proposed to hire a permanent group of security officers, to do away with assemblies and homerooms (where students might gather), and to cut lunch periods to twenty minutes.

Divide and conquer; deny the enemy, the children, any chance to associate freely! Emmanuel Havens, young, black, sensitive, and artistic, was in the hands of a system which fell back on such ideas as these.

Even worse Olney High School offered him only one art course, for thirty minutes a week.

Manny's mother heard about the Parkway Program and he applied. His name was pulled out of the hat, and in February 1969, Emmanuel Havens bid goodbye to Olney High School.

To his surprise, when Manny came to Parkway, he soon found himself working harder than he had ever worked in his life, approaching the basic skills of English and mathematics as though they might be instruments of his salvation.

He also found outlets for his artistic talents. On Saturdays, he worked at the Moore College of Art, a degree-granting institution on the Benjamin Franklin Parkway that opened its doors to the students in the new program. He also studied design at the Philadelphia Center for Cultural Studies, at 45th and Spruce streets, more than fifty blocks from Moore College. Manny was covering a large part of the city, but between the two institutions he received training that could hardly have been offered by the art departments of the finest prep schools.

Through a visitor to Parkway, the San Francisco Art Institute learned about Manny's ability and his aspirations. In the spring of 1970, he flew to the West Coast at the Institute's expense. Manny had reason to hope that a scholarship to study in San Francisco or elsewhere would eventually be his.

This is the story—the opening chapters, at least—of one boy, rescued from a traditional city high school, his horizons expanded by the luck of the draw, whose talents were given a more reasonable opportunity.

5

Student, Teacher, and Program Evaluation

It often seems that what is learned is less important than whether it can be measured. The measure may be quite unscientific, or it may be of something which has little educational significance, but there is a constant pressure to reduce learning to numbers, or, at least, to letter grades. The insistence on this kind of evaluation represents a psychological type which often uses the rhetoric of measurement as a means of maintaining control, but educationally it can scarcely be taken seriously.

If evaluation is to be of any educational worth, it cannot be regarded, as it is in most schools, as a postmortem that takes place after the student has died. Evaluation must become an integral part of the total learning process and not an appendage to it. True evaluation takes place on a day-to-day, or, more accurately, a minute-to-minute, basis, but this is possible only in a learning community structured to encourage spontaneous feedback and which thereby permits interaction. Above all, it should be remembered that the student must learn how to evaluate; evaluation is a subject matter for him, and he learns it only by doing it. Therefore, he must himself participate in the evaluation process. It is not something that is done to him.

The final danger of the current philosophy of evaluation is that it arranges the student body in a hierarchy, and in ranking students, it divides and splits them. The practice may make control easier, but it does not noticeably improve the learning process.

Parkway's way is the abolition of marks, grades, or class standings. A student either earns credit for a course or he does not.

Some people call this a pass-fail system, but, in fact, the terminology

[74]

of passing and failing is not employed in the Parkway Program. In its stead, there is a system of written evaluations.

Teachers evaluate students.

Students evaluate courses.

Students evaluate themselves.

Students evaluate teachers.

Parents evaluate the entire program.

But not necessarily in that order of importance.

Teachers evaluate the work of the students in terms of the form illustrated here. The completed form goes to the student and to his

---

THE PARKWAY PROGRAM
EVALUATION OF STUDENT'S WORK

STUDENT:_____TUTORIAL_____

SUBJECT:_____

COURSE TITLE:_____

Units of credit granted (if any): 1 unit = 120 classroom hours
1/10 unit = 1 hour per week for
12-week term

ATTENDANCE_____

Part One (To Be Completed by Course Instructor)

DESCRIPTION OF COURSE CONTENT:

EVALUATION OF STUDENT'S WORK (including academic, social, and emotional growth)

STUDENT'S SIGNATURE_____

_____
Instructor's Signature

_____
Unit Head's Signature

[75]

parents. Copies are made available to his future instructors and to college admissions officers.

Does it tell more or less than the traditional report card? The reader can judge for himself from the following samples of actual Parkway evaluations (portions of which are in italics for emphasis).

Course: Uptight about Math. Evaluation: Colette is a pleasure to have in class. This young lady puts forth a conscientious effort, completing all assignments and taking good notes. In addition, she works well with the elementary children.

Colette has an excellent understanding of the basic skills in mathematics. *I think, perhaps, that she was misplaced in this course and should pursue more challenging and complex topics in mathematics.*

Course: Law in Pennsylvania. Evaluation: Mary's performance in the classroom has been consistently excellent.

She followed all class discussions and displayed, both in writing and orally, a good understanding of legal terminology.

Her attendance was very good and her class notes were complete and well organized.

Aside from a reminder to her that reading will improve spelling, I have little else to add. She is quite a mature young lady.

Course: English. Evaluation: Josh has an unusual talent for writing. Together with a little commitment, he can produce some beautiful, imaginative work. *It's too bad that Josh sometimes succumbs to whims and doesn't finish what he begins.*

Course: Bookmaking and Binding. Evaluation: It could be said that Robin and Dan worked until the very last minute on their book, *The Lonely Witch.* The book is a magnificent effort by both of them. The combination of Robin's story and Dan's illustrations resulted in a meaningful experience (and product) for both. The 36 pages of linoleum cuts took many hours of patience to cut and print. *Although they could have saved themselves many hours of last-minute work to reach their deadline by budgeting their time more effectively,* I have nothing but praise for their finished product. Long live *The Lonely Witch!*

Course: Basic and Business Math. Evaluation: Joanne showed good attendance and *a willingness to work when pushed.* She got a better understanding of fractions especially and also practice with simple operations. She is still confused about parts of basic math and is slow with abstract concepts.

Course: Hopi Indians. Evaluation: Janet is much too worried about receiving credit and sometimes she will do work only to appease instead of for the enjoyment inherent in pursuing the subject. She is learning, however, that school "work" many times is both enjoyable and interesting. Her discussion of the topic "The Hopi and the White Man" showed a good comprehension of what she had read. She could have supplemented her class sessions with other research and perhaps have tried to provoke related discussion.

Course: Biology. Evaluation: *I was at first deceived by Marc's slowness of manner. I interpreted this to indicate a lack of interest. However, throughout the course he has shown a high level of interest and motivation.* His performance in laboratory and field trips has been extremely good. I am very much satisfied with his work.

Course: Photography Core. Evaluation: David can easily develop into a good student when he learns that he can learn from things which he dislikes. He is beginning and hopefully will continue to be open to new ideas and concepts. *Often he rejects too quickly, without thinking, things that could turn out to be real learning experiences for him.*

Consider the students whose evaluations were just given. If Colette and Mary had received A's, would that have told as much about them? Would a mediocre B— or C for Josh (who did not complete his work) have been as helpful to him or to his future teachers as the evaluation was? Isn't it clear that Marc's evaluation will help others understand this slow but interested and highly motivated boy? Could a 70 or a 75 grade have achieved the same result? Would any traditional mark or grade have said as much about William as the following evaluation by his tutorial leader?

William came to tutorial with basic problems in the area of reading and writing. After realizing the problem, we established a program of individual attention to furnish a better groundwork in these areas. William submitted weekly written assignments for evaluation, and he read special assignments constantly. His attitude towards this work was studious. He kept up with assignments and seemed to make a moderate amount of progress in reading. However, a great deal more work needs to be done. William worked well in group discussions, and at times showed definite leadership abilities. He is a sincere young man, who must learn to take more responsibility for his own future and work to be in possession of the basic skills. He can learn to read, he knows this, and he must learn to overcome the frustrations of learning those skills.

The foregoing is typical of extremely significant evaluations that come from the tutorial leaders. Consider these as well:

Robert and I developed a good relationship. We listened to each other and learned together. He shared in the activities but could have made more of a contribution had he been able to control his likes and dislikes. He needs to become far more tolerant than he is now.

Randy is a very active and usually enthusiastic member of our tutorial. He likes to have his own way and manage the group. He could be more effective if he would learn not to let his wishes predominate, and then try to find out what the group wants, and manage that, instead of just his own wish. I think Randy has grown more frank this semester. I like this in him. I think that Randy has it in him to do great things, but must face and control himself before he can begin to accomplish them.

Joan has the potential to make many worthwhile contributions. Her behavior was greatly influenced by those who lacked self-control. She needs to develop independent thought and action. She participated in every activity of the tutorial group, but not fully. I would like to have seen her more involved.

As we have said, evaluation is not a one-way street populated by teachers. Students, too, evaluate themselves, their courses, and their instructors. These appraisals of their progress and learning become part of the permanent record. Here are some evaluations by students:

Course: Bookmaking and Binding. Evaluation of Course: I think the course was very good. It was fun and interesting. I liked learning about lettering and design. It was a good way to learn how to plan time and design. Description of Personal Progress and Learning: I learned a lot about books and magazines that I never knew before—like how they are planned and layed out. I learned a lot about planning & design &

budgeting time. And also writing. Dan & I did a book, *The Lonely Witch*, together & learned how to cooperate. We made two copies. I did a lot of linoleum cuts for the book & really got good at cutting & printing them. I learned how to cover and bind books and what it feels like to accomplish something really big and worthwhile.

Course: Basic and Business Math. Evaluation of Course: The course was not as interesting as I thought it to be, because she kept giving us the same thing. Nothing new did I see, and the only reason I kept going was because I needed it and the credits. Description of Personal Progress and Learning: I felt as though I fell back because I wasn't getting the math I needed.

Would you learn from that, if you were the teacher? if you were the teacher's unit head? Of course you would. Now consider what another student said:

Course: Cities and Suburbs. Evaluation of Course: The course had trouble getting off the ground and I think that was the start of our problems. We didn't know where we were going or what we wanted to accomplish. We talked half-heartedly about some things, but it seemed as if there was no real goal or objective. . . . A lot of kids were lost who really shouldn't have been.

The speakers were good and I learned a lot from them, but they did not really fit into a pattern (they were not used to achieve some end goal). Nothing in the course was really held together. We went on trips, discussed what we saw, listened to speakers, and talked among ourselves. But in the end none of these things went together and pointed toward anything tangible which was accomplished. I feel we should have read Harrington the first week and started out doing some writing. . . .

Description of Personal Progress and Learning: The course opened up a lot of new things to me. I think Harrington's book was mainly responsible for this. I really gained a great deal from reading it. I never really realized what it was like to be poor and how many poor people there are in our country. I'll never know what a life of poverty is, unless I live it, but I feel I did see a lot from this book I never saw before.

I also began to understand some about city planning and redevelopment. I never thought about people planning redevelopment. I understand more about the workings of City

Hall. I realize I gained a lot of things that I cannot verbalize on, but I know that my learning did not point in one direction. It was a lot of jumbled realizations.

I think I had a lot of expectations about the course and felt let down after the first few weeks didn't move along. Then I lost some of my original interest and became lax about attendance — but I still cared about the course.

I'm very confused about my role in the class and also that of the faculty. I am disappointed in myself, but also feel that I am not entirely at fault. After reading my evaluation, I saw a part of myself which usually isn't pointed out to me — and a part I do not like to think about. Just those few words, written for me to read, were a part of my learning. I did gain from the course, but I guess not in the way I had expected to.

Course: Math. Evaluation of Course: I think the course was very interesting and the things we did in class was good. Description of Personal Progress and Learning: My progress was good but I think that if I could start where I stop at before, instead of going to another sheet, I would probably would done much better.

Students evaluate their teachers on this form:

STUDENT'S EVALUATION OF THE TEACHER

NAME OF TEACHER:_____

COURSE TITLE:_____

What were the best features of the teacher's teaching?

What were the worst features of his teaching, and what suggestions can you make for his improvement?

_____
Student's Signature

These evaluations were not treated frivolously. Criticisms and suggestions were seriously given but reserved for the eyes of the teacher and his unit head only. Here are a few examples of what the students said about their teachers:

Course: World War II. Evaluation of Instructor's Teaching: When assigning books for the class to read, she seems to have read many of them, which I think is very good. Her teaching is very good except for a few things.

She moves quite a bit during class. (pacing up & down the floor during class.) She skrims quite a bit at times when seated in class. She seems to be to dramatic, like she may make a statement, and while saying what she has to say she makes all types of movements as though she's acting it out in a play or something. The given assignments should have been more interesting.

Course: Elementary French. Evaluation of Instructor's Teaching: I had Karen last year. I dropped the course because I cannot function as I see fit in a chaotic classroom. This year the controll is there. It is not a whip in hand type of controll, but enough controll to handle the students who like to flex the mucles of their minds in a off the subject way. Some how she is able to lead these thoughts back to the original subject. I can see quite an improvement in Karen, and I like it. This is my most enjoyable class.

Course: Advanced English Skills. Evaluation of Instructor's Teaching: The best feature of Lisa's "method" was that she emphasized on opinions and insisted that everybody had one. She (Lisa) seemed to focus on discussion and opinionated composition. I think the course could have had a lot more visual and a little less verbal.

Finally, parents evaluate the Parkway Program and their children's progress in it. The following form was used for this at the end of Parkway Program's first semester:

Dear Parent,

We are coming to the end of our first short session at Parkway. We are new and growing; we have had our bright spots and difficulties. We need your help to look carefully at this past spring. Please respond to the following questions.

1. In what ways do you feel that your child grew this spring? (This does not have to be directly connected with school.)

2. What is important to you in your child's education?

3. What of this education is Parkway providing, what is missing?

4. Please share any added comments, joys, problems, anything that meant something to you as a parent.

On behalf of the staff,
thank you,

John Bremer, Director

The response by parents was generally favorable. One mother wrote:

> Our son enjoys the school situation—particularly where the school is and the freedom from confinement to one building. We think he is slightly freer, more candid, and happier at home also.
>
> It is hard to undo the effect on a child of his years of prior experience in a lock-step type of authoritarian academic environment. In the Parkway Program, a child with his newly found freedoms has a difficult time adjusting. The problem with most formal educational systems, on the other hand, is that they try to teach a child mastery of some arbitrary subject before he is interested in it, and certainly before he is ready for it.
>
> You seem to be going in the right direction. Just keep doing what you are doing. . . .
>
> A final thought: the absence of marks within the Parkway Program is accompanied by a corresponding absence of examinations. How then can the students learn to do as well as they might in the College Board's Scholastic Aptitude Test (SAT)?

The answer lies in the curriculum. Parkway offers a course on College Board Preparation, with "tips on test-taking, practice in taking sample tests, gimmicks, and games for vocabulary-building." This course may contribute little to learning how to live, but its inclusion is better than prostituting the entire course of study to what are thought to be the demands of the colleges. That this is a more sensible way of dealing with college entrance is suggested by the fact that, in the authors' experience, every single graduate of the Parkway Program who has wanted to go to college has been accepted.

The only full-scale appraisal of the program by independent critics was carried out in June 1970 just before the resignation of John Bremer, the original director. It was undertaken for political reasons — and, probably because it was clearly in favor of Parkway, the survey was not made public by the superintendent of the Philadelphia school district within the following year.

SURVEY OF THE PARKWAY PROGRAM FOR
THE SCHOOL DISTRICT OF PHILADELPHIA
June 8-12, 1970

Survey Team

1. Mrs. Mary Carter Evans
   (formerly Principal of Radnor High School, Radnor, Pa.,
   formerly President of the Middle States Association)

2. Mrs. Mary Chapple, Executive Secretary
   Friends Education Committee, Philadelphia

3. Mr. John Spriggs, Dean
   Student Personnel
   Cheyney (Pa.) State College

4. Mr. Charles Gilmore, Division Director
   Social and Behavioral Sciences Division
   Community College of Philadelphia

5. Dr. Elwood Prestwood
   (formerly Assistant Superintendent in charge of Curriculum,
   Lower Merion (Pa.) School District)

6. Dr. Albert Oliver
   Professor of Education
   University of Pennsylvania

Purposes

The chief purpose for the establishment of the Committee was to provide the Superintendent with up-to-date information concerning the nature of the Parkway Program. In order to give some direction for this rather broad assignment, answers were sought to such questions as the following: What are the philosophy and objectives upon which the Program is based? As the Program has developed, has it moved in the direction of its philosophy and objectives? Just what is the Program's impact on the students? Just what is the impact on the teachers? What are the reactions of parents to the Program? What types of relationships exist among the students and between the students and their teachers?

In Philadelphia, as well as in many other large urban areas, those who discuss secondary schools look to such topics as drop-outs, dope, gangs, overcrowding, integration, basic skills, "irrelevance." How does the Parkway Program look in terms of such matters as these?

Limitations

It must be recognized that the Committee has operated under several handicaps. The Committee was assembled on short notice near the end of the school year. The last week of school before graduation is not the time to gain an accurate picture of any program. Some scheduled classes had finished their regular work. A six-person Committee had to try to cover a far-flung (geographically) Program in two days of concentrated visitations and conferences.

For school evaluations the usual procedure is to have the school group spend some time in self-study and in writing up its own findings. Then a committee comes in to review these statements against experienced observations and looks critically at the school's self-perceptions. In this situation this method could not be used; so the Committee had to rely on a sampling of activities. Meetings were held with all Unit Heads, most teachers, and some parents. It was not possible to talk with all students. While the sample was not "random" (statistically speaking), it is believed that it was fairly representative.

Procedure

The Committee of six first met on Monday, June 8, to review the assignment and to lay out a plan of operation. It was agreed that the Committee would be divided into three teams of two members each—a team to visit each of the three Units in the Parkway Program. Each team was to try to visit both conventional academic classes as well as some of the electives offered by community participants. In addition, arrangements were made to talk to students, teachers, and parents. Conversations were also held with each Unit Head, and the Program Director was contacted on several occasions. Two members of the Committee attended the Parkway Program graduation on Monday evening, June 15.

The focus of the visitation came on Wednesday and Thursday, June 10 and 11, but Committee members also arranged for interviews with institutional participants on other days throughout a one-week period. The Committee members then met on Tuesday, June 16, to report, to organize their findings, and to prepare this report.

Organization of the Parkway Program

The Parkway Program, under the direction of John Bremer, has three autonomous Units—Community Alpha (1801 Market Street), Community Beta (125 North 23rd Street), and Community Gamma (6th and Buttonwood). Their respective Unit Heads are Mrs. Anita Hackney, Mrs. Argentine Craig, and Mr. Cy Swartz. All of these people and the Director were very helpful in providing information and in responding to the various questions which were asked.

The detailed operation of each Unit differs somewhat, but there is a general pattern underlying each of them. For example, there are about nine full-time paid teachers in each Unit and each teacher has at least one Intern assigned to him. Each teacher, and this includes the Unit Head, is responsible for a "tutorial." Each tutorial contains about fifteen students and this serves as the home base for that particular tutorial group. Most classes are scheduled to meet in two-hour blocks, and the tutorial is basically a two-hour session that meets two or three times a week. In addition to taking responsibility for the tutorial, each teacher handles other classes. He also is responsible for organizing, supervising, and following up the elective courses which have been set up with cooperating agencies in the community. Great importance is attributed to the responsibility of teachers for members of their tutorials. This involves both individual and group counseling, tutoring, and many conferences on a one-to-one basis.

The schedule for each day tends to be somewhat different. It is up to the student to plan his time accordingly. When he does not have an actual class period, the student must decide what is the best use he can make of his time. Sometimes this means tutoring; sometimes he goes to a library or resource center; sometimes he talks with other students; sometimes he undertakes individual study; and sometimes he just relaxes.

In addition to the course plan mentioned above, there are "management groups." These are designed to be working units consisting of students and staff organized for the purpose of handling a specific Unit's "community" problem or project. Management groups are an outgrowth of the concept that the management and the operation of any community are the responsibilities of each of its members. Thus the student is offered the opportunity to be directly responsible for decision-making and operation of an aspect of the community life in his Unit. Some of the management groups dealt with such matters as lunch sales, government, library, social officers, parent-communication, drama, and newspaper. While this phase of the organization seems to have merit, it apparently is not as effective or as extensive as other features. It warrants restudy.

Another feature is the weekly "town meeting," which was established so that the members of each unit may air their concerns and cooperatively seek a solution. The meetings are conducted by a staff member, by an intern, or by a student as the need or interest dictates. All are expected to attend, although attendance tapered off a bit near the end of the year. Among the topics discussed were conditions at the Unit headquarters, the strengthening of the tutorials, and basic skills instruction.

In short, there is structure to the Parkway Program. It is not the type of conventional structure with bells ringing every fifty minutes as students are herded from room to room in the same box-like structure. The structure rather is a basic framework of learning and teaching which calls for the cooperative development of a plan for action based upon needs and purposes. While it is apparently the intent to have each Unit work out its own plan of operation, there would seem to be merit in having greater coordination within each Unit as well as among the Units.

Philosophy and Objectives

There are several ways to determine the effectiveness of a school. One way is to use a set of pre-established criteria and then to examine any school against those points. A second way, and one used in the area known as the Middle States Association of Secondary Schools and Colleges, is to look at a school in terms of its own stated goals and beliefs. This latter approach was used by the Committee. There apparently is no concise statement of philosophy and objectives in the literature of the Parkway Program. More important, at any rate, are the functioning philosophy and the functioning goals. From the writings of the Director about the Parkway Program, from observations, and from discussions with individuals in the Program, the following student goals were deduced:

To become a person who is effective in an urban society — continuing after formal schooling.

To develop the skills of management which are the source of power in the community.

To help understand oneself and one's environment.

To develop the basic skills of language and mathematics — stress on listening and speaking.

To learn to be responsible for one's own education — i.e., to become "self-propelling" and to accept the consequences of one's actions.

To enable those who are capable and interested to go on to college or other post-secondary education.

To develop the ability to cooperate in teams.

To become a better, more active citizen.

To learn what must be useful in life.

To become inquisitive and "open" individuals.

To develop initiative.

To discover the nature of the social organization of which one is a part.

To become process-oriented.

Among the beliefs upon which the Program is founded is the conviction that education must become more open. The most obvious result of this belief is to remove the students and classes from the conventional rectangular-boxed school building. To learn about a community one must get out into the community. Verbal descriptions are not enough. Hence, the Parkway Program has quickly been characterized as "a school without walls." This is obviously true, since students meet in small groups in a tremendous variety of locations all over the central part of the city. More fundamental, however, and much more difficult to discern, is the openness that comes by putting the student in an environment wherein he has a chance to discover and to express himself. This is why the Program stresses informality, why students and teachers call each other freely by first names, and why there is a minimum of "checking up" on student actions. Rather, the teacher and the student define the task cooperatively, and the student is expected to take the responsibility to see that his part is carried out properly. The going out into the community for classes is based on the assumption that action is important, since we do not really learn unless we do something, unless we get personally involved.

Program Offerings

To implement such beliefs as those stated above, a variety of courses are made available to the students. First of all, it should be pointed out that courses are offered to meet the basic state requirements for high school graduation — that is, English, Social Studies, Mathematics, Science, Health and Physical Education. Some of these courses are more or less of the conventional type (such as Algebra I); others are elective courses which have been developed through co-operation between the students, the faculty, and community organizations. For example, the Zoology at the Zoo can be found in one Unit, as well as Market Research or Introduction to General Psychology. There is a Basic Writing Workshop as well as Creative Writing, and one course has the interesting title "Reading Black, Thinking White."

The school year has been divided into three quarters (originally, a fourth quarter to be held in the summer was envisioned), and for each quarter each Unit develops a catalog of its course offerings. This allows a tremendous amount of flexibility, and it engenders student interest by utilizing the psychological principle of "psychological ownership." For example, the 1970 Spring catalog for the Beta Community lists fifty-six different offerings. There are about 100 courses in each of the current Gamma offerings and at Alpha. For a school that believes in flexibility, variation, and community relatedness, this certainly exhibits a significant step in that direction. However, it should be noted that all of these courses have not materialized, and future offerings should be scrutinized in the light of past experiences.

For most of the students the participation in course development is a new venture. Questions need to be raised as to whether or not they are identifying and selecting what is necessary to help them in everyday living.

Outcomes

In this report's comments on *Purposes,* mention was made of several topics associated with secondary education today. How does Parkway fare in terms of these items?

Drop-outs. There are almost no drop-outs from the Program.

A few have elected to return to their schools (prefer the security of bells ringing, need close supervision, feel it is too far to travel, desire to be near friends). A number of students, several from "prestige" high schools, reported that they were doing poorly and/or were ready to drop out; now they wouldn't think of leaving Parkway. Of interest, too, is the "mental drop-out," i.e., the one whose body attends school but whose mind wanders from lessons. As one Parkway graduate put it, "After eleven years of schooling I just started to learn this year!" One suburban boy, after four years of "failure" in his home school (highest mark before was "C") now finds himself accepted at three universities.

Drugs. The boy just mentioned gave up drugs when he "found himself" at Parkway. The students indicated that there was some drug use among the students, but all declared that it was far less prevalent than in their former schools. As one boy put it, "There is no reason to turn to drugs when you are interested, secure and occupied."

Gangs. There are gang members at Parkway but little gang conflict or terrorism. A gang representative reported: "With guys coming from all over the city this is no man's turf."

Overcrowding. With the city for a "classroom" and with community Units of about 150 students, there obviously is not the congestion nor the confinement found in schools of two, three, or four thousand. Everyone you talk to will eventually comment on the value of the Parkway approach in that it allows you to feel more like a person rather than a faceless member of a herd in a congested school. Here everyone knows you; everyone cares. This is a principle of psychological environment which is fostered by the physical environment of the Parkway.

The graduation ceremony itself exemplified the *personalization* possible with fewer members. Each graduate was introduced by his Unit Head who had a personal comment about him—an opportunity which is not possible at a graduation involving several hundred students.

Physical Education and Health. The Program's philosophy implies a well-rounded person. State requirements call for experiences in the areas of health and physical education. If walking has any virtue in these days of sedentary life, then the students get plenty of exercise. One boy kept a careful record of his walking to and from activities and found that it averaged four miles a day. (Incidentally, one Committee member declared that he hadn't walked so much since he was in the Army!)

[89]

Each Unit developed its own courses and activities. For health there were such offerings as "Introduction to Health," "Child Care and Development," "Drug Abuse," and "Human Sexuality." Frequent use was also made of various community agencies. In case of accidents or severe illness the student was referred to a nearby Medical Services Center.

The physical education opportunities included swimming, basketball, bowling, karate, folk dancing, and gymnastics. It is up to each tutorial leader to work out the weekly roster of his students and to see that they get the necessary health and physical education experiences. Nevertheless, the Committee got the feeling that there was a tendency to let the walking be the basic answer to "physical education."

Integration. The lottery selection process has provided physical "integration" in that there are students of different races, creeds, color, and socio-economic background. Of greater importance is the social integration. There are no reports of any serious clashes between blacks and whites. The upper age groups mix well; those in younger age groups tend to cluster with their own kind but without hostility toward those not in their own group. In an important sense, integration has been achieved city-wide without busing!

Basic Skills. Do the students learn to read and write? It should be kept in mind that many students come to the Parkway with high-level competencies. Others come with poor achievement marks and/or low scores on standardized tests. Through the tutorials and from the close contact with the students, the teachers (and interns) spotted those with difficulties. Some people could read; but they were so disenchanted with school that they didn't read.

One Unit gave a phonic skills test at the start of the year and another near the end of the year. "Significant gains" were reported. Another Unit secured the cooperation of the Reading Clinic at the University of Pennsylvania. A Gates Reading Test and an informal reading inventory (clinical) was given to any who wished. Those who scored low were given a chance to get special help. Several teachers and Reading Clinic trainees worked with students. However, there does not seem to have been a careful follow-up of the diagnosis and treatment.

The teachers as a whole felt that the students were performing better regardless of previous school records. They felt that the reading levels were up chiefly because (a) the activities at Parkway reinforce verbal skills; (b) the direct interest of individual teachers gives pupils the personal attention which they need. Improved written expression (style and vocabulary) can also be found in comparing the self-evaluation reports throughout the year.

Both teachers and parents reported that a number of students who resisted reading before now began to read freely — especially paperbacks and newspapers.

Somewhat less positive is the fact that limited testing provides less "hard" data than some would wish. Also there is the recognition that teachers may be willing but often lack the expertise to help the underachiever. Some start has been made on staff development along this line, but an expansion of this training is desirable. The number of workshops and tutoring sessions appears to be below what is necessary to satisfy all needs.

In spite of these reassuring factors, it seems that there is still some dissatisfaction with the skills-development approaches.

Relevance. The whole program is based on the concept that education should be *in* the community not just *about* the community. Students select a course because they are interested in the subject, because it makes sense. Thus it is not surprising to have students state that courses "became alive." Much of this entire report reflects the observation that the Program has already taken important steps toward relevance.

Post-Secondary Plans

One common measure of success of a secondary school program is to look at what happens to its graduates. Only 8 graduated from the Parkway Program last year, but about 80 received their diplomas this June. Of those who wanted to go to college, all but one had been accepted for the coming year. The colleges (and universities) involved are as close as the Community College of Philadelphia and Temple University (which has the most acceptances) and as far away as the University of Wisconsin. In all, twenty-two different post-secondary schools have been reported as accepting this year's graduates.

Of course, entrance into college is one matter; how well they succeed is more important. Hence, it will be important for the Parkway administration to plan a systematic follow-up program for the coming years.

Of interest, too, is the desire of the students to seek colleges that operate in the same spirit as Parkway. That is why a number selected Goddard College in Vermont. That is why the college counselor is preparing a list of colleges that are characterized by the same freedom-responsibility that is found at Parkway.

Not as clear are the post-secondary plans of those not going to college next Fall. A number plan to travel (several going to Israel). One young man is entering the Peace Corps and two are joining the Navy. Several are getting married. At least half a dozen are going to work in business and industry. More attention must be given to counseling the non-academic student.

Horizons are opening up for these young people, and all seemed confident that they could take the next step successfully. Time and the results of Parkway studies will tell just how successful the graduates are.

Citizenship

Every school professes to develop "citizenship"—often an undefined term. At Parkway the students become functioning citizens in their own Unit community through action—participation in course development, open discussion in town meetings, dialogues in tutorials. They learn how a city operates (or fails to operate) by getting out into the city. They become involved in their own community improvement projects. In the tutorials, they talk freely about current events—taking any side without fear of reprisal but learning to be challenged.

There are personal qualities important to "good citizenship." For example, one is immediately struck by the OPENNESS—no hierarchy. Respect is earned, not demanded. Everyone uses first names with a sincere simplicity. Nothing is locked, no door is closed against student or visitor. When free, students as well as teachers can drop in on each others' classes or go to the resource center for a variety of reinforcements: vocabulary, spelling, mathematical games, phonics survey (a combination of the Botel and Philadelphia's method), and understanding of College Boards, or help in how to take tests.

HONESTY—a complete lack of hypocrisy in class or in students' and teachers' evaluations of each others' work. The teacher's written evaluation of a student's work is discussed with the student and added to his cumulative file. Building on strengths, these evaluations are aimed at helping the student know himself rather than measuring him against an arbitrary standard. The student's evaluation of the course and of the teacher is for the teacher's growth and is given to him to keep personally. Several teachers mentioned the helpfulness of their students' comments in improving the course and their own performance. These student evaluations also served in some cases to reassure interns or new teachers that some specific thing they had done was right.

There is heartening evidence of WARMTH and TRUST between faculty and students — and among students. Everyone is learning. Teachers can, and do, discuss freely their doubts and failures with their colleagues; and students are helpful about each others' problems. Students feel free to call their teachers at home if they need to, and teachers phone parents and/or students when they feel it would be helpful. There is a strong sense of community, a spirit of genuine cooperation.

Attendance

Teachers keep roll on their own classes and on their tutorials. The figures are sent to the Unit Heads, and monthly the data are forwarded to the Alpha Unit where the Administrative Officer collates all the figures. The results run close to 90%. In April it was 92%; in May, 88%. There has been some decline in June as the school year runs out.

Credit toward graduation is tied to attendance and to performance in classes. Thus some, whose attendance lags, will get only partial credits.

It should be recognized also that some teachers are more diligent than others in checking attendance and in following up those who are absent. Some students wander into class late or leave early. This usually happens in an atmosphere of permissiveness rather than with the customary scolding of the individual or sending a "pink slip" to the office.

On the elective courses, as might be expected, the attendance is "spotty" depending upon the interest generated by the person in charge.

Students do cut classes, but they declare that cutting is less than they used to do. The philosophical question to be considered is whether or not adults should be overly concerned if a student prefers to "rap" or to play cards instead of attending a class. Shouldn't he learn to take the consequences of his own decisions?

[93]

Parental Attitudes

It is recognized that the Committee talked with only a few parents, but there was opportunity to look at comments which others had written. Also the teachers reported on some of their contacts with parents.

At first, many parents had anxieties about this "new school." For some youths this meant going far from their homes to a new territory. There was apprehension about wandering through the city. Fears tended to disappear as the year went on. While parents raise questions about details or about personal matters, the consensus seems to be one of overwhelming support for the Parkway. A few of the comments are as follows:

"He was ready to drop out before Parkway. Now he is working so hard that he will do three years in two."

Father: "The relationship with my son is on a sound base now. This has been a learning experience for the family, too."

"He used to get by by faking, by manipulating people. He has shifted the responsibility to himself. He reads and studies constantly now."

"At first my son was terribly disappointed until he got it through his head that nothing was going to happen till he made it happen."

"Will she get enough of the basics to get into college?"

"He was good in elementary school, bad in junior high. We almost lost hope. Now he is a different person. His tutorial leader, the smaller group, honest student evaluations have given him a whole new image."

"I found her easier to talk to at home. Now she'll talk about school. She never used to."

Attempts are made in all Units to keep in close contact with parents, and the descriptive evaluations provide a more effective interpretation than the conventional letter grades. Home visits by the teacher are arranged at the request of the teacher, the student, or the parent.

Faculty Growth

What is the effect of the Program on its teachers? Testimony by teachers and observations by students affirm the belief that it takes time to become a Parkway teacher. Teachers are not used to freedom. Teachers are not used to giving pupils genuine responsibility. Teachers are not used to having students take leadership in planning lessons and courses. At Parkway teachers learn all this by experience.

It is an Educational Commandment to "Know thy pupil." At Parkway this is not only possible; it is a necessity. Students agree that this has been generally accomplished when they say, "Here teachers really care about us. They are willing to take lots of time to listen."

Teachers have come to know what it means to make the curriculum "relevant." If their classes don't make sense, they will be told.

Since there is much to be learned, every opportunity should be taken to increase staff development. A few students felt that certain teachers tended to become complacent, thus they were recommending that all teachers should be screened every year.

To make this, or any program, work, you must have strong teachers. In this case teachers have to be flexible, imaginative, and resourceful. Above all, they must be adults who care about young adults. The individual student must be the center of all learning activity — a philosophy easy to accept but much more difficult to implement.

Tutorials

A basic feature of the Parkway Program is the "tutorial." Here a teacher and an intern regularly meet with the fifteen students assigned to that group within the community Unit. The purposes, as announced in the fourth edition of the Parkway brochure (p. 6), are threefold: "1. To act as a support group in which counseling can take place; 2. it is the group in which the basic skills of language and mathematics are dealt with; 3. it is the unit in which the program and the student's performance is evaluated."

Administratively, each Unit handles the tutorial in slightly different ways, but all meet at least twice a week (two-hour blocks) with consideration being given to hourly, daily sessions. Each group works out its purposes and procedures. One teacher noted, "It took time to find the clay; now we're building the model."

The success of the tutorial seems to be uneven, since much depends upon the leadership of each group. Learning to communicate (both listening and speaking) has been a main achievement. Mutual exploration of ideas and issues has been another. It is here that a number of students apparently have moved toward the major goal of "self-discovery."

Most agree that the handling of the basic skills can be improved, and several alternatives are being explored. Reading and math groups might very well be formed from each tutorial, especially for those who need the help. One proposal is to schedule the tutorial the first thing in the morning and then to have skills workshops held immediately afterwards.

Near the end of the year interest and attendance in the tutorials seemed to lag. Perhaps the "halo effect" began to wear off. At any rate, the tutorial concept warrants further study and experimentation. It does not seem to be accomplishing all that it is designed to do. Perhaps the purposes should be changed, but certainly both teachers and students need more guidance to realize the potential of this important part of the Program.

Evaluation

The Parkway Program makes extensive use of the curriculum development principle that there should be on-going evaluation. Through the tutorials and town meetings the students and the teachers (parents are also free to attend) are constantly looking at what they are doing. Weekly staff meetings may be attended by students, and anyone may propose an item for the agenda. In addition, the Unit Heads meet every other week with the Director.

For each term each student participates in a course evaluation. While each Unit develops its own evaluation forms, there are the common elements of: course goals (as seen by the teacher, as seen by the student), course description, texts and collateral readings, written discussion (by both teacher and student) on such matters as attendance, class participation, ability to express ideas, leadership, independent study.

There are also descriptive-type forms used by the staff to evaluate each student's work in terms of academic, social, and emotional growth. Then the student is asked to write his evaluation of the course and the teacher.

The Committee had opportunity to examine some of these evaluations, and some of its judgments grow out of the statements noted in this report.

Institutional Participants

Inherent in the Parkway Program is the concept that it is *in, by,* and *for* the actual city community. This involves not only physical facilities (such as a church where groups may meet) but also human resources. Thus students and teachers have explored the community to find people and agencies who would offer a "course." Radio stations, newspapers, churches, museums, banks, city agencies, insurance companies, hospitals, universities (and colleges), the Red Cross, the Urban League, and a host of businesses and industries make up the list of opportunities. A teacher is then given responsibility to keep in contact with the institution (or person) offering the course.

Apparently some discussion is made about the course purpose, and at the end the institution fills in the evaluation sheets the same as the regular teacher does.

In such an arrangement the opportunities to expand the curriculum are tremendous, but this does not guarantee effective teaching. People can be very knowledgeable but not be able to transmit their ideas to others. Some tried to use conventional lectures and the Parkway youth, now attuned to participation, either drifted away or told the instructor of their preferences.

There are obvious difficulties in coordinating, communicating, and supervising such varied operations. The teachers are aware of these problems and, with the students, are seeking to improve orientation, continuing contacts and follow-through. Interest is high, but there have been some disappointments on both sides. Here, then, the Committee finds both strengths and weaknesses.

Facilities

The Beta Unit is housed in the office area of an abandoned warehouse (125 North 23rd Street). Originally, the second floor was also used, but state officials closed it for student use since there were no adequate fire escapes. Students flow freely in and out of the street-level area, which contains staff offices, a small resource center, a room for lockers, and inadequate toilet facilities. Everyone has to be vigilant to see that no smoking goes on inside the building. The Unit is looking for alternative headquarters for next year.

The Alpha Unit (1801 Market—second floor) is housed with the Program administration. The visitors to the latter cause considerable cross-traffic with the students, but some visitors seem to like to have the students around while discussions go on about education. Nevertheless, separate facilities might be considered.

The Gamma Unit has its headquarters in the abandoned Paxson Elementary School at 6th and Buttonwood. This building was scheduled to be torn down, but late word is that this will not be done at the present time.

Each Unit headquarters has a small resource center which seems inadequate. Plans are being considered to expand and improve these resource centers. Contacts have also been made from the School District's Library Services to effect greater use of school and Free Library services. Certainly more can and should be done with learning materials and resources.

Overview

The June 20, 1970, issue of *Saturday Review* features "Alternatives to the System in Education." In this era of great change, school systems must have alternatives. Philadelphia has the Parkway Program which daily brings visitors from all over the United States—visitors seeking approaches that will humanize their schools. Thus in its brief history the Parkway idea has already become an inspiration, if not a model, for educational change. Yet it is not for everyone. The informality and the air of casualness is appealing to some; others have a philosophy which sees these as vices rather than as virtues.

There is criticism about the Program from within the Program and from the outside. It is hoped that these judgments will be channeled into criticism in its best sense, i.e., evaluative and constructive criticism. In times of change, individuals find their security (both ideological and practical) threatened. In such situations they may condemn surface features rather than exploring underlying elements. With the Parkway Program there are inherent qualities which the Committee believes to be sound and desirable. At the same time, there are errors of human judgment; there are fumblings of experimentation. However, the Parkway Program as a whole deserves further trial. It *is* a desirable alternative. Most important is the fact that the staff and the students at Parkway are keenly aware of their problems, and they are cooperatively seeking ways to find answers.

Now is the time to study systematically the experiences of the past year. Now is the time to tighten up administrative details.

The students have found freedom and they like it. It is more difficult to find the responsibility that should go with freedom. Now is the time to study further the actual attainment of the high-level goals which the Parkway Program envisions.

The distinguishing characteristic of the Parkway Program is in its human values. Cities are going to be increasingly difficult to operate in the future — if, indeed, they survive at all — and the self-reliance, humanness and maturity level encouraged by the Parkway process of education seems to the Committee to go far toward qualifying its participants for usefulness in a demo-cratic society.

6
Finance

The usefulness of money in education is declining. It can no longer command the personal and material resources it once did. This is partly because educational resources are much more expensive than they used to be, and in this sense it is not the usefulness of money that has declined but rather the amount in relation to the resources. But there has also developed a general distrust of the educational establishment. People with creative views of teaching are less willing to be bought and paid for, especially in view of the low caliber of educational leadership they see today. In Philadelphia, as the school district flounders on from financial crisis to financial crisis, people are beginning to ask themselves whether their *present* level of taxation can be justified in terms of the results.

For example, in the proposed operating budget of the school district of Philadelphia for 1967–1968, the sum of $15,650,000 was allocated for debt service—that is, for interest on borrowed money (mainly for buildings). In 1968–1969, the sum of $20,700,000 was allocated, and in 1969–1970, the amount was $27,900,000. In two years, the debt service had increased by more than $12 million—all paid out of taxes. What were the results? The *Philadelphia Magazine* in June 1970 devoted an article to one of the high schools:

> this youth . . . the one who could not read more than three words at a time without getting stuck . . . will get his liberty this month when he stands tall in his cap and gown and receives a diploma of graduation . . . signed by the principal, with . . . the superintendent . . . and the board president lending their names as accomplices.
>
> The crime, of course, is that [he]—like Johnny before him—can't read. To those who have kept in touch with the excuse for a school system we have in this city, that is no startling

revelation. It is not even anything new. That's what is so bad about it. It is getting worse before it is getting better. This month, thousands [of students] all over the city will be turned loose on society with a 12th grade certificate for a 4th grade education. That little piece of paper might even land them jobs. Maybe that is good. Maybe it is a fraud.

The people in the school system are aware of all this, of course. [The superintendent] keeps saying he has this plan to change everything around, but that he can't talk about it yet because he first has to make sure that the proper organization and monies are there, and he is not sure when that will be.

The taxpayers of Philadelphia, by this time, have discovered exactly when the superintendent is going to talk about "this plan." In the meantime, they are not about to accept a higher level of taxation. This issue has created a vicious cycle which apparently cannot be broken. No plan, no money; no money, no plan. Perhaps if the superintendent were to divulge his plan, the taxpayers would rally round and provide the money—and then again, they might not. It would depend on what was in the plan, or on whether there is a plan at all.

This not uncommon situation only indicates that talk about money is not very popular in education and also that it is hard to believe given figures. Sources are unreliable and their interpretation all depends on how one figures costs. In addition, errors are common, quite apart from politically motivated attempts to disguise the figures. For example:

1. The school district of Philadelphia refused to credit the Parkway Program with money or services received from suburban school districts for the suburban students participating. The money was simply absorbed into the general fund.

2. The records were so badly kept at the school district administration building that even in May 1970, John Bremer was informed that there was still about $20,000 from the original grant on hand, although the condition of the grant had been that it be used in 1969 (as it had been).

3. With actual cash purchases, problems arose. The first set of invoices, valued at about $1400, were sent to the administration building to account for cash received. Fortunately, somebody saw them—but then they mysteriously disappeared. Where did they go?

These difficulties sometimes arise out of obstinacy, incompetence, or downright malice and occasionally out of simple human error. But in dealing with finances, one must be very careful. In this chapter, the method of computing figures will be stated when possible; the reader will have to judge the value of the computed figures.

When John Bremer arrived in Philadelphia on August 1, 1968, to take up his appointment, he discovered that, contrary to a commitment from the superintendent, there were no funds to plan and initiate the Parkway Program. Fortunately, his own salary had been committed out of the Federal Elementary and Secondary Education Act (ESEA) Title III funds so that he himself was paid, and supposedly there was money for a secretary, although this was never used. For a time, the program shared one of the most experienced secretaries in the school district, Bess Newburn, but the time was very short and the small cost was absorbed elsewhere.

About ten days later, when confronted with the lack of funding, the superintendent merely remarked that the program (whatever it was) should run on volunteers. The director, not feeling that this was what he deserved—and certainly not what he expected—decided that he would have to raise money himself. To this end, he drew up a preliminary proposal (included as Part V of the Parkway Program Brochure and reprinted in the Appendix to this book) and began the task of informing people what Parkway was going to be all about. The first step was to inform the members of the school board, who expressed amazement when they learned that there was no funding. They were sure that the superintendent had said money was available. But it wasn't, for reasons that will be clarified later.

On August 22, 1968, Bremer sent the following proposed budget to the Ford Foundation asking for $182,000. The projected budget for the first year of the Parkway project included costs for operating the program with approximately 120 students and for planning and preparing for the academic year 1969–1970 with approximately 600 students.

Salaries:	Director ⎫ paid under ESEA Title III	
	Director's secretary ⎭	
	2 Secretaries	$ 10,000
	1 Administrative assistant	10,000
	Faculty (8 teachers, including extra time)	72,000
	Faculty (30 teachers, summer only)	35,000
	Contributions to participating institutions	20,000
	Consultants	2,000
Supplies:	All school supplies, including books	10,000
	Office supplies and equipment	5,000
	Publications for internal and external use	5,000
Transportation and travel		3,000
Miscellaneous		2,000
Contingencies		8,000
	Total for the year 1968–1969	$182,000

The Ford Foundation, with whom Bremer had worked before on a project, was sympathetic, but at the request of the superintendent the amount was limited to $100,000 so as not to take money from two other Philadelphia projects. On October 9, 1968, the following amended budget was submitted to Ford and verbally approved. This projected budget for the first year of the Parkway project included costs for operating the program with approximately 120 students.

Salaries:	Director ⎱ Paid under ESEA Title III	
	Director's secretary ⎰	
	2 Secretaries	$ 10,000
	1 Administrative assistant	8,500
	Faculty (8 teachers, including extra time)	50,000
	Contributions to participating institutions	15,000
	Consultants (services donated)	—
	Rent	5,000
Supplies:	All school supplies, including books	5,000
	Office supplies and equipment	2,500
	Publications for internal and external use	2,500
Transportation and Travel		500
Miscellaneous		1,000
	Total for the year 1968-1969	$100,000

Unfortunately, it was tied to the two other projects, which were not ready for submission until much later. Eternally optimistic, however, Bremer decided to begin the planning of the program and sent out the following memorandum:

To: Members of the Executive Cabinet   October 30, 1968

From: John Bremer, Director
Parkway Project

After presenting an outline of the Parkway Project to the Ford Foundation, I have been assured of $100,000 to fund us for this academic year. Unfortunately, we cannot receive written confirmation of the funding until at least the fifteenth of November. Since we need five to six weeks to complete the final stage of organization, it would be unrealistic to plan the admission of students before the beginning of January 1969. Under these circumstances, I intend to wait until the beginning of the next marking period, namely, Tuesday, February 4.

We have a large number of offers of assistance from the institutions along and around the Parkway, and I see no difficulty in our operation for the rest of this year. The educational offerings of the institutions are being worked out in detail at this time, including the time and space factors.

As soon as we receive written confirmation from the Ford Foundation, I will announce the opening date and begin the process of student and faculty enrollment.

Since we need some space of our own for various purposes, I have discussed with Mr. Poindexter, Mr. Perks and Mr. Finney the possibility of moving to 1801 Market Street. The facilities on the second floor will meet our needs for some time, as long as we can make some minor changes in partitions and do something about the heating. I hope this will become our relatively permanent administrative headquarters.

Although the memorandum was sent to the superintendent and the members of the executive cabinet, there was no response. It was clear that Parkway was going to have to go it alone.

The second floor of 1801 Market Street has already been mentioned, as was the fact that its emptiness was an embarrassment to the school district. The rent was already being paid — although what it was the director did not know, except that whatever it was it was too much.

Given the level of funding from the Ford Foundation, Bremer decided that he would spend the $100,000 between January and early September 1969 (instead of spreading it out to last until December 31). His thinking was that the program should make a concerted effort to prove itself in that period and to do it in such a way that it could be supported from the operating budget of the school district in the year 1969–1970.

One major difficulty that new educational programs always face is the continuance of their funding. If a project is started with private or federal funds, it will almost certainly be phased out when the sources of those funds dry up — as they inevitably do. During the school year 1968–1969, Bremer learned why there was no money from the operating budget of the school district. To understand the reasons, one needs to understand the political structure of the Philadelphia board of education.

According to the Home Rule Charter of Philadelphia, members of the board of education are appointed by the mayor from a list of candidates drawn up by a nominating panel appointed by the mayor. The board prepares its own budget each year, but it has no taxing powers of its own; it must go to the city council to raise the money by taxation. The city council, which effectively means its president, raises money only if it approves the purposes for which it is to be spent. Technically, it is not supposed to carry out a line-by-line analysis but simply to approve or disapprove the total amount. But that is technically speaking. In fact, however, what the president of city council does not like is usually removed from the budget. Among other things, he does not like new programs—they always cost more money. Like all politicians, he enjoys publicity. He also does not agree with the president of the board of education (a former mayor of the city). So these factors combine to produce an annual ritual which has to be seen to be believed.

It is, of course, the political structure that is incorrect. It manages to produce the worst of all possible worlds. The educators say that they cannot be successful without funds, and the fund-raisers of the city council claim that they are safeguarding the public interest by resisting money wastage for fancy experiments. In the meantime, it is hard to allocate responsibility for the failure of the school district. A plague on both their houses is, perhaps, the best comment.

The funds for Parkway were removed from the operating budget for 1968–1969 as proposed to the city council, at the insistence of the president of the city council, Paul D'Ortona, and a commitment was made by the school district not to try anything else new without his approval. It would be easy to criticize the president of city council, but it should be remembered that the leadership of the school district did not exactly command his confidence. The Parkway Program was thus caught in the middle. When Bremer approached the school board president to seek his support for inclusion of Parkway funds in the operating budget for 1969–1970, he was told that it was impossible without the support of the president of the city council and that he was the man to approach. Bremer did not follow up this suggestion but waited. Later, he again asked for inclusion of Parkway funds in the operating budget, and the school board president, Richardson Dilworth, again suggested he speak with the city council president. The director replied that he was new in the city, did not yet understand the political games that were being played, and was afraid that he would cause some harm—unless the situation was so bad that no harm could be caused. Mr. Dilworth simply replied, "Yes."

Accordingly, Bremer went to see the president of the city council, accompanied by Clifford Brenner, who knew much about city hall and who originally proposed that use of the city's facilities which led to the Parkway Program (as will be described in a later chapter). After a delightful hour with Paul D'Ortona, it was clear that there was no further objection from that quarter. It also made it difficult for any objection to be raised from any other quarter, and Bremer's hand was strengthened considerably by winning his own political battle. The following memorandum from Bremer to the superintendent and the school board president put it clearly:

[105]

The Parkway Program

At the suggestion of Mr. Dilworth and through the good offices of Mr. Brenner, I met with the President of City Council, Mr. Paul D'Ortona, to inform him of the progress of the Parkway Program and of our hopes for its immediate future. In the course of the conversation, Mr. D'Ortona made it very clear that City Council's approval of the proposed School District operating budget for fiscal 1970 would not be done on a line-by-line basis. He stated he had no objections to the Parkway Program being included or expanded as long as the School District was willing to use some of its money in that way, and as long as this did not require funds beyond the over-all limit set by City Council.

This means that he will not object to the Parkway Program's inclusion and/or expansion and that the commitment of the School District to City Council not to use regular operating funds in the current year has been met.

As it turned out, the Parkway Program was included in the operating budget for 1969–1970 at a level to support about five hundred students, and it was supposed to be in the 1970–1971 budget for high school level students ($548,840) and elementary school students ($234,330). In actuality, the program continued in fiscal 1970–1971 at the previous level of five hundred students. If Parkway makes it one more year, it will be immortal.

To estimate the operating costs of the Parkway Program is difficult, since many factors are unknown or unknowable. To afford a reasonable comparison with other programs in conventional schools, the payrolls for every high school in Philadelphia were taken for an arbitrary week. These payrolls show each staff member directly responsible to the principal and paid by him (teachers and secretaries, but not custodians, for example). There are 21.7 pay periods in the year, so by multiplying the biweekly payroll by the number of pay periods, the total annual cost of personnel for each school was computed. It should be borne in mind that this represents the level of spending at the time of the particular pay period taken; there might well be minor fluctuations over the year.

The left-hand column of the following table lists the high schools, grouped by districts. Column two gives the actual biweekly salary total taken directly from the payroll. The third column shows the cal-culated total personnel cost for each school, while the fourth column shows the actual number of employees involved (mostly teachers, of course). The fifth column gives the number of students on roll; the sixth, the social breakdown of students; the seventh, attendance; and the eighth, the calculated per student cost for personnel in each school.

District and school	Biweekly salaries ($)	Calculated annual cost of personnel ($)	Number of personnel	Number of students	Racial breakdown			Attendance	Annual per student cost ($)
					B	W	Hisp.		
District 1									
Bartram	108,649.83	2,357,700	235	3817	57%	43%	0%	73%	618
W. Phila.	97,131.60	2,107,760	209	3423	99%	1%	0%	70%	616
District 2									
Ben Franklin	63,970.97	1,388,160	136	1544	95%	1%	4%	71%	899
Wm. Penn	48,602.12	1,054,670	97	1329	94%	3%	3%	74%	794
District 3									
S. Phila.	114,364.40	2,481,710	234	3301	51%	48%	1%	73%	752
District 4									
Gratz	121,535.19	2,637,310	274	4388	99%	1%	0%	72%	601
Overbrook	133,437.80	2,895,600	289	4506	85%	15%	0%	79%	643
District 5									
Edison	68,028.50	1,476,220	142	1913	82%	12%	6%	70%	772
Kensington	47,920.31	1,039,870	102	1491	60%	30%	10%	71%	697
District 6									
Central	69,761.40	1,513,820	130	2166	17%	83%	0%	90%	699
Germantown	102,265.30	2,219,160	221	3738	79%	21%	0%	76%	594
Girls High	70,965.32	1,539,950	139	2440	28%	72%	0%	92%	631
Roxborough	63,910.21	1,386,850	130	2114	14%	86%	0%	82%	656
District 7									
Frankford	69,594.54	1,510,200	135	2283	8%	92%	0%	81%	661
Olney	110,850.28	2,405,450	229	3723	33%	66%	1%	82%	646
District 8									
Lincoln	114,718.91	2,489,400	228	2673	2%	98%	0%	89%	931
Northeast	109,427.65	2,374,580	215	4036	1%	99%	0%	86%	581
Washington	126,326.57	2,741,290	254	2550	3%	97%	0%	88%	1075
Parkway Program	15,787.14	342,580	30	476	48%	52%	0%	89%	720

The comparable figures for the Parkway Program are given at the end of each column. There is one adjustment that has been made and that is that the salaries of the director, his secretary, and the information officer have *not* been included in the first column. The reason is that by the design of the program no further increase in "central administration" is necessary and that the cost of such administration should be shared among the students in a fully enrolled program and not in the necessarily small initial enrollment. (If these figures were to be included, it would increase the annual cost to about $790.)

As the table now stands, twelve schools operate on a smaller per student cost for personnel than Parkway, and six schools operate on a greater per student cost. The over-all average for the high schools in Philadelphia is $690 per student, compared with Parkway's $720. Since more than one third of Philadelphia's public school students drop out or fail to graduate for other reasons, the cost per graduate would be much more favorable to Parkway, which has an extremely high percentage of graduates.

There is, however, some variation of per student cost within Parkway itself. Consider the three units:

	Biweekly faculty cost	Biweekly interns	Annual total	Number of students	Per student cost
Alpha	4960.87	800.00	125,010.90	157	$776
Beta	3645.39	416.00	88,132.20	158	$558
Gamma	4941.38	1024.00	129,448.70	161	$804

The reason for the variation is to be found in the small cost to Beta of paid interns and the relative youth of its teachers. If all paid interns were abolished (a direction in which Parkway is moving), the per student cost could be brought down to less than $620, which would rank it fourth or fifth among Philadelphia high schools, if we are considering the personnel costs only. However, if money is available, it should always be spent on people and not on buildings, at least in Parkway's scheme of things.

But high schools have other costs the Parkway Program does not have at all. First, there is the cost of the high school building itself. This cost, according to the most recent estimate for a three-year high school for 2000 students in Philadelphia, is not quite $20 million. Since the money has to be borrowed, the interest will amount to almost as much again. The school will therefore cost the taxpayer $40 million, and if it is earthquake proof it may last for forty years. The cost per year of just the building, not including instruction, heating, lighting, and so on, is $1 million. With 2000 students, the cost per year for the building alone is $500 per student. Parkway uses virtually no money for this purpose; it pays rent on one unit only for less than $60 per student per year.

It should be remembered that building costs (that is, capital expenditures) are often calculated on a per student basis, using the total number of students in the system. It may be unfair to pretend that a student in one of the very old schools shares in the benefits accruing to a student in a brand new school. However, on this basis, the per pupil cost for buildings in Philadelphia is more than $100 — and the amount goes up each year. Either way it is figured, Parkway is cheaper.

The present cost of plant operations and maintenance in Philadelphia is approximately $100 per student per year. Parkway uses virtually none of this money, since it has virtually no space to maintain and operate.

When Parkway began to furnish the original headquarters at 1801 Market Street, Bremer, with the help of the excellent warehouse manager, obtained used furniture returned from schools as not wanted. The furniture was not pretty, but it was sturdy. No one in the schools would use it, however, and rather than have it burned or almost given away, Parkway took it. This practice has continued.

When the Parkway Program became involved with elementary school children, the per pupil cost was about $430 per year, which was about the same as the least expensive schools in District 6 (from which many of the children came) and one third less than the most expensive school in that district.

It must be emphasized again that Parkway flourishes only because of those who *give* their services, whether these donors are private individuals or corporations. If it were possible to compute the cost of these volunteers, no doubt Parkway would be very expensive; but it is not necessary to do so, since the larger community gives service when it would not give money. And what it gives is more valuable. John Bremer gave the following talk to the Greater Philadelphia Chamber of Commerce at its winter conference in January 1970:

> Do we have a learning environment? The answer is simply no. Not in our schools and not in the city. Why not? Because there is no learning without interaction and there is little chance for interaction in our schools and little chance for it in our city. The school can act and does act upon the student. The city can act and does act upon the citizen. But when does the student act upon the school? When does the citizen act upon the city in a continuous and self-sustaining way? The answer is never.

And yet learning is the process by which our city renews herself, renews herself in the sense that she makes herself new again, so that we can in a sense fall in love with her again. Over and over again, because she is the source, the major source, of beauty in our lives. Now this means that the city changes, and it is by changing that she preserves herself as a matrix of all that is good in human life.

How weary, stale, flat, and (if I may be forgiven) unprofitable seems the reality of a city kept like the fossil bones of a once potent creature as a reminder of how great we used to be.

How unjust and inhuman our lives can be in Penn's fair city that once sustained and nourished the tradition of civility. How oppressive and degrading human life can be, in a city dedicated to the rule of law. And how easily we tolerate educational disaster in a city that boasts the founding of the first public school in the original 13 colonies.

No, we do not have a learning community, a learning environment. Neither an environment that learns from us nor an environment in which we can learn or in which anyone else can learn.

The conventional solution to this problem is simple. More money, more money for new schools, for better-qualified teachers, for research, more money for materials, more and more money. Now, the importance of money should not be underestimated (particularly when you are being asked to part with it), but it should be clear that large infusions of money alone will not do what needs to be done. The educational system has been likened by some to a worn-out internal combustion engine that is so old it's almost an external combustion engine. The more gasoline you pour into it, the more smoke and the more noxious fumes are emitted. Similarly, it is said the more money, the more energy you put into the educational system, the more educational waste you produce. And that is all you produce.

Now, this is a very harsh judgment, but we should not forget that money, the cash nexus, is used in order to avoid a human relationship. It is literally a compensation given when the human dimension of the transaction is unsatisfactory and one-sided. To put this another way, money is used mainly to avoid interaction, or even more simply, by using money we usually avoid learning. But the learning environment depends upon interaction for its existence, depends totally upon interaction for its existence, so money will defeat us unless we use it very sparingly, very carefully.

There is a harder way which I wish to propose to create a learning environment. And it is in my opinion the only way. It is not sudden, not dramatic, not spectacular, producing instant results. But that should not surprise us, since we are men and not magicians. It is the way of interaction. The professional educator's task in the future is to promote interaction between the student, somebody who wishes to learn, you or I, not necessarily somebody between the ages of 6 and 16 and someone or something else, in such a way that the rewards of the relationship will insure its continuance. I am proposing that you invest not money but yourselves. If you cannot, if you will not, if you do not, the city will perish.

There are in the city some thirty-five thousand business concerns. Let us suppose that every tenth business provided a room thirty feet square, or larger, or smaller; that would mean that we could increase the number of classrooms in the city by one third or more overnight. And that space is available. Secondly, let us suppose that we were to admit that the rewards of business are not always to be measured in human terms, and that one of the difficulties corporations face is the human development of their executives. Could we not, as part of a business program, invite business executives to become more human, to become learners and teachers as a part of their regular assignment? Is it not possible to take into the business world young people to learn what business is all about not by reading in a textbook, not by reading some scurrilous attack upon capitalism, or whatever it may be, by somebody who has been denied the fruits of it, but to see what, in practice, human beings are endeavoring to do through a particular mode of economic and social organization? If they could see that, they would learn something of value. They would not deny the importance of business, they would not feel that committing their talents to business was a prostitution of their heaven-sent gifts. Let us suppose that students in the future will learn about government in City Hall, about biology in the zoo, about art in the city and in the art museums, about labor relations on the waterfront. Why can we not get students to use the city as the campus?

We need help from the students, too, and it should not be thought that this is a one-sided affair. Students are perfectly capable of carrying out large undertakings of research of one kind or another with assistance; they can do things which will help us to do our job. Why do we not provide for those things? The students can help the city.

It is also true that the per capita cost in the school district is about $1000 per student in terms of the operating budget alone. What would happen if twenty students came to one of you and said, "We have vouchers here for twenty thousand dollars. Can you give us an education, can we buy from you an education?" Could you do better than the school district of Philadelphia does? It might be possible to put teachers or people who are certified on your payroll and to ask them to split their time and their energy between teaching on the one hand and learning with you and helping you as employees on the other. It is also possible to make employees teachers, and I think every business should commit a percentage of its profits to educational purposes, and every business should sponsor some very specific concrete educational project. If you do that, you will have to expect one thing and that is that you will change, and that is why this suggestion may find itself on very stony ground. If you admit students to business, museums, the governmental offices of this city, those places will never be the same again. And we should look upon that as our salvation, but learning is always something we ask somebody else to do. The city is our only curriculum and there is nothing else we need to learn about. The city is our campus. And our students and we ourselves have to re-create that curriculum and that campus. In the future education has to be a function of the total community and not just of a group of special, specialized professional educators. In my own opinion, education is the supreme political function.

As was pointed out at the beginning of this chapter, the usefulness of money is declining in education. Parkway flourishes not because it is a bargain—which it is—but because it knows how to liberate the energies and skills, without price, of the larger community. That is what leadership is about.

But can a city support the whole school system in the Parkway fashion? And what would happen if the support were withdrawn?

It should be clear from the statistics in Bremer's speech that a city can support the school system; it does, in large part, anyway, through taxation. In the long run, it must support education in this way if the cities are to survive. The resources are there to do it if we so choose. Every community must have within it the resources to continue its own life, and education is the process by which that is to be done. Whether the larger community can come to accept this responsibility is another question, but leadership is crucial. The fact that donated services are a tax write-off will not inspire the business community—but a leader could.

If the larger community should withdraw its support, a Parkway-type program could not function. This is not a total disadvantage, since such a program structurally requires a school district to interpret its educational work to the larger community and to hold itself accountable for what it does. The closeness of the interdependence is what constitutes salvation, for education is much too serious an affair to leave to the professionals.

7

Community Education

Lisa Strick

Information Officer, Parkway Program

A question frequently asked of me by visitors to the Parkway Program is how, in the short space of a year, did the program manage to win broad-based local support and considerable national recognition? Perhaps the only legitimate answer to that question is that the Parkway Program is an educational program which *works* in a climate of widespread despair over education. However, during these conversations someone nearly always points out the coverage the program has received in *Life* or *Time* or on the national television networks and says, "Well, really, Mrs. Strick, hasn't a lot of it just been good public relations?"

Yes, it has. But not in the sense that these people normally think of public relations. Most people assume in our media-conscious culture that the function of a public relations person is to lie — or at least to be creative and selective about the truth. Many visitors to the Parkway Program fully expect from me some kind of hard sell — a "pitch" which will direct them toward our successes and away from the skeletons they are sure we have rattling in our closets. These people tend to be surprised when all I have to say to them is, "What do you want to know, and how can I help you find it out?"

Public relations at the Parkway Program means transparency and accessibility. We have not thrown screens up around our operations; rather, we have installed plate glass windows. The principle behind the practice would sound naïve if it didn't work so well: we think we have a good thing going. If people can get to see us, they can get to understand us. If they understand us, they often support us. It's basically as simple as that.

The decision to open every aspect of Parkway's operations to public scrutiny was not made easily—nor was it made without opposition. A program as new and as different as the Parkway Program was when it opened causes a great deal of attention, and this kind of attention has two sides. As sensitive as an administrator may be to the fact that public attention may lead to public support, it can be very hard to sell that to a student who has just for the four-hundredth time explained to some inquirer how he meets his state requirements. A teacher who regularly finds several observers added to her class of eight can be expected to turn a deaf ear to insistence that visitors be treated as welcome. When I joined the Parkway Program, students and faculty lost no time in telling me their feelings about the situation: "I feel like I'm in a zoo," one student said. "Throw me a peanut and I recite my roster." Accommodating observation requests came under heavy fire at an early faculty meeting: "What are we, anyway?" one teacher shot out, "an educational institution or a publicity gimmick?" Those who weren't actively against an open-door public relations policy had become, at the very least, bored with it. Six months after the program opened, I found myself trying to recruit some students to be interviewed by a local news network which had undertaken a follow-up on us. The cameras and lights were set, the mikes in place, and the interviewer poised. Several students were around and I went to work: "Hey, how about it, you wanna be on television?"

"Nah, man, I'm sick of being on television."

A jaded celebrity at sixteen.

It was just this kind of mounting dissatisfaction with a fishbowl way of life which was responsible for the creation of my job at the Parkway Program. While John Bremer believed strongly that no inquiry about our program should be turned away, he also knew nothing would be gained if the public came, only to get a hostile or apathetic reception. The public had to be satisfied. And the program had to be protected. It seemed logical to find someone who could stand in the middle and keep everybody happy.

I met John Bremer while producing a local television talk show in Philadelphia. When the Parkway Program opened, John became an instant local celebrity and I asked him to come and subject himself to an interview on my show. Without knowing it, our first phone conversation gave me my introduction to what John Bremer thought public relations should be about. I remember being very impressed with how friendly and cooperative my new Philadelphia celebrity was. Celebrities in my life were not always cooperative. The show I produced was quite demanding of them—it was live, requiring precise timing, and operated out of a studio located some distance out of the city, which meant complicated travel. Not everybody thought that twenty minutes on the air would be worth the trouble. John Bremer did, however. Furthermore, he seemed ready to go out of his way to uncomplicate *my* life: When would I like him to come? Was there anything special I would like him to talk about? Was there any advance material he could send me which might help? Later, I will return to the subject of John Bremer as the Parkway Program's greatest public relations asset — suffice it to say for the time being I liked him enough over the phone to decide I would present him in the most favorable possible light.

On the air, I found I liked John even more. He is basically an interviewer's favorite kind of guest — articulate, direct, not shy about controversial subjects. Furthermore, what he was saying, to me at least, was making sense. Trained as a teacher in college, a sense of desperation concerning the public schools caught up with me sometime during my third year, and I opted for a journalism career instead. By the time I met John I had been a magazine editor, a freelance writer, and a TV producer, yet what he was saying made me want to get back into public education as soon as possible. It occurred to me at the time that here, on my very show, was a man whose educational philosophy conformed exactly with my own. What was astonishing was that this man was actually running a *school,* in the public system, no less. It was too good to be true. I had to find out more.

Off the air, I found John as ready to talk about the program as on. Yes, it really was a public school. Yes, he knew the public school system was crazy. Yes, it really was going to work. I invited him back for another appearance, and suddenly I found myself quitting my job to become the Parkway Program's information officer. John's offer came as a surprise to me, but I suffered no hesitation in accepting it. As far as I could tell, he was running the only educational project anywhere which made any sense to me at all.

It was my first official day at the Parkway Program, however, which *really* introduced me to John Bremer's approach to learning. I remember walking in the door, up the steps past lounging students (one of whom looked up at me, grinned amiably, and said, "Hi, baby, whose friend are *you*?") and into John's office, separated from what looked to me like an indoor softball game by a shoulder-high plywood partition. "Well, John," I shouted over the din, "here I am. What am I supposed to do?" He looked me full in the face and said: "What are you supposed to do? I don't know what you're supposed to do. It's *your* job. Look around and see what you *can* do."

Clearly, this was going to be a job rather unlike any I'd had before. For the first time I had doubts. This man had found me, sounded me out, hired me, and was paying me, all to do *something,* but he didn't know what. Now, journalists are relatively independent people, but this situation had me fairly floored. I looked around. A teacher and a student were arguing about politics in a corner, and two students nearby were playing chess. A couple more kids tossed some round object back and forth over what looked like a tutoring session in Spanish. One boy came up to me and asked me if he hadn't seen me at last year's prom at Overbrook High School.

"No, I'm not a student. I work here now. Starting today."

"Yeah, hey what do you know? You look sixteen. What's your name?"

"Lisa Strick."

"Hi, Lisa. What are you going to do here?"

"I'm an information officer."

"*A what?*"

"An information officer."

"What's that?"

"I don't know."

"Well, don't worry, you'll figure it out."

This job was going to be different all right.

During my first three weeks on the job, I was given virtually no responsibilities other than to find out as much about the Parkway Program as I could. I talked with students and faculty and read every printed piece of paper I could get my hands on. I spent a great deal of time out of the office as well, following John around town. As the program's reputation grew, John's calendar for outside appointments — opportunities, as he saw them, to bring the program to the community — became crammed. I went along while he "sold" the program to an institution from which we were asking space. I attended a speech he gave to a group of college students studying education. I sat in on a joint meeting of suburban superintendents who had summoned John, as far as I could see, for the purpose of exposing him and his program as a fraud. In the process, I began to pick up on the kinds of questions people most commonly asked, and what the answers to those questions were. I decided I might soon be qualified to start answering the phone; it rang constantly, and the caller always asked for John, regardless of his mission. I asked our receptionist-secretary-den mother Tami Williams if she thought some of these people would settle for an official-sounding title like public information officer? "Why not?" she said, and the phone was all mine.

Except for the fact that I seldom had the information these callers wanted, the system worked fairly well. Most people won't be too demanding about answers, I've found, if they feel they at least have a sympathetic ear. My title was sufficiently impressive to get people talking, and anything was better than unanswered phone messages piling up on John's desk. Most of the callers' questions were repetitive and basic, but at least I felt I was making a start at some useful activity.

[117]

A year later, the phone still hasn't stopped ringing, and sometimes my desk gets nearly as littered with messages as John's used to be, but I still try to answer them all; good public relations, I am convinced, has to start at just this pedestrian level. There are times when I want to rip the phone out of the wall rather than answer it again, but someone who has been trying to get through for three days without success will not bear the program much in the way of goodwill. I try to remember that as the 1,567th parent calls to tell me why her daughter/son needs a change of schools.

The majority of calls we received were from people wishing to visit the program for direct observation; this situation has not changed much since the program opened. In May 1970, we averaged fifty calls a week asking for observation information, and most of those calls represented groups. The nature of the individuals who are interested in us, however, has changed. At first, the interest was primarily, understandably, local — parents, teachers, businessmen, and community groups. Many of these people called after having heard John speak somewhere. It is still the case that whenever John goes to some city, I can expect a large volume of calls from that city the following week. Within a relatively short time, however, the Parkway Program attracted the attention of the national press, and more and more of the calls we received were long distance. Publicity has an escalating quality: the more out-of-town press covered the program, the more out-of-town visitors we received, and the more out-of-town visitors we received, the more the out-of-town press people became interested in us. As the months went by, the visitors came in larger numbers and came from higher up on their organizational ladders — fewer local teachers, more city superintendents; fewer Philadelphia community people and more representatives from the Office of Education in Washington.

In the first hectic weeks, however, I made no such distinctions: the calls were just from people, growing numbers of people who wanted to come in and observe our classes, talk to our students, grill our director. Prior to my coming, requests from people who wanted to come and observe us had been met with, "Well, just stop in any time," but as the numbers grew, this situation became impossible. Guests wandered in and out of classes randomly, and half the time, when they showed up at our central headquarters, no one was around to talk with them. Students and faculty were all out in the community, leaving one harried secretary to divide her time between the guests and the constantly ringing phones. Given this situation, I took the most obvious step and bought an appointment calendar which would allow me to schedule visitors according to reasonable traffic patterns convenient to both the visitors and the faculty. In the meantime, John had prepared a booklet describing the program's operations.

The brochure, however, did not supply the basic information I quickly learned most visitors wanted first: How many students are in the program? How do we meet Pennsylvania state requirements, and what were those requirements, anyway? After their class visits, guests repeatedly returned to my office with these and other questions and I developed a sort of a chant of facts and figures which helped fill in the gaps. It occurred to me, however, that it might be a good idea to answer these questions *before* our visitors set out on their observation schedules. The feedback I received from visitors was beginning to show me that, out of context, a Parkway student's day was hard to grasp — it could look disorganized, fragmented, even chaotic. A class in its beginning stages could look to a visitor (used to the idea that "class" was a place where you sit in rows, keep your mouth shut, and don't chew gum) like sheer mayhem. Students lounging in our headquarters in their off hours nearly always got visitors asking, "Why aren't these children in school?"

I became more and more aware of the truth of John's statement that the Parkway Program is something which cannot really be observed — it has to be experienced. A Parkway student's day is not measured by hours and classes but by learning. Visitors who can think only in terms of what is being produced, in terms of blow-by-blow feedback, can find this situation frustrating.

I undertook the practice of scheduling "orientation sessions" for visitors about to observe classes, and the results were good. These sessions are not to "brainwash" our guests, or to indoctrinate them with the party line. Their purpose is to help visitors "experience" the Parkway approach to learning as I answer their questions. In fact, I believe I have successfully oriented a visitor only if, at the end of our meeting, he is answering most of his questions himself. In these orientation sessions it is perhaps easiest to identify Parkway's public relations for what it really is: a teaching activity. Most visitors to the program are about as capable of understanding what we are doing as is a first grader of understanding calculus; that is, he is ready to understand it only when the teacher springs his thinking from a limiting background experience. My behavior with visitors these days does not differ appreciably from my behavior in the class in communications which I began teaching a semester after I joined Parkway. I avoid pat answers to questions — instead, if I can, I throw the question right back at the questioner. Most of the questions people ask about the Parkway Program can be honestly answered only with the same two words: "It depends."

"Tell me how you organize your curriculum here, Mrs. Strick."

"Well, that depends."

"On what?"

"On the students and what they want to learn. And the teachers, and what they want to teach. And on what sorts of resources seem to be available in the community. Things like that."

"Yes, but who *does* it, all the coordinating, I mean?"

"Well, that depends too. On who wants to do it."

"Well who ends up teaching things like—oh hell, I guess that depends too, on who happens to be available with the skills needed."

"Right."

Most people start to pick up on this approach in about an hour, unless they are hostile, narrow-minded, or both. Of course, we do get a certain percentage of people who come in convinced that it all can't work—and who intend to prove it. I suppose that anyone who runs a program which in any way deviates from accepted norms must expect the attacks of hard-core traditionalists who will reject anything that's different just *because* it is different. This kind of prejudice represents a learning problem which most teachers should be familiar with: it is not unlike the student who "can't" learn math because he's "stupid" in it, or who won't give Emily Dickinson a chance because he "hates poetry." I took my cues from John in working with these people. While consistently polite (and it never pays to meet hostility with hostility), he demonstrated to me in innumerable situations that prejudice can give way only when it is confronted with a conviction of equal intensity—and better logic. On one occasion John was accosted at a meeting by a particularly hostile school official, who asked sarcastically, "Just what makes you think we need an alternate system of education?"

"Because," John said placidly, "the present system is crazy." (I have always admired John's ability to retain his convictions and his cool simultaneously in situations like this.) The man sputtered: "Why," he said, "what do you mean by that! I believe we're doing very well. Our students score in the 90th percentile in national tests."

"You are telling me," John countered, "that your students have learned how to be passive and follow directions, and perhaps they know how to read, which is an advantage. The tests, however, are no indication that your students have learned how to *think,* nor, I suspect, will they learn how to think as long as you continue to emphasize the importance of those tests."

The man was indignant. "Why," he said, "our students take those tests because they are *important.* They *must take* tests."

"Why?" John asked. The man had no answer.

Since that meeting, I have never felt intimidated by a hostile or suspicious visitor. Recently I worked out what is perhaps the most successful means of dealing with the hard-core suspicious—one in which I hardly talk to them at all. I have found that the most convincing statement I can make concerning the effectiveness of the program is to introduce a guest directly to our product—the students—and leave. Guests wise in the ways of PR people are usually astonished by this tactic: it catches the really suspicious off guard. Here I am, leaving them free to grill our kids about what's *really* wrong with the program while I walk out the door—yet I have found I can do this with perfect confidence because our students feel positively about their school. Even the most negative kid in the program will, when he is put on the spot, defend it. It seems that the more a student senses hostility in a visitor, the more protective he becomes. I have yet to have a student let me down in this respect. One afternoon a contingent of visitors came from the State Department of Public Instruction in Harrisburg. They were looking for flaws in the program—somehow success didn't interest them. Sensing that they weren't going to believe anything they heard from a public relations person, I asked them if they would like to talk to some students. They eyed me suspiciously—had I perhaps "planted" in the crowd students who were trained to give a good story? They pointed to a kid who was reading in a corner. "Can we talk to him?" they said. The student they indicated was one whom I knew to be a real complainer. At town meetings and faculty meetings he was always in evidence saying that the program wasn't working as it should. This, however, was the student they had chosen, so I made the introductions and left. When I returned, several other students had joined my visitors, but the first student was still doing most of the talking. The end of the conversation, as I overheard it, went like this:

> HARRISBURG: But can't you tell us anything you *don't* like about this school?
>
> STUDENT: Man, why do you keep asking me that question? If you want to find hang-ups, go visit the school I left last year—there they treat you like in a prison and they crowd forty kids in a class and they have kids on dope and all sorts of things. Here they care about *me*—I mean, like I may not dig everything here, but, you know, I can change it. You have to work harder here, but you get more out of it.

Later, I thanked the student for taking the time to talk to my visitors, and told him they had been very impressed with the program as a result. "Yeah, it's O.K.," he said. "*Now* can you tell me why we can't get together a drama class that *works* for a change?"

Increasingly, I now ask students to orient visitors. In the end, our reputation will have to be made not by me but by them. People will come to understand our program only when they have a chance to examine our product—and our product is impressive. Within another year, I believe that there should be no need for a "specialist" to work with visitors; this function should become part of the curriculum for the students. More and more students are beginning to see visitors much as I see them, as learning opportunities. In orientation sessions, the communication should go two ways, just as it should in class. Given the right attitudes, talking to visitors is a pleasure rather than a chore, and wherever positive feelings are present, good public relations are sure to follow.

Although most of my time is spent working with visitors to the program, clearly only a limited number of people can learn about us through direct experience. Although those who come to see us usually are our most enthusiastic supporters, if we are to win the kind of wide, broad-based support which we need, ways of reaching a far larger audience have to be found. Quite simply, what we are talking about here is politics, please forgive the expression. In the educational community, it seems, most people find politics distasteful. If John Bremer had any unshakable convictions in opening the program, one was that political support was something we would have to have, and as quickly as possible. His reasoning on this is almost childishly simple: he does not believe that any public program will succeed—or has a *right* to succeed—without the public behind it. One of the ills of the traditional public school system is that parents and community people are virtually excluded from the process of decision-making on how their children are to be educated. Since there is normally no alternative to the public schools apart from expensive private education, public educators have for years been able to get away with acting and being in no real way held accountable for the result to their constituencies.

When the Parkway Program opened in Philadelphia, all that was changed. Our teachers, our institutions, and our students (with parental consent) all join us voluntarily. We are in every way accountable to them, because if they are in any way, at any time, dissatisfied with their Parkway experience, they may leave. In John's mind, this is as it should be—the program is valid only as long as it is responsive to the needs of its membership. If the program is to remain a viable entity, however, it is also true that membership must be strong both in number and in voice: this is the persistent reality of politics which most educators seem to find uncomfortable.

It is my feeling that much of this distaste for politics is owed to the fact that most public educators lack confidence in the collective judgment of the people. Nowadays, of course, the feeling is mutual. At any rate, it must be admitted that this is a strange attitude for the officials charged with the responsibility of educating the people's children.

Since the Parkway Program's future is dependent on the continuing support of the public, John has no distaste for politics; rather, he has a positive zest for it. He has always, in fact, felt that he can probably do the program greater good outside the office rather than in it in many ways. To support the program, people must first know about us, and John has made it his business to get the Parkway idea across to as many people as possible. In setting up the program, he arranged to meet with every group which might eventually have an interest or an influence in it. He met with businessmen and parent groups and student groups. He talked to educators in the public schools and in the universities. He met with individuals, groups, and organizations. In many ways, the earliest and firmest impressions people received of the Parkway Program were inseparable from the personality of John Bremer. Jovial, conservative in appearance, dignified beyond belief by an English accent which somehow makes anything sound respectable, John "sold" the Parkway Program by laying his reputation on the line. Frequently, the climate was in his favor: parents, teachers, and students were growing increasingly desperate, and John's message sounded like a reprieve. Yet also, John proved enormously effective at cracking the basically conservative segments of the community—those inclined to mumble about the influence of "bearded hippie freaks wandering around center city at all hours." Perhaps the greatest measure of John's ability to drum up political support can be judged from the two rumors which sprang up locally about him about six months into the Parkway Program's operation. John Bremer was leaving the Parkway Program, people said. Why? One group said he was going to start a public relations firm. The other said he was running for mayor.

John was out of the office a great deal, as likely to be in San Francisco talking to the city fathers as at the University of Pennsylvania talking to an education class. He almost never turns an invitation down while there is a free hour on his calendar. More often than not, people call about visiting the Parkway Program because they heard John talking about it in Kalamazoo or Albuquerque or Toronto. His out-of-town efforts have resulted in over a dozen cities seriously considering proposals for Parkway-type schools.

John and I share an acute awareness that the single most effective means of reaching large numbers of people is through the media. It is humbling to consider that the number of people which John and I combined might reach in our lifetime is not equal to a fraction of those exposed to one national network news broadcast. If one has a sense for the political, the potential power of the media is something one cannot afford to ignore. It is exactly this fact, of course, which has made public relations big business in this country—courting and convincing the media has become a highly sophisticated profession which earns those who are good at it millions annually. The growth of the public relations

[123]

brain pool has, however, resulted in a definable backlash to which many new programs fall victim: the more people are out to get the favor of the press, the more public relations tends to become public rationalization—the more you want good coverage, the more you are inclined to whitewash. The more whitewash they get, however, the more suspicious the press, and the harder it is to get the support everybody is after. I say it with conviction because I made my living as a working journalist. Press people today are probably the most negatively oriented people in the world. They don't just report disasters—they go looking for them. And almost nothing pleases a reporter these days more than catching somebody trying to whitewash and turning that into a scandal—right on the front page.

Perhaps I have just made my former colleagues out to be a thoroughly dislikable group, which they indeed can be if you ever get on the wrong side of them. And getting on the wrong side of the media is relatively easy—but so is getting on the right side if you know how to do it.

Press people really operate on a very simple code. You be nice to them and they'll be nice to you; "nice" by media standards, of course. Being nice to the press has been relatively easy for me, since I used to be a member, and it has been a rewarding way of life for John, as coverage on the Parkway Program in every type of media through local radio stations to *Life* will show. Anyone with a normal dose of intelligence and sensitivity can learn to work with the press effectively, and I will try to set down here those general, common sense rules which usually work in such a way that my former associates will thank me rather than excommunicate me.

There are many different kinds of media today—local people and national people, of course, also print people (magazines, newspapers) and picture people (news photographers, film-makers, TV people). Each group requires a different kind of attention. There are also basically two kinds of media situations—the situation in which you are relatively unknown and are trying to get media attention and the situation (not necessarily any easier) in which you are relatively established and someone either comes to document you as a feature story or find out what's wrong with you, also as a feature story.

There is one thing to keep in mind which applies to all of these groups and situations. It is always, in working with the media, to *your* advantage to make *their* job as easy as possible. If you are not familiar with press operations, the easiest way to find out what makes a media man's life easier is simply to ask him—it varies from man to man, anyway, and most press people will appreciate your initial concern. You know, you can get to feel really badly about writing a negative story about someone who has gone out of his way to help you. Someone who's tried to brainwash you or use you, yes, but not someone who's really tried to *help* you.

It is easier to learn to be helpful to the press if you understand the kinds of pressures these people commonly work under. Most of us at one time or another have had to work against the clock to get a project finished. Media people do it *all* the time. Their professional lives are normally measured out by deadlines, and their deadlines are absolute and to the minute. For example, no matter how many stories a newsman might have to cover in a day, no matter how many places he has to be or how many people he has to talk to, the stories *must* be filed in time for the press deadline, or in time for the 6 o'clock evening news. It will not do to run the story tomorrow instead—competitive media are running it tonight, and tomorrow the story will be "killed." Feature writers and documentary-type people usually have the most leverage in terms of scheduling—but, on the other hand, an average-sized mobile film crew costs its employer around $1000 a day. These people are anxious to get it over with as quickly as possible. Your object in working with the media, then, is simple—you want to help them get their story fast. One of the most foolproof ways of alienating the press is to waste their valuable time.

Let's start with the kind of situation most programs start in. You have not, let's say, in spite of your obvious merit, been "discovered," and you'd like to be. Courting the press is a tricky business—almost nothing is guaranteed to work. Quite a lot can be said, however, on what's guaranteed *not* to work. The following generalizations are worth keeping in mind:

1. *Start local.* Of course you'd like to appear on the cover of *Time,* or even on the last page somewhere, but local media are the easiest to reach, and in many ways support of the local press is more important than national coverage. Chances are, if you are really new, the national media will be inaccessible to you anyway—but national media frequently become interested in a story via the local press coverage it has received. Generally, newspapers are the most approachable media (don't ignore small neighborhood newspapers). Newspapers have to fill up all of those pages daily; broadcasting media reach more people, but they have less time to fill and can afford to be more selective. Broadcasting people too, by the way, also often get ideas for stories from newspaper coverage.

2. *Be newsworthy.* From the above, you ought to have concluded that to get into the newspapers, you ought to be a news item. If you are

new and different, of course, you are already a news item—but are you two inches on the back page or a 1500-word feature news item? Know the difference. When bringing yourself to the attention of the press, do so in a way which makes you of maximum interest to their audiences—that's who they're really thinking about. What interests audiences, of course, differs from area to area and even from paper to paper within an area. Suffice it to say that if people are up in arms about a budget crisis, that is a good time to point out how economical you are. If overcrowding is an issue, point out your low student-teacher ratio. Your entire story, of course, need not consist of this one facet of your program, but it gives the press a handle to grab onto; it gets them in the door and gives them the "lead-in" all newsmen look for. An important "don't" in this area is *don't* bother the news media if you don't have news for them. Every local newsman knows which organizations are in the habit of crying wolf, and he avoids them. Don't flood the news desks with releases full of petty facts, and don't call a news conference to report irrelevant information (irrelevant to the press, of course—seldom to the organization distributing the information). Remember newsmen are pressed for *time:* don't waste it. Find out also what aspects of the press's operation in your area work to your favor: for example, Sunday is usually a good time to hold an attention-getting event, because Monday papers are normally pretty slim, coming right after the fat Sunday edition.

3. *Be brief; and be clear.* Whether you are writing a news release, planning a statement for a news conference, or answering questions in an interview, make your point in as few words as possible; that is what the newsman is going to have to do. Think of the way a classical news paragraph is written—in journalism classes they still teach that the first sentence should contain all of the essential information, the "5W's": Who, What, When, Where, and Why. Talk to reporters in their own spare language. If you bury your point in rhetoric, the greater the chance of their missing it. If background information is essential, write it down, get it printed, and hand it out to the media; they can read it later. Taking the time to spell it all out is committing the cardinal sin: wasting time. Being brief has another benefit—it makes you more quotable. How many times have you found a news report which went,

> When asked what he thought about the current school board crisis, Mr. X said: "Well, I've thought a lot about that, and after due consideration, I think that perhaps——and, of course, I realize that there are other points of view on this, points of view which we in public office naturally don't want to ignore because all of the interests represented in the com-

munity will bear on our future actions, but I would like to say
that, having considered particularly the recent statement
of. . . ."

At this point, the newsman stops hearing. He has only six hundred
words in which to tell his story, so he quotes the guy who said, "It's
irresponsible and insane."

4. *Be consistent and play fair.* Never, never, play dirty with the press.
Media people can be extremely vindictive, and they have long memo-
ries. A newsman who feels he's been scorned or used or betrayed by
you is entirely capable of deciding to get back. And he can. Right on the
front page.

Don't lie to the press, and don't be evasive — that arouses suspicion
immediately. Honesty *is* the best policy. When asked a direct question,
answer it. When asked for other information within reason, supply it.
(I say within reason because a newsman once asked me to give him the
personal records of half our students without their consent, and there
I drew the line.) If you have the kind of program you have to lie about,
stay away from the press altogether — you're just making it harder on
the rest of us. Consistency in dealing with the press is also important
in many ways. Press people really don't much like surprises. If possible,
designate one person on your staff as the media contact. That way,
media people always know to whom to go for information, which
makes their job easier. Also, it expedites building a friendly working
relation between your program and the local media. I, for example,
have made a point of getting to know which local reporters' "beats"
cover our field, and I try to insure consistency from their end by direct-
ing all information to these people personally, time after time. Now,
months later, they have built up a familiarity with our background and
I have a familiarity with theirs. I don't have to go out of my way to
explain all over again what month we started, how many students
we have, and so on; *they* know I won't schedule a news conference
at 3:30 because half their deadlines are at four. Life is easier all around
for both of us. John, too, has made a special point of getting to know all
the reporters who cover the program personally. He remembers their
names. He monitors the types of stories they write, which helps us
place a special story if we want to ("this sounds like a box X sort of
story," John or I will say, "so let's call his paper in on this.") Even more
important, John's friendly concern for the press has gone a long way
toward earning him their respect. Their support follows.

5. *Be attentive to special demands.* You will find that each media person
you come into contact with will have his own idiosyncratic requirements. This reporter goes for human interest and that one is big on

interviews. That paper always sends a photographer so you have to provide something visual (with so much news coming through television now, in scheduling news events it is nearly always to your advantage to play up the visual aspect of it. I've been known to remember that at the last minute and hurriedly move all the chairs for a news conference previously set up to another room which has posters on the wall or some such thing). This network uses heavy lighting and needs an outlet or two. That network is heavily unionized, so it's expensive to run overtime. If you can learn to anticipate these demands, your relations with the press will surely improve. Any little consideration, from providing coffee for an early conference to standing in the background joking with reporters for a few minutes (in my case, in my shortest skirt) contributes to your chances of winning the best kind of reputation you can get—that of an enjoyable assignment, one reporters look forward to.

Let's say you have been successful and become a big enough story that local and out-of-town press start coming to you. Most of the guidelines listed above still apply, plus one more: never pass up a chance. You have to practically be in the White House before you can feel confident that the media will wait for you. When a media man comes to you for a story, he normally has two reasons, and you know only one. You know he is there because you are a good story. *He* knows that, plus the fact that he has a feature-sized hole in his January issue which has to be plugged up fast. A man with a hole in his January issue will not be responsive to your saying that your schedule is really very crowded now and could he come do his research the first week of March? As far as he is concerned, you are less a good story than a good *January* story. After that, forget it.

Second chances to become a good story don't come often, and all the first chances count. The first chances, also, come in many forms, and it doesn't usually pay to discriminate. It has been to John's credit that he has been as ready to appear on a live 7 A.M. local radio broadcast as on a national television network. Both appearances did us good. John's belief in accommodating nearly every request from the media hasn't always been met with enthusiasm by his staff—in fact, the last time he told me we should expect the third consecutive camera crew in a week I nearly brained him with his paperweight. However, there is little doubt that this policy, within reason, pays off. The circulation of the Parkway idea through the press quickly made us a force in Philadelphia to be reckoned with. The fact that millions of people know about you won't necessarily keep you from being done in, but it will surely keep you from being done in quietly.

There is one peculiar negative aspect to receiving a great deal of media coverage which is worth keeping in mind. After you have become established through the media as a good program, the only way they can make a viable story of you is to show that you're not as good as you've been cracked up to be; the fact that you exist and that you do good work is dead news. As more and more press covered the Parkway Program, I learned to anticipate the first question from media newcomers. Somehow it was always, "Well, what *problems* have you been having?" If you understand the reasons behind increasing negativism like this, you can deal with it: the man is looking for news, so find some good news for him. Develop another proof of success — point out a new development. Find a whole new slant on what you are doing which is to your advantage before he makes one up which isn't.

Of course, no amount of good public relations will turn a bad program into a good one, but it can make the difference between a program which makes it and one which does not. A mediocre program needs public relations to sell it. A good one only needs it to make people aware of what's happening — after that it sells itself. Know the difference between telling and selling — it's a big one. Doing public relations for a program which sells itself is one of the most pleasurable jobs in the world. One other thing which relates to public relations in education specifically: if you have a truly educational program, you cannot legitimately limit your educational functions to your students. Running a "school without walls" breaks down the barriers between the students and the community, but also between the community and the students. I'll put it in the words of a recent visitor I had at the Parkway Program. She had spent over a month visiting innovative educational programs preliminary to starting one of her own, and she had been disappointed with many of her experiences.

> Many of the educators I saw really didn't seem to care about helping me to understand what they were doing. They didn't have time to talk to me, and once I came in and was left for over an hour standing in the hall. Every time, the excuse was that they were too involved with educating their students to take time out for visitors. Just because they made the distinction, I couldn't help but get suspicious — if they categorized their educational objectives that much, how good a job could they be doing with their kids?

She was right. If you define learning only in terms of students and not the larger community, it is only a short step to defining English only in terms of grammar and history only in terms of dates. If an educator is sensitive to a need for learning, he cannot limit his vision or his responsibility to those in his classroom. A true community of learning is not limited to students and teachers; it is a community in which everyone has flexible roles, teaching some of the time, and, hopefully, learning a great deal of the time. Can a program which draws a line between helping students learn and helping the community learn really be called a school without walls? Think about it.

8
The Early History

How did the Parkway Program originate?

The answer comes against a background of violence, increasing use of narcotics, underachievement, dropouts, vandalism, and arson in the Philadelphia school system—these despite every effort at improvement by a blue-ribbon school board, its president, former mayor Richardson Dilworth, and his new school superintendent.

Ineffectiveness of teaching in the schools was brought home to the public in January 1967 with the publication of reading and arithmetic test results. The skills of most Philadelphia pupils were well below the national average. Subjected to national tests for the first time, the students were found to be appallingly deficient in vocabulary, reading, arithmetic, languages, and other educational abilities.

Third grade pupils were five months behind the national average. Above that level it got worse. Boys and girls in the eighth grade were a year and a quarter behind.

Only in the relatively affluent northeast section of the city did children approach the national average. Elsewhere pupils were as much as two years behind.

In only three of Philadelphia's twenty-two high schools were 50 percent of the tenth grade pupils able to match the national level. A great number of students who were about to receive high school diplomas could hardly read.

Approached by a reporter upon emerging from the school board meeting where the test results were disclosed, a board member, Rev. Henry H. Nichols, was visibly moved. Shaking his head, Mr. Nichols observed that the schools were in "pretty bad shape."

[131]

Then came a ray of hope. Three New York educators reported to the U.S. Office of Education that Philadelphia was in the midst of "the most dramatic revolution in a city school system in the post-war period."

> Though the extent of actual change thus far has been relatively limited, the nature of the accomplished change . . . is highly significant.
>
> By moving outside the community for new and needed expertise, by seeking out and providing mechanisms for encouraging community involvement and by pioneering in long-range planning and evaluation, the Philadelphia board has set the stage for changes yet to come.
>
> That reform has come to Philadelphia schools is clear and that it is directly identified with Mr. Richardson Dilworth, the new board chairman, and his perception of his role as a "change agent" is clearer still.
>
> The circumstances leading up to Mr. Dilworth's appointment may turn out to be the most dramatic revolution in a city school system in the post-war period.

Coming to light in August 1967, in the wake of the publication of the test results, the words of the experts confused many Philadelphians.

The January announcement showed that education in the city was going downhill, yet the August report seemed to say that a dramatic educational revolution was underway. Or did it? Some people pointed out that the revolution was described as being more in spirit than in actuality.

Confronted by these conflicting claims, most Philadelphia parents — or most of those who gave the matter any attention—bided their time, waiting to see whether the school board could transform good intentions into better education.

For some of the black students of the city time was running out, however. They bided their time no longer. Motivated by concern over their educations—a concern that involved racial considerations only in part—some of them skipped classes on November 17, 1967, and marched on the school board's administration building at 21st Street and Benjamin Franklin Parkway. Converging on the building, the students, estimated at 3500, demanded courses in black history.

They also carried leaflets which went to a more fundamental issue. "If the training provided in schools is inadequate . . . for making a living," the leaflets declared, "the individual man is crippled in his effort to provide for himself and family the three basic requirements: food, clothing, and shelter."

At first, the students were orderly. Four hundred police arrived on the scene, however, and then hell broke loose. In the words of the *New York Times* (November 19), "Clubbing by policemen, attacks on by-standers by the students, 57 arrests and at least 22 injuries marked the incident."

The *Times* also reported that student demands, presented to officials within the administration building, included one for an over-all improvement in education.

This gave School Board President Dilworth and his superintendent something to discuss until it was worn slick, greasy, and threadbare! Withdrawing for a serious talk, they emerged with a statement that deplored the violence and emphasized what steps had been taken in an effort to abort the demonstration. (Students were told that any unexcused work missed would have to be made up or a zero would be received for the day.) Then they addressed themselves to the critical educational issue of our time, the issue that the Parkway Program meets.

Dilworth and his superintendent declared:

> There is no doubt in our minds that the students not only have a right to be heard, but that some of their concerns are quite legitimate. . . . Let us stress that in the display of energy and concern witnessed today on the part of high school youth, we saw real evidence of a desire to improve the quality and relevance of education. *We feel that students do have the intellect and power to help speed such improvements.* But they must direct their energies to the real issue of improving schools—which is a big step beyond mere protestation—if their energies are not to be wasted.

This statement went to the heart of the problem. Few people in Philadelphia would have any part of such a reasoned approach, however. Instead, there were recriminations between black and white, old and young, civil libertarians and the police. Eventually the educational aspect of the demonstration was submerged in the concern over violence by the students and the police. Then most adult Philadelphians forgot the entire matter, as though no lesson were to be learned from it, just as none had been learned from the revelation in January 1967 of the collapse in the educational system.

Clifford Brenner, however, did not forget the lessons of 1967. He sought a new pattern for high school education in Philadelphia, creating the opportunity for what later developed into the Parkway Program.

A former newspaperman, Brenner had served as press secretary to Richardson Dilworth when the latter was mayor of Philadelphia from

1956 to 1962. Named assistant vice president for public affairs for Temple University after this, Brenner left that post to rejoin Dilworth at the board of education. Serving first as an administrative assistant to the board president, Brenner remained to become the school district's director of development.

In a memorandum to Graham S. Finney, deputy superintendent for planning, Brenner set forth his concept more fully:

> This memorandum replaces and supplements the earlier informal draft I shared with you.
>
> I propose the creation of a new four-year high school organization to serve the Center City pupils and pupils drawn from all parts of the City.
>
> The new high school would be located physically along the Benjamin Franklin Parkway from City Hall to the Art Museum. With the Parkway as a campus, the new high school would draw upon the resources of the many institutions on or near the Parkway for required physical facilities. Examples of how this could be done are as follows:
>
> The YMCA, with its pool and gymnasium, would be the new high school's physical education facility.
>
> The Academy of Natural Sciences would contain the classrooms and laboratories for the teaching of chemistry and biology.
>
> The Franklin Institute would contain the classrooms and laboratories for the teaching of the physical sciences. Mathematics could also be handled at the Franklin Institute or, perhaps, at the Insurance Company of North America.
>
> The Free Library with its books, records and films is a natural center for the teaching of English and foreign languages.
>
> Art and art appreciation: The Museum of Art, the Moore School and the Rodin Museum.
>
> The administrative headquarters of the new high school could be in the Board of Education building. Or, if there is no space there, space could be rented at Park Towne Place, or . . .
>
> Space could be sought at any number of places along the Parkway for instructional or special purposes. Apartment houses like Park Towne, the Plaza, the Windsor, 2601, 2401, the Philadelphian, etc., all of which may have available space.
>
> But the fact is that there exists singularly appropriate space, facilities and environment for the teaching of subject matter

courses in all of the institutions. All of them have classrooms, auditoriums, etc.

In addition to regular subjects being taught at the above-mentioned facilities, specialized instruction could take place at such locations as Bell Telephone, the *Inquirer,* KYW Studios, Smith Kline & French, General Electric, etc. In short, in addition to the most beautiful campus in Philadelphia with its center at Logan Circle, and regular classrooms and laboratories in the various institutions along the Parkway, many of the City's centrally located business institutions would be readily available to the new high school, for either curricular or extra-curricular studies in the world of work.

Moreover, the new high school could have admirable "laboratories" for civics-social studies by virtue of the convenient location of City Hall, the Municipal Services Building, the County Court and the Youth Study Center, as well as the nearby State Offices Building.

It is not suggested that we get all of this free of cost. It is believed we may have to contract for some of the space. But with a regular high school costing $10 million, it is thought we can bring this new school in for a very modest amount annually. Now, as to some specific items:

Faculty: A faculty would be recruited from the school system. Additionally, we should sign up people at each of these institutions for lectures, enrichment, etc. For example, Franklin Institute people would be working side by side with our math and physics teachers. Finally, there are many very talented people in the Board of Education building who could spend a couple of hours each week with the boys and girls attending this high school, from [the superintendent] on down.

Transportation: Since the high school is a campus school, the boys and girls would walk from class to class as they do in college. But in addition, it would have several "loop" buses going from Logan Circle to the Art Museum and from the Circle down to City Hall on a continuous basis.

Feeding: Almost all of these institutions have employee cafeterias or public cafeterias. The students could be spread among them and small groups assigned to eat at Bell Telephone, Board of Education, etc.

Leadership: The success of this school will depend on having resourceful and imaginative educators and administrators at its head. Clearly, there will be many opportunities for new departures in both educational program and administrative practice. But in addition, this school should have an advisory board composed of parents, Board of Education people and representatives of the institutions which are providing space, people and other resources.

When Do We Start: We should begin operation in the Fall of 1968, with about 600 9th graders — about 200 from Center City and the balance city-wide. They should be evenly distributed as to sex, and obviously integrated as to race. Detailed selection criteria should be prepared promptly, but the new school should not be viewed as an "elite" school. A new grade should be added with each successive year, until at the end of four years Philadelphia will have a high school (9–12) of 2,400 youngsters, integrated, and livening up the Parkway with their vitality. There should be very few dropouts from this school. . . ."

This memorandum was dated November 13, 1967, but it was not until February 7, 1968, that a meeting was called by Board President Dilworth to make public the plan for what was then called Parkway High School. Representatives of several score Parkway-related institutions and agencies, including the diocesan schools, were invited to an exploratory meeting to consider the feasibility of operating a high school using multiple resources. The response was, initially at least, enthusiastic.

The *Philadelphia Evening Bulletin* was supportive, and so was the *Philadelphia Inquirer* which added its realistic cautions in an editorial it called "Non-School on the Parkway." In part, it read:

The concept of a high school, without a building of its own, drawing a student body of 2400 from public, parochial and private schools in the city and suburbs and integrating its study subjects into the operations of the cooperating institutions, is unquestionably imaginative and exciting.

It is, however, just the germ of an idea. Its practicalities have to be worked out. There has to be much more to the plan than the mere saving of $15 million or so in building construction — not to mention the additional money saved in janitor wages and the cost of policemen patrolling the corridors. It has to be shown that the non-school would furnish the students with a good secondary school education, fitting the graduates for college if they wish to continue their education, and not confining them simply to elaborate field trips. . . .

Newspaper articles, too, supported the idea, even in its outline form.

The *Philadelphia Tribune,* on February 10, 1968, welcomed the chance to participate:

TRIBUNE TO BE PART OF RADICALLY NEW PARKWAY HI SCHOOL COMPLEX

The Philadelphia Tribune will be included in a revolutionary new high school complex that will draw students from all over the city to an area centered around Benjamin Franklin Parkway.

The "non-school" school, described by the Board of Education Wednesday, will utilize cultural, scientific and business enterprises on the Parkway as a mile-long education center.

Some 2400 students will travel on a loop bus from building to building, learning from both teachers and experts in the various fields.

The Tribune is the only Negro-owned establishment which will be a part of the complex.

The *Jewish Times* also gave editorial support:

DURING THESE DAYS when imagination seems to be at less than a premium in Philadelphia, it is invigorating to see concepts such as the high school campus on the Parkway come to light. It would have been better to see some of the details presented with the original plan, but the thought conjures visions of great education for the children of this city. Support for the idea has been given generally. A follow-through is expected to support this.

And the *Evening Bulletin* reported the publicly expressed support of the diocesan system:

MSGR. HUGHES HAILS PARKWAY SCHOOL PLAN

One of the city's top Roman Catholic educators today hailed the Board of Education's proposal for a new four-year high school which would utilize existing cultural and scientific facilities along the Parkway.

"It's an exciting new concept in the field of education," said Rt. Rev. Edward T. Hughes, archdiocesan superintendent of schools.

He said it was not yet clear "how parochial school students will fit into this new educational structure."

Some difficulties, however, had been created. The *Inquirer* carried the story:

"PARTICIPANTS" DENY COMMITMENTS ON NEW-STYLE SCHOOL

The Board of Education's announcement of plans for a highly sophisticated new high school complex in the Benjamin Franklin Parkway area caught reported "participants" from the worlds of business, industry and culture off guard Thursday.

Most of these "cooperating" companies and institutions contacted by The Inquirer said they had not been in touch with the school board on the proposal. Others said there had been talks about the possibility but no commitments were made.

And further:

According to the announcement, the "Parkway High School" would provide a four-year program of diversified, in-depth courses utilizing the resources of such companies as the Bell Telephone Co., Smith Kline and French and the Fidelity Mutual Life Insurance Co.

Cultural institutions, including the Museum of Art and the Academy of Natural Sciences, also are included in the plan.

It was also proposed that facilities in some of the plush high-rise apartment houses along the Parkway be leased for classroom use.

The latter proposal drew a quick reply from attorney Irving L. Mazer, representing The Philadelphian, a luxury apartment building at 2401 Pennsylvania Ave.

"At no time was anyone connected with The Philadelphian advised or informed, either orally or in writing that any such plan was being considered," Mazer said in a letter to Richardson Dilworth, school board president.

"The Philadelphian does not contain any vacant space which could be used for any of the purposes contemplated by the proposal."

[138]

Mazer also informed Dilworth that several tenants of the building have informed management that they would object to any such use of the premises.

Clearly, there had not been sufficient preparation of the potential cooperating institutions. The attorney for The Philadelphian apartment building drew a characteristic response from School Board President Dilworth:

> I think you and your tenants are completely justified in saying you want no part of the Board of Education, and that you have no interest whatsoever in public education. That certainly is your prerogative.
>
> However, it does seem to me that you are taking in a bit too big a field when you state you object to the use of any part of the Parkway, or any of the public facilities along the Parkway—which, in fact, stretches from City Hall to the Art Museum—for the purpose of education.
>
> If you are successful in this I would suggest that your next step be to tear down the Museum because it interferes with the view of your tenants on the lower floors.

The letters to the editor columns of the *Inquirer* also reflected prevailing sentiments:

> [1]
> To the Editor of The Inquirer: Brainstorming by educational theorists can be overdone. I agree with your editorial, "Non-School on the Parkway." Insurmountable obstacles make the Parkway scheme impractical. A school on the Parkway may make sense, but a building and other facilities would be necessary for the purpose.
>
> Students enrolled in the Parkway institution could not be permitted to monopolize the cultural facilities which after all exist for the sake of the entire community, including adults and students attending other schools.
>
> [2]
> I read in your paper the description of the proposed plan for the Parkway School. The next day I read of a statement by Mr. Mazer, attorney for The Philadelphian apartments, in which he discouraged this plan.
>
> As a mother of three teenagers, and an educator on the faculty of two institutions involved in this proposal, I thought it was one of the most exciting, progressive ideas put forth in recent years.

As a tenant at The Philadelphian, I cannot speak for the management or other tenants, but I do object to Mr. Mazer's speaking for me. No poll has been taken here, and I cannot think of a better use for considerable wasted and empty space in this building. This is one family residing here that is most amenable to this plan.

[3]

With reference to converting the Parkway area into a high school campus, since this area already has the Friends Select School in its vicinity, an additional 2400 children let loose in this section would crowd the residents out, in addition to snarling the heavy morning and evening traffic leading to the expressway.

In addition, the sight of hundreds of children running in and out of buildings all day long would discourage not only future tenants in the apartments, but also visitors to the museums.

I suggest that the Board of Education choose, instead, the Society Hill section which, too, is a cultural area with plenty of room, fresh air and no traffic congestion. This could be arranged without any friction since some members of the Board of Education live there, and I am sure would be glad to open their sumptuous homes to the children, free of charge.

The scene from the towers is excellent, with a clear view of the river and boats, and the children would not be worn out at the end of the day with so much traveling.

It was, of course, inevitable that the humorists try their hands. The following appeared in the *Philadelphia Inquirer,* Wednesday, February 14, 1968:

PINBALL CULTURE ON MARKET ST.
By Joe McGinniss (of the *Inquirer* staff)

Last week's announcement by the Board of Education that it was planning a new High-School-on-The-Parkway, utilizing existing buildings such as art museums so that students could be exposed to culture they otherwise would never know was there, was only part of the story.

What the board did not reveal was the second part of its plan, which is to organize a similar institution on Market st., between 18th st. and City Hall.

Like the Parkway school, the one on Market st. would take full advantage of the cultural and educational opportunities afforded by buildings already in public use.

"This is a terribly exciting proposal," a board spokesman said Monday, "and we are terribly excited about it." The spokesman did not wish to be quoted, however, for fear of reprisal from the powerful pinball industry.

"We are hoping to make pinball a major part of the curriculum," the spokesman said. "With three of the finest emporiums in the East located in the heart of the new complex, we feel Philadelphia has a unique opportunity to become a national leader — no, make that *the* national leader — in this field."

The spokesman added, however, that proprietors of the establishments involved — Sharon's Fun Spot, Pennyland and Variety Corner — had expressed concern about the influx of students disturbing their regular clientele.

"We been building a trade for 30 years and we don't want it ruined by a bunch of kids who can't even find the coin slot," one of the proprietors said.

"This is a problem," the board spokesman admitted, but he stressed the fact that students would be using the machines only during school hours so that the regular night-time trade would not be disturbed.

"In addition," the spokesman said, "before allowing the students to actually use the machines, we will give them a six-week orientation course that will cover not just operating procedures but the history of American pinball with special emphasis upon Philadelphia's magnificent heritage in this area."

The spokesman said that currently the board's chief concern was financing the pinball part of the program ("We can't expect the kids to use their own dimes") but added that through recently improved communication with City Hall the board hoped to obtain funds from Mayor Tate.

"But pinball is only a part of the master plan," the spokesman said. "In the same three emporiums, students will be able to play skeeball, to take instant photos of themselves, with four separate poses for 25 cents, and, hopefully, even to watch soft pretzels being made."

The new educational complex also will occupy space in the Puppy Palace, the bus station ("We feel an important sociological breakthrough can be made through sustained observation of the rest rooms"), the Sun Ray Drug Store, Flagg Brother Shoes, the King of Pizza ("Not so much for the pizza as for the jukebox. King of Pizza has one of the finest jukeboxes in the city") and the three movie theaters in the area.

"Primarily, I think, we will use the Studio Theater, because its films consistently deal with subjects of great relevance to the high school study of today: For instance, the current double feature, 'World of Flesh' and 'Sex Perils of Paulette.'"

There is some concern here, the spokesman admitted, because not enough Negro actresses are involved.

In conclusion, the spokesman said that the new multiple turnstile subway entrance on 15th st. would be utilized by the school.

"We've wanted for a long time to get more kids down into the concourses and the new entrance is just what we've been waiting for. We feel that now, for the first time, we will be able to tap a vast, untapped recreational area.

"All in all," the spokesman said, "we are delighted with the Market st. plan. And we feel that the people of Philadelphia will be delighted, too. It is just one more example of what a progressive, imaginative, far-sighted board of education can do.

"Philadelphia has many unique cultural and historical resources and we intend to take advantage of more and more as time goes on."

As can be seen, reception of the plan to utilize the buildings along the Parkway for a high school was mixed, but on the whole, Philadelphia was favorable — and not least because the media were favorably disposed.

In the four months that followed the February 7 meeting, and the attendant publicity, very little happened to advance the project.

What Clifford Brenner would have done with his idea of using Parkway facilities had he stayed with the school district is not known. One can only speculate, since Brenner had left the school district before the February meeting. When Richardson Dilworth became school board president, a number of intelligent and imaginative people who had worked with him over the years continued to help and support him. When a new superintendent was appointed, however, the situation changed. According to the *Philadelphia Magazine* of June 1969,

The prominent Dilworthians in the administration building when [the superintendent] arrived — Donald Rappaport,

John Patterson, Cliff Brenner—were soon in the background and then out.

In place of them, the article continued, the new superintendent "picked the top bureaucrats as his own men. He left the old Establishment intact." His top managers were "the entrenched of the entrenched."

John Patterson—along with William L. Rafsky and Donald Rappaport —worked on the task force created by Dilworth even before he was sworn in as president. The *Philadelphia Magazine*, in the same article quoted above, noted:

> The task force did a monumental job. As a kind of ex-officio multiple superintendent, it really got the school system moving. . . . It not only made recommendations, it put those recommendations into action. Many of the innovations for which [the superintendent] later got credit—like special kindergartens—were all accomplished by the task force.

Patterson also had worked on the Parkway idea and had written up outline speeches for the February 7 meeting. But he too was gone.

The planning was thrust upon Graham Finney, the deputy superintendent of planning, and, as had been pointed out in the newspaper editorials, an idea is all that there was. "We are planning from ground zero," said Finney, who was swamped with work trying to launch a major capital program to build new schools.

During the period, however, Richard de Lone, an administrative assistant to the superintendent, had been talking with various institutions and summarized the general situation in a report dated April 2, 1969. This contained a great deal of important information, some possibilities, and a number of recommendations, but it saw as a key to a number of problems "the kind of program we have and the willingness of the museums, industries, et al, to participate. This makes it all the more imperative that an educator-head get on board." De Lone began his search for such an educator. He himself saw some of the possibilities that the use of Parkway buildings opened up, but he too was busy with many other tasks, and he made his contribution by finding the man to direct the Parkway project.

John Bremer visited the school district of Philadelphia originally on February 28, 1968, at the invitation of Gail Donovan (Levinson), an administrative assistant to the superintendent. As superintendent of one of the three decentralization districts in New York City, Bremer had been invited to participate in a one-day conference for administrators. Significantly, it was Ash Wednesday.

Gail Donovan passed the name on to Richard de Lone and John

Bremer visited Philadelphia twice more in May. After a brief meeting with the superintendent, he spent a lot of time with de Lone and then later met with the members of a board set up to select the director of the Parkway project: Athelstan Spilhaus, at that time president of the Franklin Institute; Monsignor Edward Hughes, superintendent of the diocesan school system; William Wilcox, executive director of the Greater Philadelphia Movement; George Hutt, member of the Philadelphia school board; John Patterson, educational consultant; and Clifford Brenner. They recommended that John Bremer be appointed, and on June 24 the board of education formally made the appointment, effective August 1, 1968.

The new director inherited a rather complex situation, documented only by the status report prepared by de Lone and a few newspaper clippings. Other documents were collected later, including the original memorandum from Clifford Brenner, whose relation to the school district and to the project was by this time vague and unintelligible. The criticism of some wealthier Philadelphians, for example, some of those living in the high-rise apartment buildings along the Parkway, had alerted the City Council to political danger, which was only magnified by the vision of "hordes of students" (black students, of course) "running up and down the Parkway." Actually using public land! It was for this reason that there were no public funds available for Parkway when Bremer arrived. The superintendent's attitude was not very helpful; de Lone was obviously phasing himself out, and within three months Graham Finney resigned as deputy superintendent of planning. It is doubtful if anyone in authority at this time, apart from Bremer, took the Parkway Program seriously.

Henry Resnick wrote in *Think* (November–December 1969):

> Bremer was so soft-spoken and mild-mannered that some observers within the central administration wondered in the beginning whether he could handle the politics of the job. Soon, however, their fears were set firmly to rest, for it became clear as time went on that, in the words of an educational consultant close to the program, Bremer has been "the right man in the right place at the right time."

The situation was made more difficult for the new director because of his lack of knowledge of the political situation within the school district. Bremer stated: "It was obvious that there was no over-all education policy—no view of education, even; it was equally obvious that only Dilworth's power kept the superintendent in office—and that Dilworth had to back him, politically, for he had brought him in. As a consequence, with nothing to be loyal to, all the new people were leaving—and I was arriving." The situation had all the hallmarks of disintegration and dissolution—and it seems as if only the strong dedication of people to their habits kept the system going, but it was the old system. Whatever went on in the administration building was like a ripple affecting, momentarily, the surface of a large and deep lake. And then it was gone forever.

The superintendent had not been particularly helpful and had rejected any help that Bremer might have given him in dealing with the larger problems of the school district. As a consequence, Bremer realized that he had to go it alone—and it was a not unmixed blessing, since if he did work by himself he would at least escape the ill will that the superintendent had generated for himself among some sections of the community. The difficulty was that the more successful the program became, the greater the hostility from the superintendent. Time was short, however, and Bremer decided to go ahead.

By August 14, 1968, a document had been written which outlined what Bremer intended the Parkway Project, as it was then called, to be about. This was circulated to various people, but there was only one written acknowledgment and no comments or suggestions were offered. The memorandum was used to solicit support from various institutions in Philadelphia and also for fund-raising purposes. It is reprinted in Part V of the Parkway brochure in the Appendix to this book.

During this period, Bremer was helped by the friendship and support of people like Finney and de Lone, but particularly by two college juniors, Neil Kauffman and Carla Meyer, who were spending the summer working in an intern program at the administration building. Neil was, in fact, the first employee of the Parkway program and Carla the first volunteer.

Moving methodically but rapidly, Bremer's intent was to use the suggestion of putting a high school in the Parkway buildings as an opportunity to do what, in his opinion, was really required. All that had been suggested to Bremer could be characterized as a dismembered high school. No doubt, it would have been considerably more than that if Brenner had been given a chance to develop the idea. But he was gone, and with Finney and de Lone on the way out, where were ideas to come from? Bremer saw that while using the Parkway facilities he could attempt to transform the nature of public education by redefining the social and administrative organization of education within the Parkway program. And that is what he did.

The problems with the original proposal vanished as the plan ceased to be thought of as a school and was seen as a program. A major problem was solved by making the administration of the program part of the program, that is, something the students did. By localizing, transportation was unnecessary. Employee cafeterias were already overcrowded and could not accommodate the Parkway students, so this also became a problem for students to solve.

Although Bremer's document outlined some basic principles, the details of the organization were not fixed until many meetings with students, parents, teachers, businessmen, and administrators had taken place. Bremer clearly had the initiative—he called the meetings and proposed the agenda—but crucial elements were hammered out in public. Many parents felt that if they applied early, their children had a right to attend. But it was in a public meeting, with Bremer arguing for the first come, first served principle, that a group of representatives from the Urban League persuaded the whole meeting that only a city-wide lottery was just. Some of the parents were there and they saw the justice of this idea. All Bremer had to do was to acknowledge this and make policy what he had always wanted. Not everything worked out so well.

Bremer described it in this way:

> On occasion I have a sense of what is best in the situation, but *my* sense of what is best will only get in the way unless it is shared by others. If I propose it, it may well divide the group; so all I do is to put people in a problem situation where they persuade each other; I may make a contribution or two, but essentially they present me with their conclusion. It doesn't matter whether I had already arrived at this conclusion or not —they arrived at it, so it is theirs. If I have arrived at it, it then becomes ours. If I haven't, then our education—mine and theirs—goes one stage further back, and we start again."

Bremer held sixty-seven separate meetings in September. After that, the number increased. But the Parkway program became a public property. People wanted to hear about it, to discuss it, to make a contribution to it. It was news.

9
The Later History

The news about Parkway spread and excitement increased when the support of the Ford Foundation was assured and confirmed by letter in early January 1969.

Fortunately, Bremer now had help. After the vacation, his New Year was considerably brightened by the appointment of Tami Williams as administrative officer and secretary. The two of them occupied one of the coldest rooms in Philadelphia — with windows broken — at the back of the second floor of 1801 Market Street. The front part of the building was in partial use by a commission that originally was expected to finish its work in December. They moved out shortly after Parkway moved in.

There were problems. The Parkway program had four different phone numbers assigned to it in as many weeks. There was no typewriter. There was no mail service. Apart from all that, communication was excellent.

And there was more help. In the fall, a man from Antioch College, Rick Hall, had dropped in to talk with Bremer, and between them they had arranged for seven co-op students to help Parkway get started. Shortly after the New Year they arrived, followed almost immediately by two students from the University of Massachusetts. The little back room was getting crowded, but the rest of the second floor soon became available.

An announcement was written to be sent to every eligible high school student in the school district. (This letter is reprinted in the Parkway brochure in the Appendix to this book.) That in itself was a major feat.

Faculty were canvassed and the eighty or so applicants were screened,

[147]

as described earlier. It was a considerable accomplishment that the faculty were selected and appointed by February 4.

The general interest that Bremer's talks aroused throughout the fall and the exploratory conversations he had had with various institutions needed to be followed up, and specific commitments had to be made in preparation for the students' arrival on February 17. It was a busy but rewarding time. More than 2000 student applications were received, and the lottery was scheduled for January 31. Dan Shapiro, an early, enthusiastic, and loyal supporter recorded the event:

> Now back to the project. Today is the day of public drawing of students, a very hectic day. One of the interesting things is that twice as many applications came in from Central and Girls High. These are the two high schools set up for high IQ academic students. It's interesting, but unsure, why this high ratio of applications is happening. One could take an educated guess. By two o'clock the television cameras are coming in from all the stations, newspaper reporters are here, people are starting to come in. We are set up with a number of tables lined up in the back of boxes. I guess there were about 200 people, students, community observers, and about 40 from the press. John [Bremer] gave a short speech. Then George Hutt, who was substituting for Dilworth, and is a member of the board himself, said a few words and pulled the first name out of the box. Each district than had a student representative in order of districts. The students drew 14 names out of the box and read them aloud for the TV audience. It was all very exciting. Finally, after all these months, we have actually committed ourselves to our students. When they had all gone home, we settled down to send out letters of acceptance to the students. Then we chose the alternates in the same way, made up lists of the alternates, sent out letters and scheduled Saturday for writing postcards to all of the non-accepted.

In his remarks (also in the brochure in the Appendix) at the time of the drawing, Bremer emphasized his determination that students for the Parkway program should not have to meet any requirements except that they be of high school age.

Bremer, the appointed teachers, and the interns then faced the problem of what to do, of how much to do. It was decided that there would be a three-week orientation period for students and faculty alike. This would give people a chance to get to know the city, to get to know themselves, and to think about what formal courses they wanted to take. It also gave the cooperating institutions a much-needed extension of time in which to organize.

The three-week orientation period began, in the first week, with a systematic exploration of the campus, that is, the center-city area. This area was divided into four quadrants for tours by as many groups of students and teachers until each group had covered each area on foot, guided by maps the city's tourist bureau furnished.

Dan Shapiro described in his journal the first day of the first week:

February 17 — This is our first day. The students have arrived today. The schedule for this week is enclosed. It includes the trips around the city in the morning and the tutorials in the afternoon. Sat in on Cy's [Swartz] tutorial today. During the tours, some students were told by the police (who hadn't heard of our program) to "move on." We now have ID cards for all the students and this will probably blow over. This event had happened after the group had just come down from a tour of City Hall. Cy discussed with his group what orientation week is about and what the roster is going to be like. The students decided with Cy that the first order of business is to find a meeting place, and there was a big discussion about finding a place that would be like a clubhouse with a refrigerator that they could paint themselves, etc. Cy also talked about the requirements of the students to keep a log. There was some discussion when one student wanted to know why *they* had to find a place. This was an excellent opportunity for the students to bring out their feelings about the program. Sitting around in a circle, discussing the problem, and getting to know the students was a very interesting experience. It turns out that we have a very high percentage of dropouts, some who have already dropped out, some planning to drop out, and others still in the system but who in effect had dropped out, because they paid no attention in class and cut as often as possible. Everyone is a little edgy, and there is tremendous diversity within the group, that is, within age (we have 9th — 12th graders) and certainly in background, ranging from the white suburban student to the black ghetto student, indiscriminately mixed in these tutorial programs. It's interesting to observe the different reactions to the problems that come into the tutorial and how the students and staff react to the reaction. It impressed me that the white suburban students are much more at home in verbalizing and understand concepts of organization and how to conduct themselves at a meeting, and somehow assume that this is a fact of life that everybody does and should know. Many of our students are uncomfortable in the new surroundings, feel that they don't know how to express themselves; they are shy and seem to have been so brainwashed before coming to us that you expect any minute for one of them to raise his hand for permission to go to the bathroom. They are not quite sure they can trust our program yet and will be allowed to do and say things that were not allowed previously. After the tutorial, I got a chance to talk to some of the teachers. Penny, who is our young art teacher, was telling me that on the way to the art museum, which is about eight blocks from where they started, as she was walking she saw strung along the Parkway many of the students who were on their way there and they waved to each other, and then gradually caught up with each other, and it was like a very exciting meeting in a foreign country with friends, even though this was the first day. They began to collect together outside the art museum, and while they were waiting for the other students to come, they talked and played around on the fountain outside, and for a while had their meeting outside. Then they went to the facilities that the art museum had given them.

The second week, with its films, more tutorials, and continued attention to the roster of studies, brought some reduction in tension. Dan Shapiro noted in his journal for Monday, February 24, 1969:

The morning 9–11 was spent watching a movie called "The Jungle," filmed by a gang in Philadelphia. Also saw "The Family of Man." In the afternoon, I went to a tutorial run by Mark and Jeanette. This is being held in the cellar of the Catholic Youth Organization. One of the students there had brought a guest who was dropping out of the Philadelphia school system and was trying to find a way to get into the Parkway program. The tutorial took this on as their own concern, and there was a very interesting discussion about how they could help this boy. He told us he was dropping out of Ben Franklin because he "couldn't learn anything," that the teacher "just sits there." All of the students told him how great the Parkway program is. Asked him what he would do if he did drop out. He wanted to know if he could transfer. The students were very sympathetic and have a great deal of understanding of how the system squashes the students. They talked about how and why we chose our students. Many of our students were ready to drop out of the system anyway. There was quite a learning thing going on here as the students tried to understand that Parkway program could only take a certain amount of students on and that's all we could handle, and at the same time trying to figure how we could get this particular boy in because we know him now. There was a conversation about what we would do if we were in John Bremer's position. The only outcome was that a group of

[150]

two or three students decided they would go with this boy to John Bremer and discuss their problem.

The discussion then turned to a room that some of the students had seen, that could be used for their tutorial, and was much better than the one now being used. They also talked about the tutorial not being voluntary but mandatory in the Parkway program.

Spoke to Dorice, another tutorial staff member, afterwards. She feels now that the students are getting along much better and so is the mixture of students and staff. Also thinks that maybe the three-week orientation is a little too long and that the students are anxious to get into a regular class situation. Mark feels that the kids are loosening up because they're bringing up things that interest them instead of staff trying to force significant discussions.

The third week of the orientation period was given over largely to the final selection of courses to be taken ("rostering") and to a project in which each student commented on his first weeks in the Parkway program. Collected and published in book form by the students, this was an early step in their constant analysis of the new learning community of which they were a part.

How did the young people choose their courses? What took place after the initial "open-house" discussions with the teachers?

To begin with, there had been a parent-teacher-student evening meeting just before the Parkway program opened, and at this time each student completed a form, answering these questions:

Do you plan to go to college?

Would you like to go to college?

Are you interested in pursuing any post-high school training (business, trade, vocational, and so on)?

What foreign language have you studied? how long? when?

Are you presently studying a foreign language? which? how long?

What language are you interested in studying in the Parkway program?

What sciences have you studied?

If you plan to continue your studies in science, what areas interest you most (be as specific as you like)?

Are you interested in getting work experience?

Are you interested in helping elementary or handicapped children?

With this form and the student's school records before him, a staff member of each pupil's tutorial group sat down with the youngster to review his history and his aspirations.

Then the student tried his hand at making up a personal roster for the first semester, after which the staff member reviewed it with him, checking to see that state educational requirements were met (college requirements also, where pertinent) and that the proposed work load was not too heavy.

Nancy Greenberg described this procedure and its sequence:

> After two and a half weeks of getting catalogs, descriptions of courses, and conferences with the teachers, I finally had to make out my roster. For the first time in my school life, I will be taking classes that I chose completely on my own. Film making—not just English, math workshop—not an ordinary geometry class with thirty-five other kids, are two of the courses I'll be taking. But when I sat down to put these and more courses on my roster I found that I couldn't fit in one class I needed. For two and a half hours, I slaved and tried all sorts of time combinations but I still couldn't fit it in. I was really worried about it but at the town meeting, John [Bremer] asked for specific problems in roster making. My Spanish problem was brought up and because a few kids had the same trouble I had had, the times for the course were changed.
>
> I think the thing that's so great about this is the fact that something was changed for a student, even though it might inconvenience a teacher and take time to figure out. This proves to me that Parkway is for the student and not a stone institution with old teachers.

The Parkway program was on its way. For student Ruth Kleiner, it was a moment for reflection and appraisal:

> The first three weeks at Parkway program have been spent getting to know our campus, each other, and most of our faculty. The first week was mainly made up of walking tours through the city. The theme running through the second week was that of *Romeo and Juliet*. We saw "The Jungle," a movie filmed by the Twelfth and Oxford Gang. We discussed similarities and differences between the two. On Wednesday, the school divided up into groups to prepare for our "celebration" on Friday. The groups covered many different topics: drama, music, dance, language, art, and newspaper. This week, the most important thing on our minds was the decision of courses. Since we missed Monday because of snow,

we have had less time to plan our rosters. At least ninety courses have been offered to us so far. There are institutional offerings, faculty offerings, and courses given by outside experts. It's rather frustrating to have to make choices from all that I can choose from.

Several of the students have said that they feel that these first three weeks have not served any useful purpose. Maybe some of the things we've been doing haven't been so awfully exciting. But then, that may be almost deliberate. We've all come from schools with very structured surroundings.

We really looked forward to the freedom of Parkway program and pictured ourselves strolling down the street and window shopping and just taking it easy. These three weeks might have been to wear us out, or show us that taking it easy isn't the easiest thing in the world for most of us. On the whole, it might have been the way to get us ready for the new way in which we will be learning.

But I think three weeks *has* been a bit too much. I'm tired of the slow pace everything has been moving at. I am anxious for courses to begin. Monday, the first day in "class," won't get here too soon.

There were others who agreed that three weeks of orientation were too much. When a second unit of the program was opened in July 1969, the students were given two weeks to get their bearings. Again they were divided into four groups (a pair of tutorial groups made up a walking group) and sent out to tour the city. Again time was spent selecting courses, attending tutorials, and taking part in town meetings. But this time orientation culminated at the Electric Factory, a rock concert hall with electronic sound and light facilities, where the young people met in a setting to which their generation is indigenous.

For an hour and a quarter they attended a show featuring the sounds and sights of urban life and of classical and urban art. Then each student wrote or graphically portrayed his response to the show in the context of his fortnight in the Parkway program.

When Parkway opened its third unit in September 1969, there were two weeks of orientation again, and once more there were walking tours through center city. This time, each group studied one area of the city in depth, however, reporting what it had found at town meeting. In this way it was hoped that the students would be prepared to take elementary school children through the city, explaining some of its wonders. More will be said about this aspect of the program later; for the present we will observe that the evolution of the Parkway program's orientation period reflects a basic principle—to learn is to change, and there must be constant change based on what is learned.

After the orientation period, the program settled down to its task of helping students learn. It soon found that, having caught the imagination of Philadelphians, it was going to have to conduct its affairs very much in the public eye. The media in Philadelphia provided good coverage and soon afterwards reporters came from out of town. One of the first of these was Stratton Holland of the *Toronto Daily Star*, whose fine article was published on March 15, 1969. Shortly after this, the program was written up in *Life* and the *Saturday Review* in the same week. The reporter and photographer from *Life* were superb, and the students would not let them go.

Since the Parkway program was ungraded, some of the students were "in the twelfth grade" when they entered. By June they had completed the requirements for graduation, but the board of education had been unable to provide the requisite diplomas. The ceremony was postponed, although the eight students were technically graduates. Two of them wanted to go on studying with Parkway even though they had graduated and asked Bremer if this were possible. He said yes.

Another test of the program came in June. Bremer felt that the school district was slowly but steadily disintegrating, that there was no leadership, and that with the continuing pressure from City Hall, the time for expansion of the program was running out. He decided, therefore, to move ahead as quickly as he could. The dangers of doing so were obvious, but so were the dangers of not doing so. The move to expand was encouraged by the number of students applying for the June lottery. They numbered very close to ten thousand.

As a consequence of this very obvious vote of public confidence, six hundred names were drawn at the June 22 lottery held on the John F. Kennedy Plaza in central Philadelphia. Three units (Beta, Gamma, and Delta) of 150 students each were made up, and another 150 names were drawn as alternates. After discussing the situation with faculty and students, Bremer decided to open the second unit, Community Beta, in July. This unit was fortunate enough to have Tina Craig, one of the original faculty, as its unit head. Its premises were at 23rd and Cherry streets.

As this was done, the original group of students and faculty at 1801 Market Street became Community Alpha, and about half the students elected to study through the summer—at least until mid-August. Under the leadership of Ralph Kendricks, a special summer program was devised—not a remedial program but a regular Parkway program. Students could concentrate in one of a number of areas, and about twenty students were paid, out of Ford Foundation money, for working a number of hours a day in the various branch libraries of the Free Library of Philadelphia.

While this new organization of units and unit heads was being created, Bremer was facing a number of problems. First and foremost was how to detach himself from the students and faculty of the newly titled Community Alpha. It could hardly work satisfactorily under its new head, Ralph Kendricks, if Bremer was still around. Unfortunately, Bremer's office remained at 1801 Market Street, which was an error. Second, administrative arrangements had to be made with the administration building of the school district so that the newly created unit structure would maximize autonomy for each unit. Third, plans had to be made for the location and opening of the third unit, Community Gamma, in September. Fourth, after a fairly active year, John Bremer needed a vacation.

After the impressive response of students in June, Parkway had screened and appointed faculty for the coming year. Although there had been no advertising, there were about three hundred applicants out of which eighteen were appointed. To screen that number of applicants in the Parkway fashion was itself an organizational feat of some dimensions, but it was capably handled by one of the original Antioch interns, Jeanette Marsh, who returned for a second tour of duty.

The difficulty of locating premises for the unit headquarters of Community Gamma has already been described (Chapter 1), but the arrangements were made fairly late in the summer, and Bremer and the unit head, Cy Swartz, another of the original faculty, decided to postpone opening until September 15, slightly more than a week late. A meeting with the students and parents of Community Gamma was held on September 10, and there seemed to be no insurmountable difficulty.

Summer term had ended for Alpha and Beta on August 15, and a week later, with some misgivings, Bremer left for Nova Scotia for a week's vacation. It was not enough, but the needs were pressing. In his view, the future of the school district was nothing but travail and frustration, and with the financial situation deteriorating as a result of the educational disaster stemming from what seemed to him to be inadequate leadership, the prospects were growing dimmer, particularly for new, innovative programs. It was a now-or-never situation.

Part of Bremer's plan for expansion involved the creation of a non-geographical school district, the Parkway Volunteer School District, which anybody could join if he liked the kind of program it offered. It would enable everybody who had applied through the lottery to be accepted, sooner or later, and, above all, it would provide a natural and voluntary solution to the segregation of the existing eight school districts. As long as the school district of Philadelphia was structurally segregated, no amount of fussing and bussing was going to do any good. By artificially working with quotas, harm was done—by wasting money, by offending people, by wasting students' time and energy, and by putting people in situations where confrontations were almost unavoidable. It is the structure that is racist, and that is what must be changed. Parkway had enough of a political base to begin this change, but it had to be seen as a district, a programmatic district. One major obstacle was the fact that it was only a high school level program. It made no contribution to the elementary level, and Bremer decided that he had to show that Parkway had something to offer young children. The unit head of Community Gamma, Cy Swartz, had been chosen partly because of his interest in the possibilities that a unit of equal numbers of elementary and secondary students afforded. And that had been an element (reported in Chapter 1) in the choice of premises, which were finally the now-famous Paxson Parkway.

Community Gamma was supposed to be three hundred students strong, half secondary and half elementary, and the program it developed had to encourage and assist the working of the older students with the younger. That was the mandate that Cy Swartz and an excellent group of faculty had to carry out. And carry it out they did, at tremendous personal cost.

The story of the Paxson Parkway cannot be told fully, although the general pattern is clear. There were additional factors:

1. Bremer, the president of the school board and the superintendent were all involved.
2. The elementary school children came partly from the locality of the old Paxson School (but very few children lived there because it was a redevelopment area that had suffered drastic bulldozing) and mostly from the Germantown area in northwest Philadelphia (otherwise known as District 6).
3. The Germantown children, or rather their parents, had been given the usual administrative runaround by the district superintendent of District 6.
4. This group of parents had run an "illegal school" in a house and were accused by some of not wanting their white children to go to school with black children. It is more likely that they resented the style of education offered in their local school.
5. The principal of one of the schools, an unsuccessful candidate for political office, decided to remedy the injustice involved in the criticism of her school implied by the fact that some parents wanted to withdraw their children from it.

6. An independently wealthy lawyer, who it was widely rumored wanted to occupy one of the vacant seats on the school board, was thought by many to capitalize on an opportunity to crusade, and he was an officer of this school's Home and School Association. He had also wanted his child enrolled in Paxson but was too late.

7. Into this highly charged emotional atmosphere a black newspaperman stated that "a large group of retarded students were ousted from the [Paxson] school to make way for those in the new innovative program." As a matter of public record, the school had had retarded children in it the previous year, but because the building was to be demolished shortly, they had all been transferred by a decision made by the board special services director in April.

But who was going to listen to facts? The following documents outline the history as it was seen by some of the participants. They may convey something of what went on.

First, there was a letter from the disgruntled parents, dated August 31, 1969, to the school board president, with a copy sent to the superintendent:

Dear Mr. Dilworth:

A number of parents of elementary school children in the Germantown area have decided that we must seek an educational alternative for our children. We believe that their education should and can be greatly improved if we move in bold and imaginative ways. One of the traditional options for a group which feels this way is to enter or form a private school. We reject this option, not simply because of economic factors but, fundamentally, because we believe in public education. We think that public education should incorporate the widest variety of alternatives.

The particular style of education with which we have experimented is a combination of the infant school and Parkway models with a significant degree of parent and student participation at all levels of operation and decision.

Our children are from a wide variety of racial, ethnic and economic backgrounds. The parents, for the most part, are professional, business and service personnel. Many of us are or have been school teachers (9) within the Philadelphia system and elsewhere.

We have given weighty consideration to our decision. This spring we initiated a six-week pilot program and withdrew fourteen of our children from public school in order to experiment with a model. Actually, we did not enter into this experiment with a model in mind; rather, it grew out of our experience. Both the children and we like what happened, and we think it offers a viable alternative for many others besides ourselves. We are so convinced of the value of this that we will continue, if necessary, the course of action begun last spring.

However, on the basis of your record, we believe that you, the rest of the Board of Education, and the superintendent all affirm this kind of innovation and desire to incorporate such a program into the system. Therefore, we request your positive response to our situation. There appear to be at least several ways in which this option can be supported and thus avoid the onerous cloud of illegality under which we lived this past spring.

1. Our group could provide the nucleus for a Germantown elementary Parkway school. We have spoken with Dr. Bremer and he has encouraged us in the matter and suggested we write to you. Enclosed is a list of 39 children (13 of whom are black) who are committed to this program should it become a reality.

2. We could become a district experimental program. (We have spoken with Dr. Kelner about this.)

3. We could receive direct per capita funding.

Undoubtedly our request for sanction and funding from the school district poses problems from your viewpoint. On the other hand, our firm commitment to the highest quality of education for our children will not allow us to believe the difficulties are insurmountable, and we are willing to work with the Board in any way which will make our goal a reality.

To that end, several of us are willing to meet with you and/or any members of the Board or Administration as the need arises. We await your favorable response.

Second, there was a letter from the superintendent (with copies to all board members) confirming a telephone conversation about the letter from the disgruntled parents. In the letter the superintendent agreed that parents should continue conversations with John Bremer exploring possibilities of a Parkway-type elementary school which would include some of their own group of children. It was further offered that it was very natural to put together the parents' concern and John Bremer's plans for an elementary school component of Parkway.

From October 10 through October 19, Bremer took a second week of vacation, only to discover upon his return that the elementary school was under intense attack, its critics complaining that the students had been improperly selected so as to disturb the racial balance of the school from which some of them came. What is more, no one in the administration building of the school district was mounting a defense against the attack. Bremer at once wrote the following:

A brief account of the Events Leading to the Establishment of Community Gamma of the Parkway Program at the Old Paxson School

Late in June 1969, at a meeting with the superintendent, I drew his attention to the possibilities of expanding the Parkway program to include students of all ages, particularly elementary students. After our discussion he agreed to our expansion into the elementary field.

During July and August, I tried to locate a group of students who would be willing to participate in a joint elementary-secondary unit. The major difficulty was that we had no fixed base since it was impossible to use the Spring Garden Institute (as had originally been planned) and we ended up in August with a commitment to utilize the old Paxson School awaiting demolition by the Redevelopment Authority.

Since the old Paxson School stands in a redevelopment area, there is very little neighborhood and very few, if any, children living close. Under these circumstances, I asked District 3 office for help in finding students but was told that on the whole, District 3 was a receiving area for students from all over the city and had no overcrowding which our program could mitigate.

At some time in August, I had been approached by a group of parents in the Germantown area asking if I could help them in providing a different kind of educational program for their elementary school age children. At that time, I had referred them to the superintendent and president of the school district. When I could not easily and quickly find a group of children for our joint elementary-secondary unit, I recalled this inquiry and so phoned the superintendent to ask him, since the time was very short before the beginning of the school year, whether we could not use that particular group of children. He agreed that under the circumstances, it was appropriate to do this. I, therefore, invited the group to participate, provided that it was honestly integrated. (The final breakdown was 47 white, 50 nonwhite, over-all).

The Parkway program was operating under some difficulty because of the change of facilities and the shortness of time; it was also difficult to see how a city-wide lottery system could be applied to elementary school children who could not be expected to arrange their own transportation from all over the city. I feel very strongly that elementary educational programs should be neighborhood programs. I also feel that parents and students are entitled to the kind of educational programs which they approve within the limits of normal funding.

Since the relation between the elementary and secondary level programs is unique to the Philadelphia Parkway Program, it seemed advisable to institute the program as soon as possible so that parents could see what its possibilities were. It has always been our intention to offer this kind of program to as many students as wish to participate within the limits of money provided by the school district. We have requests from several other groups of parents who would prefer this kind of educational program, and I am willing to work to provide them with the kind of educational program they want consonant with the policy and funding of the school district.

The next day, a letter from the superintendent was delivered to John Bremer by one of the board's chauffeurs. It drew attention to the misunderstandings that had arisen over Paxson and held out the hope that some meetings scheduled by the superintendent would clarify the situation. It also claimed to reiterate the conditions under which Paxson had been approved. These included, it was stated, the involvement of the district superintendent and principals of affected schools and also the board of education itself. The superintendent denied any commitment to provide transportation. The letter concluded, "but the purpose of this letter is to make absolutely certain that any previous commitments between us are perfectly clear.

"As in the past, my door remains open to you and the powers of my office are available to expedite in a good way what we all consider to be an innovative program which promises to show the way to a new kind and quality of education for the children and young people of Philadelphia."

Bremer responded:

October 23, 1969

I am responding to your chauffeur-delivered letter dated October 21st, which reached me at 4:25 P.M. on the same day. It's always difficult to view retroactive legislation impartially, don't you think, so I will not comment on your statement at this time. I have sent you my own view of what took place.

The events leading up to the establishment of our third unit (Community Gamma) of the Parkway program and the public response gives us an educational opportunity which, if your last paragraph is anything but words, would receive your open and active support. I do not think that the Parkway program is suitable for every student and we would criticize prevailing school practice because of its exclusiveness, its claim to possess the only way. Parents and students who approve of our kind of education will benefit from it. Those who do not approve, will not. It does happen that there is a large number of parents and students in Philadelphia who would like to participate (not only in our high school level program but at the elementary level), and I have tried to point out to you that unless we accommodate the majority of those who want to participate, the program will perish because of its own attraction.

On many occasions I have sought an opportunity to confer directly with the board, since matters of policy are clearly involved, and after several wasted mornings, I finally discussed the program for 15 minutes in the early summer. At that time, I suggested that we create a programmatic school district (not geographically based) open to anyone in the city who wants to join the Parkway program. I am still urging this as a first step.

To explore this possibility requires a lot of conference time which I would be delighted to spend with the board if it so wishes. The wishes of a large number of parents and students are unmistakable. Why can't their energies and aspirations be used on behalf of their own education? If parents and students want to join, why not let them? If the board will approve, I will not be slow to move. And the matter is urgent; either the Parkway program will become more generally available or else it will die.

You seem to work on the assumption that the present system can be made to work if assisted by administrative retraining programs. I do not share this view. We can only preserve it by changing it. There are many good teachers and administrators available who are permanently frustrated by a system which uses large quantities of energy to maintain itself, instead of helping students learn. I am proposing that we set up another kind of system, alongside the existing one, so that parents, students, and teachers can participate in the Parkway program. In that way it will liberate their energies instead of tying them up. Why not?

What Bremer did not say in his response was that the "retroactive legislation" was made up of alleged conditions. There was little doubt that "the purpose of this [the superintendent's] letter is to make absolutely certain that any previous commitments between us are perfectly clear." The superintendent needed to be protected—he was in deep trouble and wanted to pass the buck. But the "previous commitments" were not previous; they were stated for the first time, and they were not "between us" but were unilateral, for Bremer had not even heard them before, let alone agreed to them.

The *Philadelphia Daily News* published some excellent stories by Lou Antosh. The following one, published on November 25, tells how Bremer, in order to save the program, was willing to accept responsibility. He hoped that by taking the heat off the superintendent the latter would rescind the order he had issued on November 18 to close the Paxson elementary program.

[SCHOOL SUPERINTENDENT] DEAF TO "HALLELUJAHS" FOR PAXSON PARKWAY

The soul-stirring tones of the "Hallelujah Chorus" filtered into the Board of Education meeting, but the music was a bit premature.

Dr. John Bremer didn't make his appearance until a few minutes later, standing in the midst of his young supporters, who applauded wildly and stomped their feet. ("What is he, a messiah?" joked one School District employee.)

Dr. Bremer is the director of the experimental Parkway Project, and says he is trying to stay out of further trouble with what he calls the "larger organization." He is talking about the Board of Education and Superintendent of Schools . . . , the powers who are closing down his Paxson Parkway elementary school.

The Paxson Parkway School is a program for 97 elementary school children, an extension of the Parkway Program, designed as a "high school without walls."

[The Superintendent] has suggested budget cuts which would close down the Paxson Parkway elementary program. The Parkway students and their parents showed up yesterday at the School Administration Building, 21st st. and the Parkway, to ask why.

As they spoke, the sounds of religious songs rose to the second floor meeting room. Outside the building, some 60 members of the All-Philadelphia High School Choir sang a series of numbers to protest proposed budget cuts which would eliminate their Saturday rehearsals.

"We were promised we would have this school," said Carleton Badger, a student at the Paxson Parkway School who stood eye-high to the microphone. "And now two months later (the school began in September) they want to close it. Why?"

"That's a very good question," responded Board Member Gerald Gleeson, who said, "The Paxson School was opened without the board's ever being consulted about an elementary program."

After the sign-carrying youngsters had their say, Dr. Bremer walked to the podium, smiled shyly as the hundreds of students clapped, then went into his talk.

Dr. Bremer noted he first came here to develop the Parkway Program, an experimental "high school without walls" which now has three units in three separate locations with 390 students. (One of the high school units is housed in the Paxson School at 6th and Buttonwood st. with the elementary program.)

Even from the beginning, said Dr. Bremer, his relationship "with the larger organization has been difficult."

Some sources claim Dr. Bremer expanded the Parkway project to include elementary students without informing the board that he was using methods of selecting pupils which differed from the high school program.

Dr. Bremer said yesterday that "as far as I know, at no time did the Board of Education pass a resolution to start the (original) Parkway Project at all."

Dr. Bremer said that when he thought it feasible to start the

[163]

elementary program last summer, it seemed within the mandate given by the board for the Parkway Program.

"It is very clear to me that whatever happened is, at least in part, my error," said the English-accented educator who admitted selecting the elementary students in a way not satisfactory to the board.

"I would urge the board not to punish the students of the program for my administrative error."

But [the Superintendent] said he had decided to "terminate the Paxson Parkway Program at the winter recess time and unless I am overruled by the board, my decision will stand."

He said the board was told the details of the elementary program and the board and administration are not at all happy with the selection process.

Parkway Project high school students were selected citywide by lot, but Dr. Bremer reportedly selected half the elementary children from the Germantown-Northwest Philadelphia area.

As a result one of the schools in the Northwest area "is further segregated and is practically an all-black school as a consequence," [the Superintendent] said.

The students hooted [the Superintendent] at this point, one of several times they became disorderly.

[The Superintendent] also claimed some of the cost of the elementary program could be stricken from the operating budget, but suggested creating similar programs in the northwest area.

Dr. Bremer was asked after the meeting how he could operate an elementary school without authorization to spend the necessary funds.

"I'm in a position in which I really can't answer that question satisfactorily without getting into more trouble," he said. "I've got one aim, that's to keep those 97 kids in the program. There are promises and promises about what to do in the future, but look at reality."

Asked if his "difficulties with the larger organization" would prevent him from working in the program, he said, "If I thought it would do any good, I would resign." He indicated it wouldn't and he won't.

"The principal of one school decided to make an issue of this," he said.

Board President Richardson Dilworth did not gavel the session closed until most of the audience — and board itself — had left.

After the public board meeting, which was not successful, Bremer received a telegram from two of the Paxson elementary students:

Dear John Bremer, We think you are a really great man. You did something very hard today but must have hurt you very much. Thank you for letting us learn about the system we have to fight. We never knew learning could be so hard or hurt so much. You are really a good teacher because you know how to help people want to change the world. We will always remember what you did.

Love

And also a letter from their parents, dated November 24, 1969:

Dear John Bremer,

Thank you for today's speech!

It was an honor to watch and hear a great and good man defend his people while speaking such painful truths.

Your message shocked us all — because our family preferred to believe that the Board reneged on a one-year commitment, and reality is difficult to digest. It did, however, make us re-awaken to the tremendous commitment we feel to alternative methods of education. You helped us see that each parent must ultimately provide education for the kind of life they believe is the most honest expression of self-awareness and individual growth.

Whenever you feel discouraged, just realize that *you alone,* singly and symbolically, have done an unbelievable amount in less than two years to shake loose tradition and change this city. Remember the 10,000 teenagers awaiting to join your program — remember how many children and parents have dared to believe learning can be fun because of you — and know you are doing a marvelous job *in spite* of the system.

Thank you especially for inspiring our children to be like you.

Our warm best wishes fly to you —

Love

[165]

Meetings and protests went on—and for a time so did Paxson. Lou Antosh of the *Philadelphia Daily News* wrote:

BUSY HUM OF PAXSON SCHOOL WILL SOON BE SILENCED

They say at the Paxson Parkway School that the building is the least important thing. The place looks it.

The corridors could use some sweeping and the windows some cleaning. Inside the cluttered office, a coffee urn occupies one chair, facing a brimming wastepaper basket. In one classroom you'll even find an old sink atop a desk.

Cy Swartz, head of the Paxson Parkway unit, who prefers a hideous ski sweater to the standard shirt-and-tie uniform, tried to explain the difference at Paxson the other day but was interrupted.

"What's your favorite color?" asked a small voice down near ground level. "I hope it's not blue. Everybody is picking blue."

Beverly Ivens, who is 5, had strolled into the office with her pad and pencil to interview people, a favorite pastime of kids at Paxson Parkway. She recorded another blue by checking her list, then wandered away to the next person.

Beverly had explained the difference at Paxson Parkway. More than anything else—books, audio-visual aids, expensive equipment—they rely on people at Paxson Parkway.

When some 100 children reported to the new elementary parkway program last fall they found behind aged wooden doors at 6th and Buttonwood sts. a strange new world with an emphasis on people rather than on bells, straight lines and commands for "Silence!"

There is little silence at Paxson. The building hums like a plane before takeoff as the small people move from room to room, interviewing others about pets or colors, playing in the wooden block room, sitting with a teacher or a parent volunteer for small group or individual instruction.

In Alan Badger's previous school, "you would have to sit most of the day in your seat. You would get tired."

At Paxson, class trips are frequent and varied. One group learned about the school bond referendum, visiting areas where new schools were needed and by visiting the polls on Election Day. A world culture class visits travel agencies to learn something about December in other parts of the world— what's it like?

The unique atmosphere of the Paxson School is a result of the mingling of elementary and high school students in the same building and, at times, the same classroom. Swartz calls it the only "interlocking school experience in the world."

The class of 130 high school students housed on the second floor is one of three groups of secondary units in the "school without walls" in the area of Benjamin Franklin Parkway. They partake of the original free-form Parkway program for secondary students, such as earning English credits by working at the Theater of the Living Arts, or commercial credits by visiting a restaurant.

But many of the high school students also work with the smaller kids on the first floor tutoring in math and foreign languages and bolstering their own knowledge in the process. Teenage students are learning that children are people, not pests, and the family atmosphere is evident throughout the school.

The Parkway program has been lauded in various national publications, including *Life* magazine. Many people have praised the program. Few, if any, have criticized it.

But the Paxson elementary program on the parkway will be shut down this month on the order of Superintendent of Schools . . . [who] says there is a possibility of beginning similar programs in the future, but this particular one must close. He gives various reasons, none of the stated ones being Dr. John Bremer.

Dr. Bremer, sandy-haired Englishman hired two years ago to begin the Parkway program for secondary students, is charged by some with being too enthusiastic. Right now he is furious.

"It seems hard to see how sense can be made of closing down a program which is good enough to be restarted," said the 42-year-old educator, whose youthful face cries out for something hipper than a plain, dark, button-up-the-front sweater.

Bremer is a rebel. He believes the educational system is not doing the job, not a popular view within the system.

"You cannot solve the problems of education through the existing system," he said. "Even people who support the system say it requires at least 50 percent more money to produce the results they think they can get and the money just won't be available."

Bremer is bucking the system. He has ambitious hopes for this new program, hopes that have not been echoed by the Board of Education.

"I don't think our type of program is suitable for every student, but it is for those parents and students who want it," he said. "I would like to see a Parkway school system set up in which everybody who likes our system can participate."

The elementary program, set up by Bremer the Rebel, has gotten a lot of national publicity. Now he talks of expansion. Bremer's emergence as an educational force may have rubbed the administration the wrong way, and the closing controversy has laid bare some bitter personal clashes.

If the nation is looking to the school, few responsible officials in this city seem to care. Swartz claims no board members have even visited the elementary program to watch its operation.

Announcing his decision to close the elementary school, [the Superintendent] said the board was not fully aware of Bremer's activities in starting the operation.

Could Bremer actually hire teachers, spend money and run a program without the board's knowledge?

"I do not have control over the school district. I cannot open and close a school or appropriate a bus," Bremer said. "Draw any conclusion from that that you like."

[The Superintendent] also said that when Bremer began the elementary program, he did not choose children by lot, as was done in the high school program.

Bremer replied he needed elementary children for the school last August and found none in the neighborhood, a redevelopment area. Since parents in the Germantown area were pleading for a Parkway school of their own, Bremer took a group of children from that area.

A principal of the Henry Elementary School charged the Parkway group took white students from her school in Germantown, making it nearly all black.

Bremer ripostes that 12 of the 20 children taken from the Henry School were transferring anyway. He points out that the Parkway elementary program is racially even.

[The Superintendent] also said the program would be shut down partly for economic reasons. But no one has ever said how much money will be saved. Questions remain unanswered. The figures are not available, officials say.

Bremer says the approximate personnel cost per pupil at his elementary school is about $430, "about the same as the

Henry School and considerably lower than some other elementary schools."

"If people were annoyed because they couldn't get into the elementary program, we can take 40 more students right now," Bremer said.

"If they give us more resources, at the same per capita cost of $430 per pupil, we'll take any number of students, any number at all," he said.

Unless the decision is changed, however, there will be no other students enrolled and the current pupils will go back to the older kind of school—"the kind where you sit all day."

Groups, like the East Mount Airy Neighbors Association, pressured the board to overrule the superintendent's decision—but although there were many signs that the board was displeased and knew that it had been deceived, to overrule the superintendent would have been a vote of no confidence.

The *Philadelphia Inquirer*, December 11, 1969, reported:

MT. AIRY ASSOCIATION CITES "THREAT TO CHILDREN" GROUP FIGHTS TO KEEP PAXSON SCHOOL OPEN

The East Mount Airy Neighbors Association has urged schools superintendent . . . to reverse his decision and allow the controversial Paxson-Parkway special school to continue operating.

In a letter to [the Superintendent] the organization contended that terminating the program at the end of the year, as now planned, will submit the approximately 100 children involved to "traumatic changes" that would be "counter-productive to their education."

Similar letters were sent to Richardson Dilworth, president of the Board of Education, and to other board members.

Besides the association's appeal for saving the Paxson program, parents of children attending the school, many of them from Mount Airy, reportedly are still trying to persuade board members to overrule [the Superintendent's] decision.

At the board's meeting on Monday, three parents pleaded for the program, while others have written board members to make similar pleas.

But time is running out.

As [the Superintendent's] decision stands, the last day for the
program at Paxson School in North Philadelphia is Dec. 19,
when the Christmas vacation begins for the public school
system. When classes resume Jan. 4, the children who had
participated in the program will have to be in other schools.

With the operation of the school generating increasing bitter-
ness within the administration and among some parents,
[the Superintendent] announced Nov. 23 it would be termi-
nated at the end of this year.

He cited these five reasons for the decision:

—The school board had not been "apprised of the establishment of the program beforehand."

—Its operation costs the administration additional funds.
(He didn't estimate how much more.)

—Paxson School is too far from District 6, in which most of
the children live, to have the proper "impact."

—The transfer of children to Paxson has had an adverse effect
on the racial balances of the schools they formerly attended;
it has led to "further segregation."

—The board was displeased with the method by which the
children were selected for the program.

It was this latter point that probably contributed most to the
attacks on the program. Many parents who may have wanted
to place their children in the school were angered when they
learned of its existence after the program was underway.

On Christmas Eve, in Bremer's absence, a phone message was
left at his home from the superintendent: "A Happy Christmas to you.
Will you just tell John that Paxson will be closed, and ask him to call
me back when he gets in."

So the Paxson Program for elementary school children closed, and in
spite of all the promises from the superintendent, it has not been started
again either within Parkway or within the conventional school districts.

The blow was bitterly felt. Bremer was disappointed, since his hopes
for a programmatic school district were ruined, he had been unable to
protect the program adequately, and 97 elementary school children
went back to uncongenial learning situations. He also learned that
Parkway could not depend on the superintendent and that it had to
develop a political base quite independent of the school district. That
then became his mission, and from January to June 1970 his one pur-

pose was to prevent Parkway from being taken over by the superintendent's system and to establish it on the local and national levels so that it could survive Bremer's possible resignation.

At the end of January, Parkway appeared on NBC's "Today" show. On the same day, the *New York Times* ran a near full-page feature story by William Stevens. Morale had begun to pick up, and a chance accident provided a new opportunity for the reaffirmation of Parkway principles. The accident was that suddenly, without any warning, the printed diplomas, requested the previous April for the eight June graduates, were delivered to Bremer. Since it was the end of January, Bremer decided to hold a graduation ceremony on the anniversary of the program, February 17. The U.S. Commissioner of Education, Dr. James E. Allen, agreed to come and make the presentations and to give an address.

John P. Corr reported in the *Philadelphia Inquirer:*

> "The ideas, spirit and success of Philadelphia's Parkway [program] may spread through the nation much as did the Founding Fathers' fervor for independence, 200 years ago," the U.S. Commissioner of Education said. . . .

John T. Gillespie of the *Evening Bulletin* took a different theme from the speech:

> "At a time when other schools are experiencing disruption, it is heartening to witness what the Parkway has achieved," Dr. Allen told pupils and faculty. . . .

In the *Philadelphia Daily News,* Lou Antosh, under the headline Parkway Graduation — CUM LOVE, reported another aspect:

> Philadelphia's famed Parkway Program, conducting its first graduation ceremony — birthday party at the Art Museum, proved there just ain't no room for Pomp and Circumstance in the Age of Aquarius.
>
> There was a lot of talk about innovative education. There was the traditional awarding of diplomas and dialogue with beaming parents. But the underlying theme was love and kisses.
>
> Even the U.S. Commissioner of Education, Dr. James E. Allen, accepted a smooch from one of the glowing girl graduates, thereby revealing his stand on school bussing. . . .

[171]

Later, Dr. Allen said only people "who act like persons in relation to others can begin to put a dent into the urgent problem of modern education.

"The interesting thing about the Parkway Program is that many of the reforms which other communities across the country have only been discussing, have already been instituted here," he said.

The superintendent was not even there to hear these words.

The graduation was a success from every point of view—and so, apparently, was Parkway. There were editorials to confirm this publicly:

The *Daily News* on February 20 wrote:

HOPE ON THE PARKWAY

Is it too soon to evaluate the merits of this city's unique Parkway School program? Perhaps.

It is hardly surprising that a number of Philadelphians looked with skepticism on the program when it was first proposed and put into motion last year. It is experimental and there are many citizens who automatically frown on innovations.

There is no question that the "school without walls" is popular with the students who have been enrolled there. They love it. Most of their parents presumably agree.

The Parkway program is a radical departure from traditional school concepts. The Parkway School's first graduation program gave promise that the experiment is working.

Dr. John Bremer, who conceived the high school project, believes it should and will be expanded in the next few years. What's more, he hopes that a short-lived experiment in extending the concept to elementary grades should be revived.

We believe Dr. Bremer's optimism is justified. But another year or two should prove the point one way or another.

The *Inquirer* wrote on February 21:

THE PARKWAY HIGH SCHOOL SUCCESS STORY

Philadelphia has reason to take pride in its Parkway High School and the first small graduating class of eight students. Whatever may be the ultimate destiny of the fledgling institution, it has a number of significant and worthwhile accomplishments to its credit already.

[172]

It has attracted nationwide attention and in the process served as an inspiration on the same scale.

Other cities are experimenting with the same or similar approaches. In some cases, perhaps, with more success but in others with no success at all.

As was expected there are both pluses and minuses for the Philadelphia experiment.

But, on the balance, we believe that the pluses far outweigh the minuses, and this in itself is a remarkable thing, for the school has burgeoned from an enrollment of 143 a year ago to the point where it now operates in three units of 250 students each.

It is probably safe to say that no new high school in this city or any other has ever been organized so quickly with less confusion or more enthusiasm and sense of purpose.

The presence of Dr. James E. Allen Jr., U.S. Commissioner of Education, at the ceremonies was in itself a measure of the influence the project has exerted outside the community, and a confirmation of his thought that the spirit of the Parkway School might spread through the nation after the manner of the ideas of liberty and equality in the Declaration of Independence.

To paraphrase another revolutionary war slogan, however, the fight to prove the permanent worth of the Parkway School idea has only begun.

The enthusiasm of the first year must be sustained over the long run, and the mistakes avoided. With two other school communities like it already begun in other city centers and three more planned, the school authorities may be inviting disillusionment and false hopes.

The Parkway High School's instant success may not be easily duplicated just anywhere or with less dedicated direction and teaching personnel.

KYW Newsradio and television both presented a good editorial:

> In the midst of all the bad news about Philadelphia school taxes two happy events have slipped by almost unnoticed. They are good news for taxpayers.
>
> The first involves the unique Parkway High School—the school without a school building. It is a high school which the taxpayers will not have to build at the usual cost of $12

million. It is an experiment which uses scientific, civic, cultural and business institutions that already exist along the Benjamin Franklin Parkway. Students will be getting the benefit of these rich community resources at no expense to the taxpayers.

It's an exciting opportunity for education geared to the real world. The new school is drawing students from all over the city. And, for the first time, exchange students from a suburban township.

And Donald Barnhouse, of WCAU-TV, on February 17, gave a very perceptive analysis:

A news story like this really stands out in a day when we are accustomed to school buildings that cost millions of dollars. Here is a high school opening with no school building at all, as such. Can it work? Is it possible that such an idea can really get off the ground?

Looking at history, at the past experience of humanity with schools and buildings, we find that education is not as dependent on buildings as Americans might have come to assume in the last generation or so. For the first several thousand years of human civilization, of course, education never had any buildings of its own. The world was the curriculum, and being out in the world was the laboratory experience. As for the more abstract schooling, the education of the mind, that took place in discussion, conversations that could take place anywhere. Sometimes these conversations took place on long walks in the countryside, sometimes strolling up and down in a beautiful city setting, occasionally indoors. This tradition of education stressed the teacher and the student, not the location. It was centered in the relationships between people. As recently as the past century in America someone said that the ideal education would be Mark Hopkins on one end of a log and the student on the other end — Mark Hopkins being a particularly brilliant and stimulating individual.

It is still true in our elaborately structured educational systems of today that this kind of special personal relationship is the key to an outstanding educational experience. If you're lucky, you recall at least one such teacher you may have had, a person whose classes made you forget the walls, the school, the building, and seemed to draw your mind into vast open spaces where frontiers of knowledge and imagination opened, a teacher who knew the subject and loved it, a teacher who knew you too and had some personal feeling for you beyond your being a name on a class list. It is teachers like that who make education work, and the finest buildings will be very ordinary schools, or even poor schools, unless we can find ways of discovering and attracting that kind of teacher.

No one can be sure *now* whether the Parkway School will be a success or not. But it will depend more on the teachers than on any other single factor. Having no building isn't a marvelous sure-cure formula, but it's not a crazy impossible idea, either. It might really work.

Another heartening piece of news was that the idea of Parkway was catching on. *Education U.S.A.*, for example, wrote in January:

> *The "school without walls" concept is catching on in major cities across the continent.* Chicago has scheduled the opening of its on-location Metropolitan High School for Feb. 2, 1970. The school will have no conventional building. Instead, students will do their class work in hospitals, theaters, museums, newspapers, and in local businesses and industries. The prototype "school without walls" is the Parkway School, which opened in Philadelphia last February. Chicago's Metropolitan High will draw its first freshman class from schools throughout the city. It will operate on a pilot basis for the first year. The curriculum will be divided into three areas: skills, humanities–social sciences, and natural sciences. Students will be taught by the school's certified faculty and personnel from participating organizations. Other cities, such as New York, San Francisco, and Toronto, are reported to be considering the "school without walls" idea.

With the program going well educationally, these events — and the reporting of them — began to solidify Parkway's position and to make it appear safe from any possible future attacks. In the next several months, there were articles about the program in a large number of magazines and journals: *Time, The Atlantic,* the *Reader's Digest, Orbit, Media & Methods,* and several others.

There were many calls on John Bremer for informal talks, lectures, and consultation. He tried never to refuse. It took him away from the program, which disturbed some people, but he knew that this was a weaning process, hard and difficult but absolutely necessary if the program was to stand on its own feet, without him. But it also had the effect of giving Parkway a national — and even international — reputation. This gave it the freedom to be itself and removed forever from the political interference of the superintendent, as witnessed by the search for further funding.

After the establishment of the program, it was natural enough to ask the Ford Foundation for continued support, at least, for the expansion of the program. In January 1970, Bremer had prepared an outline of a proposal to submit to the Ford Foundation and had held preliminary talks with them. The board of education had discussed the proposal, and its members were clearly confused about what it would mean to adopt it for formal presentation to the Foundation, except that it meant expansion of the program both in numbers and into the elementary and middle school years. And they had just allowed the superintendent to close Paxson. Whatever else, it would mean an endorsement of Bremer, and, perhaps wisely, they queried the worthwhileness of the program and suggested an evaluation. The superintendent was in a dilemma—he wanted to bring money into the system, but did not want it to give more freedom and power to Bremer.

Some time later, when asked for a proposal to submit to the Ford Foundation, Bremer sent his original document back again, this time for discussion with the superintendent and the executive cabinet. In the discussion with Bremer, they took the attitude that the board had turned this proposal down, at which point Bremer remarked that he had no reason to approach Ford if that was the case.

This left the superintendent somewhat restricted, since Ford knew what was happening and would certainly raise questions if the director of the program was ignored. However, his hand was forced and the superintendent prepared his own proposal (without consultation with or the knowledge of Bremer) and put it before the board on Monday, May 11, 1970. Bremer was invited to the meeting and was asked what he thought of the proposal. He replied that it had been drawn up without his knowledge and he had seen it briefly over lunch the previous Friday when an assistant to the superintendent wanted to find out about the program he was writing a proposal for. Board members then raised questions with the superintendent as to why Bremer had not been involved. There was no satisfactory answer. Again the matter was put off, and on May 20, at the suggestion of Robert M. Sebastian, one of the board members, Bremer circulated his original proposal with an emphatic statement against the superintendent's proposal (which would have been educationally disastrous, since it proposed a one-year program in the junior year, after which the students would be returned to their schools for senior year and graduation).

The outcome was that no proposal was submitted to the Ford Foundation. The Parkway program, and Bremer, could clearly prevent external forces from controlling it and using it for other purposes. The price was no funding from outside—but perhaps that was an advantage.

In accordance with his plan of putting the Parkway Program on its own feet, Bremer had told the superintendent that he thought he should consider changing his role with respect to the program, that he should cease to be director and remain only as a consultant or perhaps should sever connections altogether. Although told in confidence, this matter was soon public knowledge and the Parkway community had to face the fact that its director might leave. Bremer discussed the situation with faculty, students, and parent representatives and tried to make clear their political function. He then tried to keep out of the way, even though he had not determined what to do. If it would help the program he would go — or stay.

As the events of May and June started to unfold, it began to be clear that another year at Parkway would only mean continuing conflict with the superintendent, and Bremer believed that would mean unnecessary trouble when the program needed a time of quiet in which to settle down. By the end of August when he had been away for six weeks, he had decided to resign.

The program had raised its own money (through an admirable group of parents) for a summer program and had also found an acting director who seemed acceptable to Parkway and to the superintendent. It might well work. The only way to find out was to do it.

Before leaving Philadelphia in June, John Bremer had seen the second Parkway graduation, also at the Philadelphia Museum of Art. There were eighty graduates and more than five hundred in the audience. The superintendent was not among them.

Robert Rafsky, of the *Evening Bulletin,* on Tuesday, June 16, reported the event:

> Waving a peacock feather (for beauty), and several sheaves of wheat (for fertility), Diane DeKalb marched up the canvas-covered grand staircase of the Art Museum last night.
>
> Behind her, some 80 young men and women walked and stumbled into what may have been the most unusual graduation ceremony in the history of the Philadelphia school system.
>
> It was the first large-scale graduation for the Parkway Project, the city's year-and-a-half old "school without walls. . . ."
>
> "More than half of the graduates will go on to some form of higher education," director John Bremer told several hundred of their relatives and friends. . . .
>
> It was typical of the school — which gives students long written evaluations instead of grades — that something was said about each graduate last night.

Every student who had applied to a college had been accepted, most of them by their first choice. Most of the others had a clear sense of purpose and were on the way to accomplishing it. What more could be asked of an educational program?

A few days after the graduation, and a few days before leaving Philadelphia, Bremer was honored by the Philadelphia Chapter of the American Institute of Architects — a rather improbable body to give an award to a man promoting schools without walls. But they understood.

AIA

The Philadelphia Chapter/American Institute of Architects

**ACCOLADE TO
JOHN BREMER, EDUCATOR**

For bringing to Philadelphia his conviction that good education is something that happens to kids, not something packaged and passed out by teachers;

For making us agree with him that schooling is everybody's business . . . and that if we want better results we'd all better lend a hand;

For making real and viable the notion of the Parkway Projects, and proving beyond any rational doubt that these — and thus other — alternatives to the traditional educational system have much to recommend them;

And finally, just for being John Bremer — too honest and persuaded to be other than outspoken when a call needs sounding.

/s/ *Henry Shurick*
President
June 18, 1970

Bremer did not return to the Parkway Program, and its third academic year of operation began without him. Apparently, he was right; it could stand on its own feet.

PART II

The Parkway Experience

10

From a Student—Lynn Schultz

I could write pages and pages about the condition of the Philadelphia school system in general. Being in it and messed up by it for quite a few years, I've collected my share of stories. But I think that the increasing vandalism, kids graduating without being able to read or write, and kids in junior high (even in the semisuburban school I come from) shooting smack do a pretty good job of reflecting what's going on. No matter what the purpose of education is, there are too many kids who aren't fitting into those big buildings anymore. There are too many kids who can't figure out why there is someone standing at the front of the class pretending to be something he's not, pretending to know too many things he doesn't and trying to tell them what to do. There are too many kids who are being stepped on or walked over because they can't believe it and they've been trained not to question, because no one will show them or even admit to them that there are other ways; the kids who have been conditioned into passive acceptance and the ones who just will in no way fit in. People are doing other things, though; saying "no" and leaving, saying "yes" to themselves and building. This means life styles, this means education, and it means politics.

For a long time I was aware of the shit that the school was laying on me, that it was not what I wanted, and not what I needed. I spent a long time trying to fight what was happening and work for change in the school through student organizing and through politics. But I was still a part of the system I was fighting. I was still in it and still felt threatened by its authority. The reality of its authority is constantly perpetuated by fear; fear of expulsion, low grades, and so on. As long as you have that fear you're still a part of it; and being a part of it feeds the system and keeps it going.

Cutting school was, for me, the beginning of getting out. I cut school for weeks at a time, spending my time in town at the library, at museums, sometimes with my friends, and sometimes just walking alone. That really started my transformation period between simply not accepting to actively being against what was happening in school and looking for and trying to build something new.

This is where Parkway picked me up. I wasn't sure what to expect, but it was a chance for a big change and a chance to do a lot of learning. I am purposefully not mentioning dates and time, because it can be more effectively measured by things that happened. On the one hand there were no limits and you could work as fast and go as far as you wanted, on the other hand you were confronted with starting something new, working with other people and facing their problems as well as your own. The people I was meeting exposed me to subjects and media I had never worked with before (a regular widening of horizons) and seemed to know different things. I met people who through their things helped me develop my interest particularly in film, French, poetry, and music. This enthusiasm grew from the personal contact and the really good relationships I was developing with the people there. Most of the work I did, however, was on my own. My class-type education was class communication. Everyone was busy working out problems (and probably facing new ones). We spent a lot of time getting to know each other, getting to know why we were there, and getting to know a lot of the things around us. Some kids came to try something new, some to get away from the old, to work, to goof, some just because they'd been flunking out, some because the law said they had to be in school. Kids were confronted with a lot of real problems and people who couldn't give a damn were faced with ideas. One thing for sure, nothing ran smoothly, someone was always on your ass for something.

At the beginning there was a lot of awe inspired by the press, etc., by being new, by being out of all the old shit, and for having a whole city to work with. Things took shape slowly, kids started attending classes and stopped attending classes. There were a lot of things kids had to decide for themselves, that's about one of the hardest things to learn how to do. It is much easier to look for substitutes for old standbys and to ask people to tell you what to do. Theory began to crash head on into what was happening. Parkway wasn't working with little kids who are open to trying new things, there were mostly kids who had in many different ways been fucked over by the system. It was like trying to break years of training, trying to sort out and cut out a lot of crap just to be sure there was a person underneath who wanted things of his own. It took constant evaluation of what was going on and searching for ways to make things go right and maybe overcome a little of all the bullshit that was flying. I might have been able to learn from those problems, but how much is it for someone who can't read? Should you discipline kids who are messing around and who really want it? What do you do about the stealing problem?

One day I was talking to a kid who came from South Philly High. He told me that he was going to leave Parkway because there weren't any rules to break. You couldn't have any fun. He left.

In an economics class the teacher was going to let us learn whatever we wanted. We didn't know anything about economics and had no idea where to start, let alone what we wanted to know. We spent weeks trying to decide if we should decide. Finally the teacher got together a basic theory rap—we had a lot we could talk about.

On a really warm sunny day, after swimming in the Logan Square fountain, I went to tutorial. We worked for maybe an hour in the cellar room in the art museum. There were some guys playing drums out back and a girl dancing. Pretty soon we were all out back, just dancing and sitting on the grass by the river. We had been working on writing and binding our own books, which were supposed to be finished by the end of the term. They were.

In the summer, Parkway opened a new unit. I had mono, so I don't know too much about what happened. Tina was the head of the new unit. She had been a really good teacher. A lot of the good people from Antioch split too. When I came back I found renewed chaos, but this time the enthusiasm wasn't there to pull it through. Things had been changed around quite a bit. John took the more removed role of director and Ralph became the head of our unit. It was pretty easy to blame a lot of shit on John. We had new tutorials, a lot of new teachers and interns. We no longer looked at Parkway as comparatively better than our old schools, so its faults and problems were even more evident than before. There was never enough money for the equipment we needed.

Because of all the hassles a lot of kids were accepting leadership/teacher-type roles. But whether or not they were getting what they wanted and fulfilling their learning needs was questionable too. Somehow a median must be found, where it is not just a small group accepting the teaching roles but rather an interaction of a large group. These problems and a general lack of energy and morale made it harder and harder to take being around 1801. I went to most of my classes, where the majority of time was spent talking about what was going wrong and how to change it. There was an awful lot of talking. Most of the work I accomplished was independent projects. The only time work would get done in class was when everyone decided to stop talking and do work. Things in general, though, just seemed to be up in the air and a lot of problems had to be worked out on personal levels. I spent a lot of time just being with people around 1801. We had town meetings, etc., to talk about what was wrong with the whole school.

"Kids aren't coming to class."

"Well, that's because no one tells them to!"

"No, there's no sense of community. Parkway's a community."

"Yeah, kids have to make each other come to class."

"Well, classes are bad, anyway; we have to make the teachers . . . blah, blah, blah. . . ."

"Don't you see? The question is what is a community."

"Look, do we even want a blahblahblah?"

O.K. You know where that kind of talk is at. The thing that is bad is that the ideas are right, they just don't go with what's really going on. They don't take into consideration all the indoctrination that's come before, all things that must be fought against because they are so prevalent in other surrounding systems, and all the obstacles that must be overcome. It all takes an incredible amount of time. There has to be enough time to look around at what you have, to learn to ask, to try new things, to see what you like, and just generally to see what there is. At Parkway there wasn't enough freedom or time. It was infinitely better than other schools, but you were just getting little tastes of this and that, without being really able to grab. Things were influenced by people wanting to see the "products" (something they won't see for a very long time, since school is just a small part of a process—a general flaw); to evaluate these products, by thinking at one point you can stop the process is just a progressive way of writing report cards and setting artificial goals.

With all the chaos going on it was time for me to split. Things inside my head were buzzing and I was totally frustrated, trying to work out my problem, working with other people, and not being able to accomplish what I wanted. Parkway was versatile enough to let me work out an independence far away. I was loaded with questions about "education," about theory and reality, and about priorities. One thing I realized is that education is a part of a whole; education, as I perceive it, is a form of communication, as well as communication being a form of education. What this means to me is that a school should be a place which seeks to find the most effective forms of education, constantly changing to fill the needs of its students. Part of the problem at Parkway is that working for the radical change it is, the board of education will not allow it to move at the pace it must. There is a big difference and conflict of interests and ideas. How can the board of education, which is so tied up in maintaining the status quo, really support a school that wants to say "your status quo is a myth" and fulfill the needs of students as it sees fit. It seems evident that the two systems recognize different needs. Learning is change, change is growth. There is too much politicking, too many immobile thought processes in the board of education, to allow the schools to move at the rapid pace the changes in society demand.

Now I am living up in Vermont and working at Goddard College. I am trying on all levels to build the kind of environment I can live in. For me that means learning book stuff, taking in information, and working on developing my interest (communication). I'm also trying to work out living problems and things with other people; a way of being self-sustaining and creative. But external forces are working against this, which means I must also work on a defensive level, creating alternatives in media and protection. When people are being killed by police, National Guard, etc., and you don't hear about it, you know something is going on. Education is learning how to handle it.

11

From a Student–William (Mannix) Smith

I am deeply concerned about the Parkway program. In my old school the black students couldn't talk to the white teachers because they were teaching like 45 classes a day and they didn't even have ten minutes to spare. At PP the relationship with the white teachers is starting to be "on time." You can rap with teachers and open up, while in the old school you had to worry about the structure. Like you had to say "sir" and you couldn't take the time to talk about what happened to you and your girl last night. A white teacher walking into an all-black class couldn't get around us, but here I've had the experience of a white guy getting through to us, being close to us by rapping to us and telling us about himself and about his girl. And, well, we've come to trust him.

At Edison I couldn't read or write. It seems that they pushed me through school, and weren't concerned about me. In some kinds of ways I was ashamed I couldn't read. I'd ask for help but they didn't have time for me. Because of this, school was a drag. I guess it was *partly* my fault. They passed me, but I shouldn't have been passed cause I couldn't read and write. One day I got a letter at Edison telling me about a program, Parkway, where they would take me even if I couldn't read and write. So I jumped at the opportunity to get out of Edison because I hated it. And for the first time people were concerned. I think it took about three months for me to open up because I was afraid. For the first quarter I had a teacher who taught me reading with four other students. Anita spent about thirty minutes with me each time. Other classes assumed I could read. Anita went to Gamma (the third Parkway unit) and then I didn't have anyone who I could really talk to. When people assume you can read, you have to fake it and you feel ashamed. And when they find out, you feel bad. Sometimes they pass you, sometimes they ignore you, and sometimes they don't want to have anything to do with you. I couldn't hide it anymore; I was getting kind of old—and ashamed or not I wanted help. But still, I was ashamed to ask for it. Anita came back to Alpha in September. She asked if I wanted to go to Penn's reading clinic. I was glad to hear from her. But mother said I had to work that summer, so I didn't go. She thought Penn really couldn't teach me how to read, so I should work. And that's what I did. I came back to school in the fall and told Anita. I guess she kind of spread the word I couldn't read, and then people kind of got concerned about me.

And then in Parkway we had tutorial where kids could teach other kids individually. Some kids were concerned about me, some were not. They took time in tutorial to teach me the basic structure of reading. I got my hopes up high that I could learn to read some day. I still didn't trust people yet. One day I made a mistake. I was light-fingered. I took something from the school. The director asked me to bring it back. He didn't penalize me; he didn't even tell my parents. I guess for the first time I was concerned about school. I was really shocked that the director didn't call the cops. I guess Parkway was my second home— away from home.

I was still ashamed about learning how to read. I guess in some ways I was kind of scared. There was always the fear that Parkway would close down, and then how could I go back to my old school. I had made such a great step that I was afraid that if Parkway did close down, it would be the end of my reading, and most of all the end of my good friends here. I couldn't go back to that old castle Edison, because when I first went there, it was all boys and you know the old saying "boys will be boys." I heard kids talking around the pool table at Edison. I heard kids talking about how some day I would be a pool shark. Somehow I didn't want to be a pool shark, really. I was concerned how would I get to my classes and work when I couldn't read and write. That created a problem; I didn't know how big a problem it was until I floated to the eleventh grade and still couldn't read. I started dating girls older than me, and they could read, you know. We'd go to some nice places and she'd pick up a menu and ask me what did I want. Somehow you had to ask her what she wanted and play it cool. So you played it cool all the time. Sometimes you'd go to her house and have a nice time. You might get a game out and play it, but you got uptight because you couldn't read the cards and play the game. That created a problem, too. So you would go home and try to study reading but you can't learn to read by yourself. So you'd ask for help in your family.

Man, dig it. Did you ever ask your mother for help? She'd call you dumb. If you have a little brother, he'd come by and say, "I can read *that* word." It would get you down, really down. And you'd go upstairs to your room. Boy did you feel ashamed. You shut the door, turn on the radio, and try to forget that you couldn't read. Somehow, your brothers and sister would make cracks about how you couldn't read. Then you'd make cracks at them about how they couldn't do something. But the greatest problem was the reading, I guess. They'd laugh off the cracks I made, cause I was the oldest. When you are the oldest, did you ever try to ask your brother, "What's that word?" The kid brother feels sorry for you, and that hurts. And so, you get hit from your mother, brothers, and sister.

So I wanted to get out of Edison. I started cutting classes cause classes were a drag. Somehow or some way I got into Parkway. I was amazed that they had walls, cause they said that they had no walls. And then I began to dig it cause you're outside most of the time going to classes. So you dig it; here there were no walls.

I went to a school where the population was 85 percent black; now I was going to school with white suburban students from all over. I didn't know how to cope with them cause I realized that they were higher in education than me. But I could play it cool and they'd never know how dumb I was.

So I took reading at Parkway. I was kind of amazed how some of the teachers were concerned. Not pity, man; we don't want pity. I ain't telling you a story cause I know that somewhere out there, there are kids like me who can't read. Dig it, man, don't get uptight. I know you have a hard time in school if you can't read. If you can't get in Parkway, then you should create a problem in school, like I did; you'll get noticed then. Maybe they'll notice that you can't read.

In my opinion, the Philadelphia School System does not educate. It's too busy indoctrinating* and all it should really be doing is bringing out what's already inside of you. Because you are nature. I am concerned about you, whether you are a boy or a girl who can't read or write. I want you to get help. Don't feel bad because you can't read, cause there are things you can do that they can't. Dig it?

How about all your people who are going to school day after day and cutting classes and passing. Think about it. Like when you are out of school after twelfth grade and you have your diploma and you're looking for a job. Dig it, people. You get the job probably but see, you've

---

* Indoctrinating, according to Mannix, means "messing" around with people's insides, making them what they're not. He takes it to mean something like "doctoring."

been messin' up in school all this time—messin' up with the boys, messin' up with the girls. Nine times out of ten your people get fired because somewhere around the school, the system lets you all ride. The school shouldn't have you all ride. The school shouldn't have done that because you are out there now, 17, 18, or 19 years old. Now you have jobs but you're messed up.

At Parkway when I came here, like I told you last time, I couldn't read. But I got help, so I can read words now, and I thought I couldn't never. That was a break for me—a big break.

I'm looking for another step now. Sure, when I came here I couldn't read. The big step I was talking about—someday I'd like to go to college cause I know college is something for a black guy. It's really not too fair a chance with my background. I think I really have to study—all kinds of studying. At college I could mess around, sure, but when it's time to pass the exam I'd flunk and they'd know. So I got a big step in my life now. I'm going to try my best. If I don't make it, I have one thing I can do, and it pays pretty fair. I could be a florist.

I think they need more schools like Parkway. In Philadelphia, this was a big step. Somewhere around I think they're going to do away with Parkway. See, at this school they always tell us they are going to run out of money. Gratz, Dobbins, and Overbrook—they have people dropping out, some people not learning anything. I went to Overbrook on Thursday with a friend. Around 3:30 my friend was standing by the door talking to this girl. A teacher came and asked us what we were doing. Instead of educating, he was messin' around with people.

I know the people who are going to buy this article can read. I wish kids who couldn't read could have someone read this article to them. You see, this is how I learned to read. For the first quarter I thought I was hopeless. For 17 years I hadn't learned to read, and it's hard. So my teacher, Wendy, she's kind of out of the ordinary. She took most of her time, I couldn't understand, writing a book for me. She made cards for me with pictures on them. I'd have to go home and study the cards, write the words. Sometimes I miss them, sometimes I don't. On Wendy's lunch time she'd take me to Sansom Village. She'd make me read all the records and little signs. She'd help me with the words I didn't know. Boy, I'd feel down cause there's lots I didn't know, and she'd write them down. One time she brought in some jelly beans to class. She shocked me, too, cause I'm not a kid. I like jelly beans. She laid the jelly beans on the table. She had pages from a book she wrote for me, and for every word I got right, I got a jelly bean. Boy, I worked. Hard pages were worth more jelly beans than easy pages.

We need more teachers in the Philadelphia system who will not let the money excite them too much so they can live up to the word educate. See, there's one thing I couldn't figure out about Wendy, is I know she gets points (credits) for coming here, but see I know she ain't getting any money, cause it slipped out one time. I couldn't see how no teacher devoted her time to students and wasn't getting a dime. And the teachers who was getting paid weren't doing as much as her.

In the school where you are now, if you are in trouble, there's about 35–40 kids in the class. No one is going to notice you can't read; they are going to shove you over cause they have no time for you. So I say, we need more teachers like her who is not devoted to indoctrinating and who is living up to educating.

See, I'm in a class right now by myself and I say, I love it because individual help goes much better than competition in class with 45 students who can read and getting no kind of help.

Wendy, she brought in newspaper ads and if you take your girl to the movies you have to look up the time. That was really successful, looking at papers and reading the ads. That was real nice. We were talking about dating and girls and what's happening. And she'd go home and write it up. She'd say those are your words so why don't you read them. So we'd go over it. And that same day I'd know the words on that paper. I don't know how you learn to read, but sure, this is a big step. How many 17-year-old boys who can't read, learn about 50 words in one day. See, it amazes me, when she brings in something you said the next day; when you go over it, you can read some words. If you study those words, when you see them again, you will know them.

In this system, now you gonna have to get out of high school, first of all. If the system keeps going the way it's going, you are going to have to have two years of college to go anywhere if you are black. I am glad Parkway came along because I think if it didn't come along, I'd still be in Edison much worse off than I am now. And with no help at all because they would pity me so much, man, my mind would be corroded. So I am glad Parkway came along. I'm glad someone started thinking on the right side. I think in about 77 years, if it took that long, we're going to have a few changes in the system about the kids getting educated. When you get out of high school, all the kids who are fairly good—Uncle Sam has a way of taking care of all of them. You see, you're going to be drafted and sent away and maybe messed up, shot up. This I believe will happen. The guys on the corner, Uncle Sam really don't want you guys in the system. You cannot pass the test, nine times out of ten. And the ones who do pass the test, they'll get a dishonorable discharge cause they can't hack it. So I say, we're going to have all the guys on the corners left running the world cause the good guys with an education have been drafted into the war. And the corner guys are all that are left. That leaves us a world run by??? (And you think about it.)

I hope that the system changes and we have more good teachers in this system who would be dedicated to teaching and to the kids who need individual help. I believe this system should teach kids the basic things they need to know like math and reading. They are going to have to know that before they get out of the third grade. We are going to have to learn to accept kids who have this misfortune in grades and stop criticizing the misfortuned kids and give them help. It's going to have to try hard because we are used to the old system, so I know it's going to be hard for the teachers who are dedicated to teaching in the public system to change to something new, something that could help us. And the only way you are going to help us is when you change the system of education. Because the kids who are misfortuned in grades has been passed and gone out of school, and because they have been passed in the grades, they will get into trouble.

So I say, live up to the word *educate*. Please stop indoctrinating because the kids need you. Parkway has moved a big step in the word *educate*, and you should look at the step and you should say, look, that system is working, and that system is *not working*. I think kids here are more concerned about Parkway because the old structure in the schools could not help the misfortuned kids. And so, that's why kids come here. Kids do not like teachers who use their positions to rule over them. We do not like pity; we like to be respected. And the misfortuned kids don't want your pity; and that's where you make your mistake. So I say, Parkway has taken that big step, and hope you all realize that Parkway has lived up to the word *educate*. And when a school lives up to the word *educate*, I think I should take a look at that system closely because Parkway is trying to be a great big family. We are concerned about misfortuned kids. All I can say now is that Parkway really helped me and my misfortune. And now I have come to a big step, and I hope to make something out of that big step.

Parkway students utilize Philadelphia facilities like the Franklin Institute as classrooms. (Photo by Carlton Read.)

Preparing for town meeting.

Town meeting in progress.

A class in law enforcement uses a courtroom as its classroom. (Photo by Carlton Read.)

Some faces at Parkway. John Bremer (upper left).
The girl wears the Parkway emblem.
(Photos by Carlton Read.)

Parkway director John Bremer at the second public lottery to choose Parkway students, on Friday, June 13, 1969.

Students talking in the locker area of unit Alpha, which they decorated themselves.

An electronics exhibit at the Franklin Institute serves as a focus of learning. (Photo by Carlton Read.)

A student learns hospital techniques and earns social studies credits at the University of Pennsylvania Hospital.

Parkway's first woman graduate receives diploma from John Bremer at the school's first graduation-birthday exercises, February 17, 1970. Looking on is U.S. Commissioner of Education, Dr. James E. Allen, the principal speaker. (Photo by the *Philadelphia Daily News*.)

Parkway's second graduation exercises were held on June 15, 1970, on the steps of the Philadelphia Museum of Art. (Photo by *Philadelphia Inquirer*.)

12

From a Student–Richard Gordon

THE HORRIBLE REALIZATION OF SCHOOLS

For those of you who may not have realized, school is a very heavy thing to get into, it really is! Your son or daughter needs an education, this we know, but what kind? Have you ever thought about the disadvantages as well as advantages in education? Relevancy is a word that keeps popping up from students' mouths today. What is relevancy? Relevancy is something to relate to. For instance, how relevant is white history to black people? Why are they learning about George Washington? The first President of the United States, a man who owned over a hundred slaves. Benjamin Franklin—a great man with thirteen illegitimate children. Abraham Lincoln, a great man who we all know freed the slaves (supposedly). What the white history books didn't say is that Abraham Lincoln, the sixteenth President of the United States, did not free the slaves for humanitarian reasons, but because of a political feud. Afterwards he tried desperately to take the black man from America and put him back into Africa, but it was too late; we were here to stay. The history books also did not mention that most of the Presidents and white politicians (if not all) were racists, fascists, and bigots. There was never any America—no land of the free, home of the brave, and it is time that such bull be exposed. A nation of immigrants run and owned by white racists and fascists. The other minority groups were brutally and forcefully oppressed and still are. These history books and current events and articles left out a large part of reality; they lied. Surely this is not relevant education. The really great men, such as John Brown, a white man who took a stand against white

supremacy — Nat Turner, a slave who tried desperately to free his people — or currently Stokely Carmichael, who is working very hard on
International Black Unification — why are these great men labeled as
criminals, and militants, when they were working for a common cause
which was and is to gain freedom for people in the land of the free?
Something is definitely wrong with that kind of education. Surely this
does not give us a true look at the past and present.

For years the school system has been designed to be relevant only to
white students. (You would expect this from a racist country.) It taught
every student, every nonwhite oppressed student, how to be accepted
in a white-dominated society. These students were taught to be
ashamed of their selves and their proud heritage. They were taught to
stay in their "place" and that they would never become anything. On
the other hand, some schools taught the nonwhite oppressed student
that he could do anything that he wanted to do. He could even become
President if he tried very hard and wanted to be very much. This is
another *lie* taught in schools. This is education. A black man could
never become President in the United States of America, at least while
there is still a white majority. Nor could a Puerto Rican, much less an
American Indian (who is still captive on the reservation). They did not
tell them (the nonwhite students) that the United (?) States of America
is and was a racist country. Instead, our heads were filled with bull
and we believed in our country. We even sang American propaganda
songs like "I like it here" and "This is my country." We really dug those
songs, mostly because we believed them. It wasn't until 10th grade that
I found out what I was learning and believe it I was pretty mad. I was
pissed.

The school system is very bad. In fact, it's in trouble. What about the
teachers? Can anyone be a teacher? Or maybe it takes someone special.
My personal experiences with teachers — well, to most of them it's just
a job. As long as they are getting paid, they are satisfied. They don't
care about the students at all. They will be the first to tell you, "I got my
diploma, you got to get yours." Some don't even teach. (And I don't
believe that they know how.) They give you a book, tell you to read,
and give you a test on book material. This is not teaching. Books are
nice but they can't teach you everything. They also are not human. A
really good teacher will not rely on a book, because he has his stuff
together already. He is also more concerned with his students, and he
realizes that there is no average student. Every individual student has
his own hang-ups and he tries to help them. You run across these
teachers very rarely.

The Parkway Program has such good qualities that I must tell you of
some past experiences in the standard public school system. I, like

many other of my school companions, had a really rotten time in my school life. The schools I went to were filled with boredom and un-reality. The teachers were the same old "stuffed shirts" that were in all the schools. Some racist, some bigots, and just about all were "working a job." We (the students) had no motivation whatsoever. We had no leadership or guidance, either. We went to school because we had to, no other reason. All day in class we just sat there daydreaming, passing time, trying to make the best out of a rotten situation. Naturally, we tried to beat as many classes as we could, by giving phoney excuses when we didn't show up for class, playing hookey, sick, not coming to class when a substitute teacher was taking over class that day. We also needed another means of escape from boredom. School activities did the job quite nicely. If you were on some kind of team or club you could get out of school sometimes up to a day at a time. You really didn't have to worry about passing the classes that you've missed because usually your team leader would fix it up for you.

I was in the orchestra and band all through school. I chose music because it's very soothing and relaxing. I could also express myself in a beautiful way. The orchestra and band played many concerts, very often. We were always on the road traveling, and playing, at all the foot-ball games, different schools, rehearsing, practicing, running through drills on the field, or just playing in the school auditorium. We became very close with the conductor, because he was the only one who cared, really cared about us, whether because of some selfish reason or not, he cared. For this, we respected him. And even though we called him "Mr.," it was as if we called him by his first name. It was very rare when we found a teacher who really cared.

The time has come for me to tell you about my past experiences in public school. It was not until my senior year in junior high school that I began to realize that school was definitely lacking something. That year I had a great bunch of teachers. They were young, beautiful, hard-working, and full of fun. There were young regular teachers as well as student teachers. We could always laugh and joke, and when it was time for learning, we got down to business. These teachers were real; they didn't try to put us on or down. They knew what we needed, and they knew how we felt. Knowing this, they pieced it together and came out with the solution. They worked with us instead of against us. Together, we had a great year. During the year we had several hip accomplishments. First, we had the student talent show, which un-leashed the raw talent of the students of the school. I was master of ceremonies, and my pure soul just oozed on my audience. The other students, well I gave them the juice and cut them loose. The show was so good that it was held over. Next was the faculty talent show, and believe me the faculty let it all hang out. They sung, danced, and gave a terrific performance. Last of all, we put on a performance of "The West Side Story" in which I played Tony, the lead character. It was a beautiful performance. Yes, we all enjoyed ourselves that year, faculty as well as students. But the important thing is that we learned, and we enjoyed every minute of it.

After that year, in which I was doing very good, my school grades dropped drastically. I was failing school! This never happened to me before. I was always an A and B student. I couldn't figure out just what was going on. My mother got upset, my father got a little mad. I didn't know what was happening until I found most of my friends were in the same bag. We really didn't enjoy school anymore. In fact, we hated it. The teachers were lousy. There was no young freshness in them, just a sort of oldness, and empty resentment feeling. Some of the teachers were old, and they still thought they were back in the "old days." Some of them couldn't teach. All they knew how to do was assign pages in the text to read and give tests on the text. Some of the tests, if not all, were taken from the teacher's edition of the textbook. Absolutely no work on his or her part. And the rest of the teachers were there for their weekly pay. It was and is a sorry situation. Here's what was happening before I came to the Parkway Program. In sheet metal class we had a teacher who had us (the students) in check. Being a technical high school, we had to pass shop before we were able to graduate. This means the shop teacher had the power to pass or fail the student from grade to grade. He would often come to class in bad moods and take it out fully on the students. Often we were told that we would fail simply because we voiced our opinion. For a while we decided to play it his way, but when we got tired of bowing our heads down, we decided to get together and talk it over. We decided that the only way to do it is to stick together. These are the events that led up to our meeting. Our shop teacher sent one of our class brothers down to another shop to get some nails. And he got some nails all right, right up the side of his head. They chased him out the shop. We were mad. Immediately when the rest of us heard about this we grabbed hammers, mallets, wrenches, hot soldering irons, and scrap and started down there. The teacher ran in front of the door and stopped us. He told us that the first one that steps out of that door will fail the term. He also said to go and set down. We all put the stuff away and set down, still angry. After that, we were out to kill. We went down to the basement where the shop was and we cleared the hallway. Yea, we beat everything in it. Several incidents happened after that. They jumped some of us in the corridor, and we jumped some of them. One day we caught one of them in the corridor near our shop. Two of our men nabbed him and the rest of us came, with our equipment, to welcome him. We had only hit him a few times when one of our men spotted an official. We let him go, he ran, and then we ran. Things cooled down in the weeks and we cooled down with them. There had been no trouble in a few weeks. That day one of them came to our shop to get something from the teacher, but he wasn't there. He said he'd wait. And while he waited we began to remember what they had done. Talking about it our feelings arose. "He's got the nerve to come down here after what they did," someone said. The tension tightened. "Yea, and he came walking right in our shop," said another. "You remember what happened when we sent Martan down to their shop," I said. "Yea, we remember," said Martan, who was soldering his project. The intruder just stood there, not saying a word. He felt the cold breeze of tension and he didn't like it. He then decided to leave, but it was a little bit late. Already there was a crowd around him and Martan and the others that were soldering brought the soldering irons and they were red hot. "Let's have a bar-b-que," said Melvin. Quickly the outsider ran down to the other end of the shop. The door was blocked so he couldn't run far. We cornered him around a metal press and began to hit and punch him. "Burn him," they screamed. "Burn that Mother F–ker." We started jabbing hot irons at him, but he struggled like a cornered dog. Somebody burned him, and he screamed, and kept on screaming. A woman teacher right across the hall ran over when she heard the screaming and yelling. "What the hell are you doing," she said. "Shut up, bitch," somebody yelled and a heavy rubber mallet followed those words. It came hurling through the air, just missed her face and smashed through a window. More teachers came running and we got even madder. My teacher came running, with the shop supervisor right behind him. "What's going on here," he said. "Plenty," I replied. Just then the captured boy ran out into the crowd that was in front of our shop door. After we cleaned up the shop and put the tools away, the teacher and his head man spoke to us. "I don't care what happens to you people down there, I don't want anything to happen up here! This shop has a good reputation so far and I don't want it ruined!" In other words, what he was saying is to hell with us, he's worried about his shop. That happened in high school. There was another major outbreak in junior high school. Another so-called teacher took over the lunchroom and made everyone sit down and he waited until there was complete silence before he let us buy food. It takes 800 people a good while to become completely quiet. Every day before we ate we had to wait for him to give us the signal. By the time we were quiet, the lines were getting ready to close. Only a few people were able to be served. One day, we surprised him with a strike and boycott of school food. We brought our own. When he said that we could go to the lines, everyone laughed. The teachers tried to quiet us down once again, but we had been quiet long enough! Plates started breaking all over until the floor was covered with broken china. Fighting broke out. Cans and bottles were thrown at the teacher. Tables were turned over, chairs were thrown and broken. The students went wild. Some teachers ran out of the lunchroom hurt because they were hit by bottles and plates. One teacher had chocolate milk all over his head and suit. "Will all available teachers and NTA's come to the lunchroom immediately!" This was the message that came on the loudspeaker. The principal, the vice principals, and everyone else who didn't have a class came running. After that day we could go to the lines anytime we were ready.

I had been to my counselor's office trying to get a transfer from my school shop, but it seemed that my shop teacher held a lot of check. She couldn't get me out. Shortly after that I found out about Parkway and I filled out an application. I didn't let my teachers know about it until I was accepted. Then there was no stopping me. Some teachers hated to see me go because I was a good student. Others because they wanted everybody to think that they were a good high school. Anyway, I left. When I first went to the school, it seemed very strange. But after a week of it, I knew the program was a blessing from heaven, and just in the knick of time. The director, John Bremer, seemed like a realistic logical man. He knew what we wanted and needed, and the program was designed for us. I couldn't believe that there was a sane person alive in education. The teachers were so hip that they blew my mind completely away. They were people just like us, and they were for real. They introduced themselves by their first names, and that's what they wanted us to call them. Man I was so happy that I wanted to cry. This is going to be education, finally. I even called Dr. Bremer Big John or "Doc." I said to myself, "These people really want to help me." And believe me, they did. The first year was together. I called it "Aquarius" or "Utopia." We had students from all over the city and suburbs, of all different colors and backgrounds. Students that lived in the finest houses in the suburbs and from some bad houses in the slums. We had some good people, along with some racist. But we were all there for one reason, to find a better means of education, and we had a difficult task to accomplish — we had to learn how to live together — black and white. With suburbians who never knew the meaning of black — except what they read in the paper, seen in the news or heard white people talk about. Some of the black people were bitter, some because of their experiences with white people. All because they were oppressed. At first we didn't want to get too close to each other, but after doing everything together, going to classes, tutorial, and just sitting in the park, we began to develop a feeling of caring. We began to care about each other and our school. It then made me realize that our school was finally underway. We had all the qualities of a super school. We had a director — finally a man who had good sense. Teachers — finally we had real people for teachers, people who cared. And students — people fed up with hatred, stupidity, and the usual school foolishness. This — a liberated super school. Together we designed a course catalog, which contained many courses. This enabled us to take at least six different choices for a credit. We could take as many courses as we wanted and graduate when we completed our credits. It was a beautiful year, and a sense of caring and . . . love made it that way.

13

From an Intern–Neil Kauffman

ON UTOPIA AND COMMUNITY IN EDUCATION

But the Modern Utopia must not be static but kinetic, must shape not as a permanent state but as a hopeful stage leading to a long ascent of stages. Nowadays we do not resist and overcome the great stream of things, but rather float upon it. We build now not citadels, but ships of state.

H. G. WELLS: Quoted in Matthew Miles, *Innovation in Education* (Teachers College Press, Columbia University, 1964)

Since learning is a human activity — and, in a sense, the character-istic human activity — it is intimately bound up with the human group. The process of how to enter the learning process, or to be a learner, can be restated in terms of group membership — how to be a member of a learning community. What are the character-istics of a community which has as its purpose the learning of its members?

JOHN BREMER: Parkway Program Brochure (1969, pp. 20–21)

Give me a place to stand and I will move the earth!
ARCHIMEDES

I

We need to investigate new ways of looking at education. Since many people see education as the "place to stand" about which Archimedes speaks, such investigations deserve the highest priority.

Perhaps if we think about *utopia* and *community* as appropriate models for educational programs, and if we then think about the constellation of values which ought to characterize such programs, we will gain a better understanding of successful educational change. In the discussion which follows I would like to focus on the "School without Walls"—the Parkway Program in Philadelphia (PP)—as a means of clarifying these ideas and suggesting possible directions for education.

Before going on I want to mention my own bias in the discussion. Having worked with Parkway in its initial planning and having later taught there, I find an impartial assessment difficult. Nevertheless, PP's success does stand as a matter of record, even at this early date. Clearly an examination of PP can provide a rich source of insight for those concerned with the future course of American education.

II

I believe that a prime factor in the development of Parkway is that its model for learning is *utopian* and *communitarian*, as noted earlier.

By utopian I mean to suggest a concern with the farther goals of education, for the fullest realization of what education is all about: learning how to live, or in other terms, learning how to become more fully human. PP's aim, to help people live learningly, is clearly in line with those of most utopian communities, a concern with deepening and integrating one's life. John Bremer likes to quote Socrates: "For our conversation is not about something casual, but about the proper way to live."

By communitarian I mean to suggest a self-conception as a *gemeinschaft* community, organic rather than mechanical in its functioning. Such a community can present a viable matrix for personal and communal growth. The community is one whose work is mediated through personal relationships, a sense of common purpose and overarching goals.

Too often in America our models for education have been of the managerial, industrial, or military kind. I think that PP suggests that a more appropriate model would be utopian and communitarian, looking, for example, to the communities such as Amana, New Harmony, the Shakers, and so on, which appeared throughout America during the last century. With respect to the utopian community dimensions of mutual encounter, shared decisions, planning, brotherhood, experimentation, and uniqueness, PP can fairly be characterized as an intentional utopian community. Two differences come to mind in comparing Parkway to other utopian communities: Parkway does not have sleeping facilities, and most members are not full-time members of a labor force. However, even on these two points the differences are less clear. For example, the program operates weekends and year-round. And isn't learning an appropriate "product" for a "labor force" in today's world?

There is, however, a major difference in the Parkway conception of utopian community which distinguishes it from others. In the past most utopias located themselves far from the cities. PP has, on the contrary, located itself in the city and sees the city as the locus of its learnings. While greatly concerned with the growth of a "sense of community" within its membership, Parkway conceives of the central learnings of its community to be in, with, and through the larger community of Philadelphia. Thus a process takes place in which sense of community becomes interpreted as referring to a state of mind rather than to a fixed place. Such a utopia is more a "ship of state" than a "citadel."

This definition of the learning process provides the central task orientation of PP, which is presented as a boundary condition from which to work.

I believe that this definition of task is desirable from several standpoints. For one, it makes for a kind of reality testing: theory and practice, thinking and doing become related. Another, the ability to use the city as the locus of learning, makes for an inexhaustible resource. Freedom of choice is made operational, for students and faculty really do know firsthand what is available for their use. As well, it is difficult within such a program to replicate traditional classroom procedures; one doesn't have the live option of returning to his old classroom and the reassurances of the past as a way to deal with uncertainty.

At the opening ceremonies John Bremer stated that he was "pleased that you have chosen to be a part of this community." He continued, "It is our hope that in the course of our work, each of us will be able to find meaning, purpose, and joy. Together we shall explore the resources of this city and the wonders of the world."

This concludes our description of the first major complex of qualities by which Parkway is characterized. These qualities, I would argue, contribute to success in an educational innovation. I would like to continue by examining five other characteristics, which follow directly from the broader utopian-communitarian concepts and are, as has been suggested, important for the success of educational programs.

III

An important aspect of Parkway is that there is *no hierarchy of status*. Although there do exist different roles within the organization, they are not fixed ones. The emphasis is on helping people learn to play new and expanded roles and flexibly change roles as the work situation demands. The balance within the program is toward interdependence and cooperation among all. The assumption operating within PP is that people can be learners, students and teachers who can change and grow.

There are to be sure "faculty," "students," and a "director," whose central tasks do differ, but it is often not clear who is in the role of one or the other. It could be said, for example, that the main job of the faculty is developing and teaching the program. Yet the student role overlaps the faculty's, in that students present needs, go out and find resources to teach courses, actively evaluate the program, and serve on management groups. Similarly, it could be said that the director's central job includes establishing the boundary conditions as well as long-range planning, consultation, general administration, and presentation to the public. Yet both faculty and students must participate actively in reestablishing the boundaries and performing the other tasks (for example, through a public relations management group).

An observer of the program has noted that in a sense the decision-making roles reside nowhere and everywhere. Decision-making most properly resides in the work group doing a particular task, whether it be tutorial, town meeting, staff meeting, management group, and so on. Thus, on the one hand, for one person to "capture" the program would be to destroy it. On the other hand, leadership is properly shared and recognized as *emergent* within the above groups, or others of a more temporary nature.

I have noticed that Parkway discussions do not automatically change their quality when students enter a teacher group, or vice versa. There is a basic integrity to relationships within the program; unlike traditional situations, there is no need to develop sensitive antennas to allow time to change tone should a "superior" or "inferior" enter what was a conversation between "equals." Parkway is, I think, moving beyond the gamesmanship implicit in the "presentation of self in everyday life" view of the world.

In a typical classroom much energy is expended toward maintaining a fundamentally unequal social structure to the detriment of learning. Control increases the resistance of the young and destroys the possibilities for relationship, without which learning is difficult, if not impossible. At Parkway, on the other hand, all the energy is ideally focused on the work situation, so that learning can in fact be maximized.

The basic condition of equality is dramatized through the admissions lottery, where volunteer students are selected on the basis of geographic districts. Selection is not determined by past record or scores or ability to pay. Another indication of equality is the open faculty meeting, at which students can speak their minds as well as observe.

IV

The *structure* of PP can be thought of as a well-conceived matrix. Staff and students are provided diverse opportunities to "make the learning their own" and follow their interests with a maximum of support from the community. The structure is clear enough to make a statement, as it were, about the basic assumptions of Parkway and provide the necessary order for learning. At the same time it offers pluralistic avenues through which individual objectives may be met. Since Philadelphia is curriculum *and* campus, opportunities are innumerable to learn.

Let me enumerate the components of the PP structure:

A. *Faculty offerings and community offerings.* Every term each community (three self-contained units at present) distributes a catalog which it has compiled. Courses are listed, some of which are given by the full-time staff, including the secretarial staff, and others by members of the larger community. History of art might be presented by the art museum curator, probability by an actuary, gerontology by the director of the home for the elderly, and so on. Meeting times vary, from mornings to evenings, within varying blocks of time.

B. *Tutorials.* These meet three times a week, with fifteen students and two faculty, one of whom is a university intern and the other a certified teacher from the full-time staff of the unit. The groups are each selected by lot, thus including blacks, whites, rich, poor; traditionally A students, traditionally E students, and so on.

The tutorial "family group" is charged with the on-going evaluation of the entire program, mutual support and individual assistance, and the learning of basic skills in English and mathematics. Tutorials are basic to Parkway's success and are seen as the basic unit within each community. The emphasis at PP on responsibility and decentralization demands the utilization of tutorial groups to their fullest potential.

C. *Management groups.* These meet for a few hours each week and are composed of several students and a staff member. Together they fulfill necessary services to each community, whether these be for public relations, communications with parents, credit union, college information, trading post, part-time employment, or others.

D. *Town meetings.* Held weekly or biweekly, these provide the chance to meet and discuss matters of community-wide interest. Decisions can be consensual or consultative, the latter being the mode used when the decision appears to be primarily the province of one group or another within each unit. Town meetings can be frustrating, for many members become impressed with their oratorical abilities and prolong discussions beyond a useful point. Still, many important issues do get discussed, and reports suggest that as time goes on the efficacy of town meetings does increase.

Each student participates in town meeting, in tutorial, in a management group of his choice, and in faculty and institutional offerings. He chooses the faculty and institutional offerings on the basis of his interest, consistent with state laws and college requirements. Each faculty member participates in town meeting, in tutorial, in a management group of his choice, and in faculty offerings. His two or three faculty offerings are based on a combination of his interests, student interests, and state-mandated subjects (for example, trigonometry). The one faculty member per community who serves as administrator offers fewer faculty courses in order to allow some time for daily business matters, coordination, and other vital tasks.

E. *The size of each community.* Size is designed to permit a community to manage itself. Each tutorial and the faculty meeting numbers about eighteen, give or take two. This is a workable number in terms of group dynamics. Each community numbers about one hundred and forty, which is a number that allows the necessary face-to-face negotiation rather than reliance on faceless rules. With one hundred and forty as a basic self-governing module, Parkway could duplicate itself a hundred times or more throughout the city.

Each part of the structure reinforces the others. A web is spun with tremendous tensile strength. The result is a powerful force that is much different from forces present in most school situations. Throughout the program a pluralistic kind of commitment develops, one which encourages concern for the total PP community while at the same time helping the person meet his own goals.

V

Parkway has the strength of being *inextricably linked* with the larger community of Philadelphia.

The use of community as curriculum and campus is justifiable on "academic" grounds alone. After all, it would be hard to imagine anything worthy of study in the world of Philadelphia 1970 which doesn't include the community itself. As well, however, such involvement in community people and resources helps Parkway avoid the political and social dangers of past utopian communities.

Many utopian communities (and experimental schools) suffer and wither as a result of isolation from the greater society. They have to depend on a limited number of skills and resources available within their small community. Such a community often develops its own reality with little opportunity to learn survival within the reality beyond its sanctuary. Finally, such programs may be endangered by sectarianism, one-man rule, xenophobia, and political impotence.

Note that Parkway is a different type of utopian community. Its success *depends* on the outside community offering its support. The city is a source of students, staff, meeting places, and courses. A public relations and information function is intrinsic to the program, since all its members "meet the public" as a matter of course, not just on "school night" or "salute the police day."

In the planning of PP all relevant agencies were kept informed of progress, often on a personal basis. Through extensive use of media, Philadelphia was assured that Parkway was open, open to visitors anytime and open to all offers of help. As a result, volunteers daily came to offer their assistance and hundreds of visitors participated each month. I use the word *participation* with respect to visitors, because rather than being thought unpleasant interruptions, visitors were brought into the program, joined discussions, and at least temporarily joined the community.

Since Parkway offers a pluralistic approach, it can appeal to varying interests in the city. The conservative likes the low cost of the school, the businessman likes the idea of better-trained workers, the liberal wants integrated education, the black man wants quality education, the museum director appreciates crowded galleries, the journalist appreciates readily available human interest stories. The list seems infinite. Each person who participates in any facet joins the PP constituency, the growth of which is critical to Parkway's continued existence.

This pluralism helps avoid the pitfalls of an educational experiment such as the New College at Columbia University, the story of which has been described by Goodwin Watson. During the depression the New College ignored its environment until it was too late. Despite an exciting educational program, the New College folded.

As a matter of course Parkway has steadily enlarged its constituency, among movers and shakers (Chamber of Commerce, downtown commerce) and the community at large (middle and working class, black and white, city dweller and suburbanite, hippies, juvenile gang members). The part of Philadelphia that has remained most intractable includes the school district bureaucracy, some classroom teachers, and a few parents. As separate from the usual school constraints, Parkway remains a threat to those who see any deviation from standard operating procedure as a violation of trust.

Perhaps a few words should be said here on "resistance."

Donald Klein, in an essay on resistance against innovation, makes some significant points in terms of how one must respect antagonists, work through resistance, and so on. He also suggests that many people who are defenders against onrushing innovation have become isolated from the community: they have been passed by and actually "do not participate meaningfully in the changes going on around them." In fact, it may be that the values espoused by the defenders are those which are on decline in the culture, losing support as new values appear. The rest of the community, audience to the defender's activities, may be aware of this process of "departicipation" even if they do not become involved themselves except as spectators.

Now if there is anything clear about today's world, it is the rate of change, especially in relation to educational issues. Despite this tidal fact, school personnel often seem enmeshed today in issues more relevant to the forties or fifties. Without extensive preparation they may not be able to deal with change in a way which will foster the educational process. As the world is turning, they are not.

Some see administration playing a role akin to that of the foundations, serving as consultant to schools wishing help. However, it seems that many school personnel in central offices and elsewhere view themselves not as facilitating consultants but rather as prescriptive enforcers of one kind of educational system. To these people, Parkway crystallizes the failure of their educational views to be universally accepted. Programs like PP are out of control, doing things that shouldn't be done, according to their point of view. It seems irrelevant to them that Parkway sees itself as an alternative that should be available to any students who want to participate in it rather than as the compulsory answer to everyone's needs.

How can people be helped—rather than forced—to try alternative ways of doing things? On what basis is communication possible between people of different world views? How can different approaches to public education healthily co-exist? The present need is to seek resolution of these issues so that diversity responsive to today's demands may flourish.

It is noteworthy that Parkway had one major challenge to its existence during the first year. This involved protest over a nonlottery selection procedure for the elementary youths at Community Gamma. Parents of children not selected and certain school personnel in their geographic area colluded to destroy PP's credibility, and, ultimately, the program itself. A public board meeting to consider the case brought several hundred Parkway people—students, parents, staff—to protest the imminent decision to close the primary component. Pressure to maintain the unit continued through several channels for weeks thereafter.

Although the Gamma primary component was required to close, it was promised that the total program would increase in the coming year, including new primary units attached to each secondary unit, so that the future expansion of Parkway looks hopeful.

VI

The measure of health is flexibility, the freedom to learn through experience, the freedom to change with changing internal and external circumstances, to be influenced by reasonable argument, admonitions, exhortations, and the appeal to emotions; the freedom to respond appropriately to the stimulus of reward and punishment, and especially the freedom to cease when sated. The essence of normality is flexibility in all of these vital ways.

LAWRENCE KUBIE: Quoted in Warren Bennis, *Changing Organizations* (McGraw-Hill, 1966, p. 43)

Flexibility is basic to any program's success. When problems do arise, if their solution can become part of the educational process—which includes learning how to change—then the problem can be indeed open to solution.

PP is self-renewing; planning is everyone's job. Each term requires the development of a new catalog, which represents the educational program. Town meetings, management groups, and tutorials especially are charged with integration of the individual and the group and with evaluation of the program. Fast feedback is thus built into the PP's structure. Decentralization, which puts a premium on small groups of task-oriented participants, encourages maximum individualization of learning.

In a world of constant change educators must tread a tightrope between permanent and temporary structures. Some experts consider the relation of one to the other a crucial organizational problem of the time.

I think that PP is informed by a dialectic between the two modes. It provides relatively permanent boundary conditions within which diverse activities can take place. Such activities often do take the form of temporary structures. Courses themselves are temporary, as Miles points out, and PP operates on a four-quarter system to allow maximum flexibility. Many courses include a diversity of one-time activities which take place throughout the city with guest staff members. The city as curriculum and campus provides an interactive, responsive environment open to diversity in a way which is difficult for the single-building high school to achieve.

As a process-oriented, city-oriented community of learners, Parkway qualifies as one of H. G. Wells' "ships of state" rather than as a "citadel."

VII

Parkway is *supportive*. If one can imagine a warm and friendly educational enterprise, Parkway fits the description. A suffocating warmth would not be desirable, but the notion of city as curriculum and campus militates against that occurring.

As has been indicated, many citizens are supportive of PP and they often volunteer to teach, do office work, speak out about the concept to others, and so on. The constant flow of visitors, which sometimes reaches more than one hundred a week, serves as an assurance of support.

That Parkway does receive a considerable amount of support is indisputable. However, this does not mean that much of the world the staff and students encounter is not cold and alienating. It is. But since Parkway's curriculum includes learning to deal with reality of whatever kind, Parkway people learn better than many how to go about relating to different worlds. Like all people who are learners, they make a selection of the world and try to use whatever resources exist as part of a learning situation.

The internal socialization process, which begins with an extensive orientation program carried out through tutorials, helps students and staff feel at home and learn to get around in the city. It is amazing to learn how few people have a realistic idea of downtown geography or transportation.

From the first day a view is fostered, which does have grounds in reality, that Parkway is not just another school but is, in fact, something of a different order of comparison. Students become aware that they have a good thing going; frequently they are more conservative than the staff in what they call taking chances with public support.

Staff meetings are frequent and intense. They meet a real need for communication, since the program is so decentralized. Faculty ask, "How are you using tutorials?" or, "Are we allowing enough time for management groups?" or, "What kind of evaluation form should we use?" As one might imagine, comradeship becomes a palpable need in a demanding situation such as PP.

Students have a large number of advisers, official and unofficial. Much time is allocated for informal and formal consultation.

Parents are involved, too. In a real way, their involvement—from office work to evaluation of prospective faculty—decreases the oft-discussed gap between school and home. Many parents who previously couldn't communicate with their alienated children have reported that after joining Parkway their youngsters began engaging in genuine communication with them, sometimes talking for hours about their experiences and what they signify. In this way parents and students become mutually supportive with respect to their own relationship and their involvement with Parkway.

We have examined some of the important characteristics of Parkway as an example of a utopian-communitarian educational program. I would now like to spend some time suggesting how the Parkway philosophy can be implemented on a much wider scale, to permit participation for all those who wish to join such a program.

VIII

The consideration of how Parkway can be expanded is an important one. Many people have praised Parkway but then claimed that its replicability is limited due to the small number of students who can be accommodated within the downtown Philadelphia area.

With respect to the downtown area of Philadelphia—or any city—it is clear to me that several thousand students can easily be involved. Each of the existing three communities has concentrated on a particular part of center city, and as each has come into operation it has elicited new support. Without a doubt, ten or more additional communities could easily find sufficient resources for their curricula. Since few institutions contribute courses for more than ten students, the number of institutions that can offer assistance on such a small scale is quite high. As well as faculty offerings, university interns, regular teachers, and administrative staff can provide a core of offerings which make use of the city's resources without requiring as large a commitment from the various institutions. (These courses ask for rooms or guest lectures rather than materials or full-time teachers.)

Going beyond the downtown area, I see the possibility of establishing a Parkway volunteer district, which would operate throughout the city on an open-enrollment policy. John Bremer has actively sought approval for this possibility.

Through this plan there would be a great expansion of possible resources from which to draw. These resources could represent the particular strengths of the various Philadelphia neighborhoods through use of industry, retail stores, university facilities, churches, community welfare services, doctors and lawyers, university students, housewives, and so on.

A variant of this possibility would be to create communities based on particular areas of interest, such as the specialized high schools in New York City. These could offer activities appealing to heterogenous groups of students: music, electronics, health services, internal affairs, urban studies, film, and so on. The concentration would be presented as a way of entering the learning process rather than as a way of learning a trade. Music, for example, could be used as a metaphor for science, mathematics, human relationships, history, creative problem-solving, and the like, rather than only in terms of obtaining a better job.

Another means of expansion is the creation of a dual (or more) system within existing district high schools, so that students and faculty who wished to participate in a program such as Parkway could do so within existing schools. This could offer a real choice to all participants, who could include students and faculty from middle schools, local colleges, and adult education programs as well as from the district high school itself.

It is also possible to combine a Parkway program with model-city or new-town projects. Through such a combination we could work toward true community schools, or school communities. In this approach the various programs and facilities — gymnasiums, libraries, medical services, retail stores, course offerings open to all — would be scattered throughout an entire community for use by everyone. The result would be an integration of school and community in the deepest sense.

Teacher-training programs can well be brought into Parkway programs. These could involve students both from present schools of education and from the so-called paraprofessional training programs. At present university interns receive valued experience in teaching and learning, as well as serving as vital members of the faculty. An expansion of the present intern program could be developed to include seminars, films, visits, guest lectures, and the like. These activities would be made available to other staff and students in addition to the interns.

In conclusion, I have noted that today many people believe education to be the vital institution for creating a more worthwhile world. Many see education, broadly based, as the lever which the modern-day Archimedes can use to move the world.

This conception of educational force means that the challenge to the educator is overwhelming, for his work is not peripheral to the mainstream. Rather, it is seen as central to the future direction of society. Can the educator meet the tremendous demands upon his vision and creativity? How can he best develop honorable educational alternatives to meet the challenge? Finally, how can he open educational decision-making to all who would further a learning process?

As I have indicated, I believe that in order to meet the challenge, educators need to see education as meeting the whole range of human needs rather than abstracting out a few measurable or marketable tasks. I have stated my firm belief in the efficacy of thinking about education in terms both utopian and communitarian, with the qualities that follow such a conception.

We need to redefine our vocabularies as educators. We must think in terms of the "healthy," the "self-actualizing," and "eupsychian" educational enterprise. In point of fact, when we talk about the ideal self-actualizer, eupsychian or healthy one, are we not actually describing a *learner?* Is not the root task of the educator to develop ways of building educational programs which can be described as *learners?*

I have attempted in this essay to describe the Parkway Program as an example of the utopian and communitarian *learning* enterprise. My guiding hypothesis has been that it is through the development of such utopian communities of learning that our future educational enterprises will most likely succeed.

Clearly we need to know more about the whole range of educational possibilities. It is necessary for us to consider the alternatives and then test them out through the establishment of educational programs, such as Parkway, which will offer us a more worthwhile future.

14

From an Intern–Wendy Carlton

Interns have very little status around Parkway unless somebody wants them to perform a task which no one else wants to do; then, by all estimations, they are the equals of the full-time staff. Of course, neither the staff nor the interns rank as high as students in the organizational hierarchy, but it is time that students acquired a voice in their education. Sometimes, I feel, we give students more freedom and responsibility than they can handle at the time, but as a teacher, I feel a strong obligation to help them overcome this difficulty. Interns, to the horror of some and the pride of others, are not fully certified teachers. They come from several colleges and universities and remain for three to six months. I have come from Oberlin College. Interns assume sole teaching responsibility for the majority of basic skills workshops as well as a variety of classroom subjects. Frequently they are used to bolster the faculty offerings in fields where a particular unit's offerings are weak or nonexistent. When I came to PP in January, for example, I found Alpha needed a home economics teacher. So I taught gaggles of girls how to knit and knot (macrame) and stitch (yarn embroidery). But sometimes interns are not able to play all-purpose teacher and find themselves equipped with majors that don't easily lend themselves to a high school curriculum. That is not to say that there are no unusual course offerings at PP, but even the kids realize that certain state requirements must be met. And, too, the more removed a course gets from fundamentals, the greater the problem of prerequisite skills—including minimal reading and writing abilities.

The workshops I've mentioned are primarily remedial in nature and pose a tremendous problem from two viewpoints. On the one hand, they require the ability to cope with the problem of severely below-level performance, which requires diagnostic skills. In many cases these skills are acquired only after long exposure to these kinds of deficiencies. And the range of abilities in a particular class can be dramatic. It is expecting a lot of an intern to require him to analyze the reasons for a student's inability to read at high school level and then to come up with a plan for remedying the condition. When you've been spending hours in the college classroom reading Nietzche, it's hard to comprehend what it must be like to be reading at fifth-grade level. On the other hand, the intern must face the problem of motivation. If after nine years of schooling a kid still can't give the answer to 4 times 7, what makes you think that he even wants to learn? It is possible that he no longer believes he is capable of learning mathematics. For weeks I was baffled about how to get the kids to come to history class. I finally hit upon the idea of concocting educational games. One time, for example, we played "To Tell the Truth" in order to study various myths about Lincoln. It is a working premise at PP that kids are free to select their courses and then elect whether or not to attend. Mandatory attendance is a myth the faculty likes to believe in; but in reality, not all teachers demand regular attendance and participation. A very few staff people can hardly bother to get to their own classes and meetings on time. As a result, anyone who expects punctuality and attendance must work to establish these guidelines. It has been my experience that students expect you, as a teacher, to set down a working agreement for their responsibilities in the course; we fail them if we are negligent in doing so.

Therefore, I conclude, PP places interns in positions of the greatest teaching difficulty because someone once proposed that workshops require the least specific skills and experiences. I find such an argument very weak. Closer examination would reveal that workshops present acute problems to the inexperienced intern.

Throughout my experiences at PP I've noticed that there are certain faculty members who have given up on many of the same kinds of problems that are delegated to the interns. There are numerous mechanisms for "copping out." First, you can offer advanced or erudite courses which frequently can be elected only by smart, white, suburban kids. Certainly their needs should be taken into consideration, but I would ask if we are expecting much less of them than their previous high schools. PP should offer them the kind of stimulation and self-responsibility which suburbia cannot. It should give students the opportunity to discover themselves in respect to their abilities and weaknesses. Unfortunately, many of us come to realize that the brighter students learn the material almost wholly on their own or with nominal effort and direction from us. Rather than redirecting our energies which are not dissipated by the drill and repetition of less academically able classes, some people choose to coast—and let their students coast with them. Second, you can elect to occupy your time with a greater than normal share of nonteaching duties. You can play at administrative detail, community organizing, building maintenance, and telephone answering. And third, you can take the approach of fulfilling the letter and not the spirit of your teaching responsibilities. It is relatively easy to do the minimum amount of teaching around here. We are treated as mature and capable adults. We have no department chairmen or principal to answer to. But it is not only the young who misuse freedom.

If an intern can overcome his initial dismay and disillusionment with the apparent chaos, or lack of structure, at PP, he can then accommodate himself to the situation and discover some way to establish equilibrium and order for himself. It took me almost a full quarter to make this discovery.* As I found myself asking for more and more responsibilities, I acquired a variety of teaching tasks. As I've said before, I taught home economics. And since I could do a better job teaching typing than answering the myriads of phone calls, I took on Tami's typing class—in a rather unofficial exchange of duties. I taught history with a staff member because the class was much too large for one person. In tutorial, I served as reading teacher and art teacher as well as general counselor. I felt like a combination, all-purpose substitute. I never came to feel that any particular class was truly mine. It was only late in the quarter when I started to help Mannix (see Chapter 11) with reading that my days with PP seemed to have significance.

There are some classroom occurrences at PP that could take place anywhere in the city. That is, as long as the person felt strongly about the irregular but successful techniques he had developed, he could put them to use in the more conventional classroom. But the size of the typical high school class imposes certain restrictions on time, materials, and the personal dimension of a teacher-student relationship. And without PP, I never would have gained the variety of ex-

---

* If I had left PP after the usual one-quarter stay, I would have departed quite disillusioned with innovative education and somewhat bitter. I really question the fairness to the kids of subjecting them to the "changing of the guard" every three months. As an intern, you spend the first four weeks getting acclimated to PP and the last six realizing that you've hardly accomplished all you should. Furthermore, you get to feel almost powerless when you consider that in a short time you'll be leaving and the period of adjustment will begin again. You have so little time to make an impact.

periences. I find that I truly enjoy the teaching process, and the subject matter is of secondary importance. There is satisfaction in explaining a math problem when you yourself have had trouble with the subject. When a student tells you he has enjoyed your history class, there is a different kind of gratification. When a girl says you have given her much-needed confidence and encouragement as well as new skills, there is another.

PP frees you to teach. I require discipline of my students, but I am not a policeman. I demand work from them, but I do not hear them pounding at the prison bars. I gain their friendship, but I am not their pal.

Unit Alpha has had a problem with card playing and gambling. It is very sad, but many of our gamblers cannot add their cards correctly. The kids hang around Alpha between classes, and some even cut their classes. The staff's efforts to end this unhealthy situation have not been overwhelmingly successful, and the problem remains with us. It can only mean that we are not yet giving the kids enough which interests them, enough which involves them in their education.

One day I walked over to the card game and asked the fellows what else they could be doing. Their ringleader said they had some records they'd like to play, but they didn't have access to the record player. I agreed to get the record player if they would end the card playing. That same afternoon a sign appeared: "We've made a deal. No card playing for the use of the record player." The sign was complete with the emblem of the dominant social club. The kids don't always hold true to that promise, but there is a certain core of them who persistently seek me out to get the record player for them. In fact, I've brought in an old record player of mine and one of the kids has repaired it and cleaned it up for me. They'll have the use of the second record player until I leave in June.

I don't believe I am exemplifying Gestapo tactics when I break up card games; nor do I think the kids resent my doing so. At times, I think they are testing us to see if we really care enough about them to make them stop. Teaching is not just an assignment to be fulfilled within four walls, or as in the case of PP, in a school without walls.

There is another essay in this book which was dictated to me by one of my students. His story is in part mine and mine his. I first discovered that Mannix couldn't read or write when he handed me a slip of paper in tutorial. It was supposed to express three vocational choices; there were nonsense scrawls mixed with an occasional word. I was shocked—even horrified. But we got to talking, and he said he'd like some help. And so the very next day we began to work on some very easy sentences.

I cannot imagine being without the intellectual faculty to read. I am an avid reader. And here I was trying to figure out how a 17–18-year-old might learn to read. Whatever I did, I didn't want to be condescending. And where, I wanted to know, would I get the patience, for certainly it would be a slow process. Furthermore, what did I know about teaching reading? All I could remember were horrible SRA kits in seventh grade.

As Mannix has written, my doubts and questions were unfounded. His dramatic progress keeps us both enthusiastic and devoted to learning to read. I gladly spend many hours writing stories, Xeroxing song lyrics and advertisements, and pasting cards for him and another student who can barely read. This brings me to another situation which is part of the original PP design.

I was told that Mike couldn't read, or perhaps I misunderstood the speaker, and he was trying to say that Mike has difficulty reading. I gave Mike some of my pages to read and he read them with great ease. I gave him something harder and still there was no problem. So I handed him one of my favorite Bierce stories and he started to consume it. Now the vocabulary is quite hard in that piece, so we'd work on the most important words. Mike has difficulty pronouncing words, which may have led to the popular belief that he could not read; for maybe, rather than suffer embarrassment, he chose not to read. Whatever the reason, Mike is currently enjoying the horror of Edgar Allan Poe, and he's adding some words to his vocabulary.

But before Mike gets to work on his reading, he helps teach Claude, who must be reading at about a third-grade level. The two fellows sit there, Claude with his floppy cap and Mike with his black hat pulled down to eyebrow level, and they work away. If Claude has difficulty with a word, Mike will help him sound it out or make up a list of rhyming words. The first week I suggested that Mike might want to sit in while I worked with Claude so that he could see the kinds of help he could give. In a very short while, Mike was pitching in and encouraging Claude. Claude's reading is improving and so is Mike's spelling. And both guys are gaining much-needed self-confidence.

In these specific cases, the problem of motivation is nonexistent, at least in respect to my relations with these fellows. They work hard. Really, few adults would work with such concentration as they demonstrate. I use up fantastic amounts of material each week. I cannot imagine a more gratifying experience than the day Mannix brought in a book to read to me. He needs lots of help, but for the first time in his life he is not pretending to read. And Claude is a perfect example of the quiet little boy who falls asleep in others' classes but who could never get himself in enough trouble to bring his problems to someone's attention. There are so many of these kids who escape our notice. I keep wondering how they will manage in a world where substandard reading ability will condemn them to take the most menial jobs, if only they can read enough to fill out the job application. I've come to believe it is a mistake to think these kids can't read because they are dumb. In order to function for 16, 17, or 18 years without being able to read is an amazing fact. It means you live by shrewdness and your wits in order to compensate for your deficiencies. Some of the coping mechanisms which these fellows employ make the average literate person look stupid.

For example, Mannix has told me how he scrutinizes any job application for the words *Philadelphia, Pennsylvania* because until recently he could not spell even the abbreviations for himself. And usually, he could find this information on the letterhead. Wherever the application called for the date, he'd put "month/19/70." As so frequently happens, he had made an observation but had failed to learn the basis for the practice; he would simply write the year with a slash down its middle. Now who would detect that dates are still a mystery to him? And since he can't read more than a few street signs, he gets around the city by landmarks and telephone calls to his sister, who tells him how many blocks in each direction. When I asked him how he knows what is playing at the movies, he says he goes by ads, commercials, and word of mouth.

Let me speak briefly of the problem of finding materials for the illiterate adolescent. You cannot teach him as you would a young child. He would be insulted by "See Jane run," and even the most hip, linguistic-based readers are full of inane sentences. In addition to the problem of interest, there is an interesting psychological phenomenon. It is far easier to teach the word *hamburger* than the word *was*, the word *fight* than the word *with*. The pallid vocabulary of the traditional primer, with its lockstep progression, is not appropriate to these fellows' needs. Most of the materials on the market are for nonreaders as opposed to functional illiterates. Books for illiterate adults are few and relatively useless. While both the adult and the adolescent want to learn to read after many years of frustrating attempts, each brings to the problem different degrees of maturity and experience. So I took to writing my own pages; someday, hopefully, they will form a publishable primer for adolescents. The following page is quite typical of the early stories, which were broken down into several related parts.

> On Saturday we are going to the *movies*. "Where should we go?" I asked my friend. We are going to see "IF. . . ." It was

his idea. I said, *"Right-on, brother. That is a good idea."* We are taking our girl friends with us on Saturday night. I hope they are ready *on time.**

I have written stories about going to the movies, going out with your girl, getting something to eat, receiving letters, filling out job applications, and relating day-to-day happenings at Parkway. The format may be prose, dialogue, or even poetry. There may be pages with pictures and words to be matched. We also spend some time drilling on initial sounds and word families. All in all, there is an attempt to teach recognition vocabulary, pictorial-applied vocabulary, and phonetically derived words.

When I came to PP in January, I thought I had brought with me adequate credentials. I had a history major and sound academic preparation in other fields. I had spent many hours tutoring history and French at Oberlin Senior High. And my major preoccupation with educational policy at Oberlin had made me aware of the many facets of the educational process. From the richness of my personal experiences, I had a sense of security and well-being. Here, I thought, was the perfect opportunity to make my educational ideals merge with empirical reality. When it came time to test these ideals and ideas, the experience was bruising, to say the least.

But as these pages explain, I have come to find much satisfaction with PP. Throughout the worst of times, I have kept faith with the students, because I admire their determination to fight the system, which threatens to entrap them. Label the system the city or middle class suburbia or the Department of Public Instruction. The students have a kind of openness and freshness about them which should be allowed to thrive rather than be driven out. You can never be absolutely certain how a class will go, how a day will turn out; and thus, there is always an edge of anticipation and surprise.

I was back to my own high school, first quarter, to visit a favorite teacher of mine. I had the misfortune of running into my former guidance counselor. I got to talking with her, and I remarked that I was teaching home economics. "How can you do that?" she wanted to know; "You're not certified." If PP operated under similar assumptions, I would never have taught anything, let alone the variety of topics I have tackled. It would mean that I would have continued to think that the most satisfaction comes from teaching the brightest

* The italicized words were words Mannix wanted included in the story. Upon his initial reading, he had trouble or could not read *Saturday, movies, should, asked, his, idea, night, hope, they, reading,* and *on time.* The next day he had trouble with *idea, hope,* and *ready.*

kids. It means I would have maintained my scorn of vocational teachers; after all, business education doesn't usually attract the smartest students. But I had neglected to take the time to consider that good business skills, as taught through the schools, may give some students their only means to a legitimate livelihood. Of all the subjects I have taught, reading has given me the greatest gratification. When I was teaching home economics I could never quite understand the girls' excitement in mastering the demands of the stockinette stitch. While I love the electric atmosphere of questions and discussions in a good history class, I do not think my students would suffer greatly if they remained ignorant of the bonus marchers. I have always enjoyed the study of history and find a knowledge of the past helpful in understanding the effects of today on tomorrow. But if it is to come down to the question of relative importance, then reading is of far greater significance.

It has been my PP experiences, however, which have enabled me to make these discoveries. Early in my exposure to PP, one of the units put out a newspaper which contained the adage, "Teachers are students with pay." While I enjoyed this witty aphorism, I did not really identify myself as a teacher. The fact that I wasn't being paid added to my inability to identify with the statement. Now I understand the wisdom of that pen. Unless there's learning on the part of both teacher and students, there is no real learning going on. And second, I would be foolish to say that I get no pay; it's just not the financial kind.

15

From a Faculty Member–Dorice J. Wright

MY PARKWAY THING

Parkway is an experience of growing, caring, frustration, sadness, and joy. It is these very things because we are in the world of reality where learning has no special geographic setting or time. Think with me for a moment. Isn't it preposterous that we adults (I mean parents, educators, government) tell young people that they must go to a certain building (usually an ugly one) five days a week for 180 days from nine to three to learn seven or more unrelated subjects in forty-minute time slots? Is this not an assembly line, the student and teacher being the products? I am at Parkway because I did not enjoy being one of those products. This is my opportunity to learn as well as teach. Strange that I feel more and more like a learner and less like a teacher.

Every sensitive teacher is aware of the many moments that he doesn't reach a student or when he has hurt or disappointed a student, perhaps simply because he was not a good listener. Whatever the situation, it is really no different from any other human relationship — we either attempt to understand our fellow being or we don't. However, there is one frightening possibility in regard to the teacher — he is forced to play God. Actually, I have always shuddered at being placed in that role. We are all forced to be human in a community whose members are groping to understand. We are learning to be honest with ourselves as well as with the rest of the community, for if we are not, then we are held accountable for our actions. Indeed, it is difficult to lie because people are not afraid to bring you to task for an action or a statement. During my teaching experience in a traditional school

I found this to be absolutely against the norm, for there dishonesty is propagated. I wish to share with you a composition written by Toni, a student who felt that I had overstepped my boundary or pushed her a little too far during a tutorial session. This is what happened:

The day before, our tutorial visited one of Ghana's Black Star Liners in the Philadelphia Port. At our next tutorial session I asked the students to write about the ship tour or to write a short story based on being a stowaway on a liner. Toni arrived late for tutorial. Although she looked troubled, I was angry that she was so tardy and I felt a need to let her know. Having noticed that she had not begun to write, I asked, "Toni, anything wrong? Why don't you get started?" When she dislikes something her facial muscles tighten on her otherwise gentle face. She said, "I don't want to write about *some* ship. I'm going to write about a person, *you*, in fact, because you are bothering me." I was game and this is what she wrote.

MY TEACHER

My teacher Dorice is a pest because she is very persistent, very forward, and also bold. Dorice is the type of person who you think would be a guard. She guards over you, she pesters you, she pushes you. She's also a very cool person. She never gets excited. She dresses nice. She's cool because she's the type of beautiful black person who always helps her people. She may be a pest, she may be a persistent person, she may be a forward person, she may be bold, but she's the coolest person I have ever seen. She's a beautiful black person.

With a smile she handed in her paper and walked out. I was curious to read it and my reaction was quite mixed. I was happy that though it was drudgery for her to write, she did write, but the content, though written in a time of anger, honestly described me as I was to her that day—a pest.

Toni and I had reached a different level of understanding. It was real.

She taught me a very important lesson, which is that a teacher should not and cannot control what a student learns. Oftentimes, educators are so busy brainwashing young people that they deny to the students the right to be individuals, a precious democratic principle, so I was taught in school. Why should I have said to Toni, "No, you can't write about a person. You must write about the ship just as the other students." It is not the ship that matters, but the skills that are needed to describe that ship.

For too long schools have dictated, through subtle and not so subtle ways, what teachers teach and what students learn. What purpose does the curriculum guide have other than to serve as a formula for what to teach? Who selects which history book is to be used and by what class? Certainly not the teacher. My point is that we at Parkway are working toward overcoming such trivialities so that we *can* help students learn. The challenge is great, our progress slow; often we take a step back before one forward.

It is easy to become so involved in day-to-day tasks that we lose sight of the difficulty of our over-all task. Both students and faculty were part of a traditional system which placed them on different steps of the educational ladder, one at the very bottom—the learner—the other merely one step above—the teacher. Both have been told to "remember their places." From the top of the ladder information to be taught is distributed to the teacher, who then passes it on to the student, the important one who just happens to be at the bottom of the ladder. Neither has really experienced freedom and responsibility. On the one hand, the teacher receives instructions on what to teach from "higher-ups," and on the other hand, the student is told what he should learn. Strange that in such a system the principles of democracy and individualism are preached while peoples' creativity and very humanity are being stifled. If this is an accurate description of what it is in the traditional system, then our learning task at Parkway is considerable.

All of us came to Parkway with many "hang-ups" that get in the way of learning not only the academics but learning to get along with one another or learning to move about the city of Philadelphia. Let us remember that we all have brought to the program safe old ways of dealing with these problems. It is important for us to remember that we are undoing habits accumulated over many years. They will not be undone overnight. By the same token, I am not suggesting that we can sit back on our laurels and say, "Aren't we great?" Our concerns are too important for that kind of attitude.

The concerns are both great and painful. It is interesting that we in the program are its most avid critics. For example, sometimes it seems impossible for the faculty to make a decision and carry it out. Each of us came to the program with a certain style and philosophy that should be communicated to the rest of the faculty. Certainly the faculty members are not carbon copies of each other, nor should they be, but they do have to communicate and understand one another. The process is painfully slow due to our fears of really being understood, of letting our co-workers know us; after all, wasn't it a cardinal rule in the traditional setting that "we mind our own business"? Surely, in some matters there should be unity of action. Students have repeatedly told us in words and deeds to get together, but fear of trusting one another holds us back. Some of my colleagues would disagree with this prognosis, and if we were not dealing with the lives of young people I would not worry about their disagreements. But I am concerned when I observe that we are searching for escape hatches in devising administrative means for problem-solving. The nuts and bolts matters of finding out which courses are going to be offered and finding classroom space are important to the survival of the program; but what is needed most of all is a desire and willingness by us the faculty to begin listening and talking with ourselves and with students. The lesson is clearly before us and we are not heeding it. Have not school systems devised administrative channels for dealing "effectively" with their problems? We have only to look at the state of education in America and the alienation of our youth to realize that something is wrong. That lesson is merely learning to communicate with one another about the real issues, not some vague cosmic nonsense. Of course, effective communication will also result in effective action. Communication for the sake of communication is meaningless unless something comes of it.

What is it that prevents a united effort? Is it inherent in the structure, is it us, or is it a little of both? We all are here because we wish to experience a certain amount of freedom that was not possible in our former teaching situations. Our philosophies about the role of a teacher range from noninvolvement—where a teacher becomes involved only when the student asks for help—to overinvolvement— where little growth by the student is possible. Somewhere in the middle are the teachers who manage not to take the initiative from the student but merely to guide him.

Though it is said by some that these diversities in philosophies should be advantageous, still we have not come to grips with crucial issues that evolve around providing the best possible learning environment for all Parkway students. The faculty does not possess a license to do as it pleases, neither as individuals nor as a group; yet we act as if we do possess such a license. In concrete terms, our inability to make decisions and stick to them, our differing expectations in terms of work and behavior, serve to confuse students. For example, there is a group of students who take delight in gambling at 1801. The community, that is, both faculty and students, discussed the problem and decided that there is to be no gambling; however, it continued with only a small number of faculty members making any attempt to stop the gambling. The situation was discussed at length during several faculty meetings. What was derived from these discussions is debatable: that gambling was symptomatic of a lack of "things to do";

that faculty members must spend more time communicating with students at 1801; that we ask the students to offer suggestions of what they would like to do at 1801; and that we offer alternatives to students. Now, rather than play "Black Jack," some of the gamblers have turned to playing "Scrabble," "Perquackey," and chess, but this is not a complete cure.

There remain the faculty members who either do not care to or are not able to communicate with students outside of the classroom situation. All of us must recognize that our concern for a student goes beyond his learning a specific subject matter, that it's the whole person whom we should be concerned about. That a student in my history class is devoting his energies to playing "Black Jack" is my concern. Why are his energies so directed? What have I not done or what can I do to make his Parkway experience more meaningful than a deck of cards? It is to these crucial day-to-day problems of helping the students who are misdirecting their energies that we must address ourselves.

And yet, gambling is only symptomatic of an even greater problem facing the Parkway community. I speak of racism.

Although racism may not always appear obvious, it is present in many forms. Generally, the gamblers are black students. It is also true that these are the students from the inner-city schools whose basic language and math skills have been neglected. Sometimes I am not sure that my white colleagues are not practicing "benign neglect." *Why do* teachers walk past a group of students who are breaking the no-gambling rule and say nothing for fear of being called "honky"? If a student is cutting class, talk to him, talk to his parents. Show concern and *be* concerned! To say that a student will learn only when he is ready and to do nothing to help him reach that point *is* "benign neglect." To be tutoring a black student and say that you never thought that you could teach someone of below-average I.Q. smacks of racism; to say that you gave credit to a student because she worked within her capability, which *you* say is limited, also smacks of racism. Black people at Parkway do not have time for the fun and games that whites can afford the luxury of indulging in. Black youth to survive must learn how to manipulate the English language as well as the city of Philadelphia. In fact, the two should be inseparable.

Admittedly, these students and many whites came to Parkway with handicaps in the basic skills; but we cannot allow them to leave as they came. We need a concentrated basic skill-building program based on an individual or one-to-one student-teacher ratio. This approach has proved successful in situations this year. It can be expanded to include other students who have serious deficiencies. The only drawback is the faculty member who recognizes the need to build language skill but who is wary of tutoring a student in reading because reading is not his area of specialization. It is habit or fear of doing something new that holds us back from teaching and learning.

For some, Parkway provides an opportunity to understand oneself and to learn. For others, it is not that clear, but for all, it brings some learning, sometimes painful, other times gentle. It is not a panacea for American education, merely one of the alternatives that should be offered to students and teachers. What have we learned since our beginning in 1969? Like other educational programs, the amount of learning here cannot be placed on a measuring rod, yet there are many lessons to learn. Basic to all is that we must begin to look more closely at what we are doing; establish goals; and hold ourselves accountable for carrying them out. Achieving a sense of unity among faculty is indeed important to the success of the program. This in itself hits at the crux of a vital learning concept of the program for both faculty and student: How do we make choices and what choices do we make? For the teacher, it may be choosing to tutor over participating in a faculty meeting. Which is more important? Is there not value in both? The decision is tough to make, but the choice is his. It is this individualism and responsibility to the community or to that which is larger than ourselves with which we must constantly grope. The choices are often difficult to make, but they are true to life, not artificially created, and because they are real, Parkway people have to learn to deal with them.

Second to nothing is understanding and meeting the needs of Parkway students. Our students coming from highly structured traditional systems find themselves in a new situation which they have difficulty adjusting to. This has been their experience. Let us recognize this reality and act accordingly, for to do otherwise is criminal. We must cease to ask students to do what we are not willing or able to do at this point of development. At this stage of development, it is the self-directed, highly responsible student who is getting the most out of Parkway. This student is generally white middle class. Surely, part of our responsibility is to offer the necessary support to those students who have not had the experience of responsibility. I speak of the black and other inner-city students whose experiences have been consistent denial that they are even human beings, much less capable of learning. Parkway and other educational alternatives will not meet the needs of blacks and other minorities unless they take into account the experiences of these peoples. Only when people let go of their fears of being honest and trusting one another can a change come to the American educational system and to the nation itself.

What impact the Parkway Program will have on American education remains to be seen. To those of us who wish to grow, it offers the possibility for growth in a different way, and that in itself is creditable. But its success depends on the willingness of its members to recognize what it is that they desire and to work toward that end. Its success, then, will depend on our ability to support one another, to share the tangible as well as the intangible and to work at turning fear of learning into learning and distrust of one another into love and respect.

16

From a Faculty Member–D. David Evyns

It has been my experience that a "teacher" has been assumed to be one who fulfills the roles of surrogate parent, authority figure (representing state, church, and government), disciplinarian, psychologist, conditioner, stimulus, and all-around dispenser of all that there is to be dispensed. This assumption, of course, has never been verbalized or in any other way formally dictated. More insidiously, it has been dictated behaviorally; and since actions do speak louder than words, the lesson has been learned all too well. Of course, this is what hypocrisy is all about. Often one hears a person being berated because his behavior does not coincide with his words. I would suggest that this is no accident. For some strange reason, we assume the words, abstract and metaphysical though they may be, and do not give greater credence to the behavior, concrete though it may be. Really, because of their concreteness, that is, their being susceptible to the senses, I would suggest that behavior is all that we really have that is of substance. In terms of my expectancy set, I was first drawn to the Parkway Program because I felt that it was attempting to deal with the aforementioned roles in a relatively functional manner.

Enough has been written about the Parkway Program, generally. For those who wish more in that vein, I suggest they forgo reading this monograph. This paper does not intend to discuss any distinction between the abstract and the concrete, the ideal and the real, and so on. Rather, it is merely an attempt to make evident to the reader what I have inferred from the experience of the Parkway Program. I do not suggest that these comments refer to Parkway and the Parkway experience in general. More properly, I merely intend to comment upon the various modalities of these experiences: the modalities *of* (as opposed to *at*) Parkway.

My perceptions of the program are determined by my tenure at a specific community, Community Beta. Consequently, all references to the program are specifically in relation to the Beta environment, though certain aspects of that environment might assuredly apply to the communities of Alpha and Gamma.

There are many different ways to view one and the same phenomenon. The determinants of one's perceptions are legion, and a perspective that is congenial to one person may be repugnant to another. Although it might be feasible to state why I perceive what I perceive, I will not undertake this task here. I would merely like to state a few of my perceptual determinants: namely, reality is as one perceives it. Further, one behaves in terms of one's perceptions; that is, I consider one's behavior to be a function of one's perceptions. Further, one's behavior is the *sine qua non* of a learning environment.

The above should suffice as a structure for the remarks which are to follow. This paper will have been functional if I can congruently relate my perception of the phantasm called Parkway Program.

Essentially, I consider Beta to be an environment wherein the concepts of such men as Maslow, Perls, Dewey, Dennison, Watts, Kohl, Holt, Kozol, Goodman, Postman, and Weingartner can be attempted. It is definitely an environment wherein a student can perceive of himself, as Carl Rogers might express it, as faced by a series of serious and meaningful problems. One wherein a "teacher" might attempt to be congruent, might feel an unconditional positive regard for the students and accept them, and might communicate an empathetic understanding of the students' world.

Parkway in general, and Beta in particular, is potentially a context for revolutionary educational programs and projects. Given that motivation is internal and that coercion and other rigid formats tend to stifle rather than to liberate the mind, Beta is making an extremely essential contribution to education. Beta is rampant for truly innovative curriculum projects and courses. Students are allowed to learn what they like and, to a relative degree, as they like. But the most salient and essential feature of Beta's structure, which is often not seen, is that the student is called upon to learn. For those who seek structure at the program, look no further. The structure is learning!

Beta is an alternative to the traditional high school and is primarily for those who find themselves unable to function in the traditional system. Beta can be a way and means of instilling a sense of confidence and awareness of oneself. The system of failure which had formerly been established is presently being successfully undermined and, in the majority of cases, annihilated. Thus, the strongest foundation for learning that one can build is being built at Beta. The program might seem to be, at first glance, an incoherent, nebulous blob. Though the genesis of Parkway might have been a reaction, one suggests that Parkway has, from its inception, attempted to be an action—a bold, swift, and forthright action. It most certainly is ideally suited to be another "educational environment" in the sense of Postman and Weingartner.

In my perception, the first premise of Beta is that it exists as a community of learners for the education of all the members of the general community. This goal, community of learners, I find enthralling. Savor that phrase, role it over your tongue several times, swallow it, digest it. Hopefully, one might now begin to taste the audacity, the hope, the functional aspects, the dysfunctional aspects, the coping techniques (or rather, the survival techniques), the depth of emotion, the behavior patterns both manifest and latent.

Like any community, some tools are here, others are not; some skills are present, others absent; some skills and tools coalesce, but not in sufficient number. Other skills and tools do not coalesce at all.

Essentially, the major problem of any community is the harmonious adaptation of individual differences to a level of optimum functionality in terms of the entire general community.

One constant criticism of the program is that it lacks structure. This point is so conspicuous that I feel a need to address myself to it. I would give *structure* as it applies to Beta the definition one applies to *harmonious adaptation*, the definition of *behavior patterns*, the causes of given patterns, the means of abolishing given patterns, for example, failure patterns; and the means of strengthening other patterns defined as being functional. As in all communities, given the present educational situation in this country, intensive learning of the basic skills, that is, communicational-computational skills, is needed. Beta, by means of its defined structure, is attempting to address itself to just this problem.

It should also be established that the feeling is rampant that the real problems of the community are those we do not know about. Beta is marked by multitudinous, interrelated, overlapping responsibilities. These responsibilities are tenfold in comparison to other schools due to the proximity of the members comprising the community—a proximity which is not sustained by the traditional classroom schedules. I am suggesting that proximity plus constancy equal intensity! The intensity causes the problems and faults, of which we are cognizant, to be inflated to an extreme degree. In judging the program, one must not compare it to other schools but rather isolate the educational goals to which the program intends to address itself and then measure the program against the degree and depth of the achievement of the stipulated goals. Further, it would seem to me that if the goals are not obtainable, this in no way implies that the Parkway Program is totally dysfunctional. It merely implies that a given goal is dysfunctional in terms of its being obtained at Parkway. One usually does not get too upset if one cannot purchase alcohol (in Pennsylvania) at an apothecary shop; one merely goes to a "state store." But both the apothecary shop and the state store have their legitimacy. All of the above is merely to emphasize that I consider the goal of community of learners to be both the nemesis and the balm of Beta.

The very concept of the Parkway Program brings with it problems which are indigenous to it. These indigenous problems, coupled with the problems brought to the program, enhance the difficulties with which the program is faced. This, however, is an issue of vitality, which is to say it points to the program as being alive and vibrant, not to mention stimulating and euphoric. The students at Beta have come from a bureaucratic, superdisciplined environment where the structure was blatantly identified and where signs of all levels of subtlety constantly reminded one where the structure was and what the limits of the structure were.

This is not to say, as so many have — mistakenly in my estimation — that the program has no structure. All letters of the alphabet are not A. And their not being A in no way detracts from their being letters. So too, I would suggest, all structures are not traditional, and any nontraditional structure is not therefore any less a structure. All analogies limp, but hopefully the point is made.

Having posited a structure to the program, how do I perceive this structure? Observe an amoeba. The cell walls are definitely there and it might be further noted that the walls are in motion (flexibility) in what might further be described as a centripedal and centrifugal fashion. I would further suggest, however, that the movement is much too subtle to be termed flexible.

To return to the "problems." The program is definitely, in my estimation, dysfunctional for some students just as Central or Germantown High is dysfunctional for other students. The cliché of square pegs in round holes comes to mind. Given the nature of human beings, the pegs should not be carved to fit the holes; rather, the holes should be constructed to fit the pegs. One would further buttress the above position from more traditional sources, namely, Jesus, as quoted by Mark 2:27, "The Sabbath is made for man, not man for the Sabbath." Though problematic, I thus see a positive value in the program in that it is a hole attempting to fit the pegs. I feel consternation that the general powers that be in the city of Philadelphia are trying to fit all sorts of pegs into the program and saying that if they do not fit, then the program should cease to exist. I view this position as ridiculous. But then again, our perspectives are different.

The learning problems of the articulate, motivated student are of a lesser intensity at Beta than they might be in some other environments. Such problems are also of a lesser intensity in terms of the student who is less motivated and less articulate, one whose position, attitude-wise, seems to be that he has nothing to be articulate about and nothing toward which he should be motivated. These latter students do not seem to possess the initiative to go out and get a meaningful educational experience—that is, until they are given the opportunity, in which case they do so with a vengeance. Beta attempts to assist students in such a situation to find out and consider what might be a meaningful educational experience for themselves. If, however, they remain at Beta or in any other situation which is not providing them what they need, further problems are generated.

Another problem with which the program must cope is that which I term the Parkway panacea. I perceive the program not as a panacea for urban educational problems but rather as an alternative, one among many alternatives, and its greatest validity lies in just that fact. The more alternatives, the more various the educational models, and the more the latter, the more functional the educational system. There should, in my educational value system, be a "traditional" school, a rigidly structured school, a free school, and all manner of public and private schools.

Parkway is not just either/or. Rather, it possesses the potential for being neither/or and both/and. It can include various and sundry aspects of so-called traditional education and new education. Very definitely, the components of various modes of education are present at the program in varying quantities. Consequently, it is all the more difficult to judge the program in comparison with other schools. Where the goals of "other" schools and those of the program coincide, a basis for comparison exists. The rest is wishful thinking. Though it might or might not appear obvious, my feelings about the program are what some would term good. Good for me, however, merely means that my feelings are ambiguous, at best. They are intense and I maintain that feelings one holds intensely about anything are ambiguous.

This is not to gainsay the realities to which the program must be related. Beta does not exist in a vacuum. This is of foremost consideration, especially since the program purports to be more cognizant of this external world and is an attempt to perform the educational function in conjunction with the external world.

I experience Beta as a cell, the nucleus of that being the staff personnel, as opposed to student personnel. If one might revert back to our definition of *community:* It would seem to be essential that in order for the community to function at its optimum homeostatic level and there sustain itself, some clarification for a procedural rationale relative to the creation of definitions and the communication of those definitions is necessary. For example, one difficulty at Beta is that both the staff and students have difficulty in defining their structure, that is, the limits within which they can work at their optimum. Further, when once identified, members of the community have difficulty in isolating those functions which can be carried out within the defined structure and those which can be carried out without the structure. After this consideration one is faced with the further complication of deciding what justifies (is justification even necessary) going beyond the first structure (which is, in fact, nothing more than moving from one structure pertinent in its time, place, and purpose) to another structure (which may be just as functional in its time, place, and purpose).

At Beta, it can be said that there is no recognized and universally accepted decision-making process. It might be suggested that this very lack *is* the decision-making process, for it cannot be denied that Beta has functioned quite well in its present state. Nevertheless, not having identified an optimum level precludes the judgment that Beta could or could not function at its optimum homeostatic level.

Consequently, it would seem, individual staff members do not honor decisions made by the staff as a whole, which obviously implies that the decision was not made by the staff as a whole. Why? The position most often stated is that personal feelings and philosophies conflict. I do not object to this. What I do object to is the fact that the feelings and philosophies are not articulated and shared, and thus potential communication and support is thereby lost. Aside from suffering from an intense lack of sharing on the part of the staff, the sharing of teaching teachniques, resources, materials, experiences, and most importantly, support, Beta suffers from dichotomous thinking. By this I mean divergent views concerning structure versus nonstructure, authority versus nonauthority, and so on. Though I do not like to take a middle ground, especially for the sake of being in the middle, I would, nevertheless, suggest that the position of rigid nonstructure is a rigid position. The question then becomes one of rigid flexibility or flexible rigidity. Again, however, the staff is aware of this problem and has tackled it head-on. Consequently, it has become evident that the staff possesses an extreme potential to identify alternatives and definitions. The next step is to begin to move toward those definitions and decision-making processes which are compatible with the community.

Self-definition is not the final end, for self-definition is ridiculous if it is not shared—that is, if it is not communicated.

Communication among the faculty leaves much to be desired, and this leads one to be wary of "hidden agenda" which further sap the strength and efforts of the staff as a body. This difficulty becomes all the more salient when one considers that the program has a tendency to bite off more than it can chew.

In terming the staff the nucleus of the program, I do not wish to suggest that the students play no equal essential role. The point is that at Beta the personal relationship between staff and student, one which tends toward mutual trust, tends to enhance the learning process. The staff is cognizant of its behavioral influence upon the students. Some students refuse any and everything in the name of freedom. This is to be expected, since our society kills in the name of love, God, and so on. But the students at Beta experience a staff which spends upwards of ten hours a day, in some form or other, dealing with them. The students are in the precarious position of not relating to the consequences of their choices, and the choices of the moment are not fully comprehended. But the students are at least at the stage of making decisions and choosing. I wonder if this statement can be made relative to more traditional schools, where the two cardinal rules might be, memorize and regurgitate! Consequently, Beta, for some, is an opportunity to become extremely lax. I believe that such laxity is a pseudolaxity in that it is not chosen in terms of a realistic consideration of the consequences; it is, therefore, one of the functions of the staff to make this point salient for the students. Again, I would emphasize that Beta is not a community concerned with teaching; rather, it is a community concerned, emphatically so, with learning!

I believe that another function of definition and communication is that of instilling faculty and community support. It is my perception that most persons learn most from behavior. Consequently, calls for support from students for other students fall on deaf ears when the students look at the behavior of staff to staff and see no support. Incidentally, one of the boons to learning is to have open staff meetings. Faculty meetings should always be open to students. In traditional schools, for example, instead of giving detentions, a teacher might merely tell the student being reprimanded to report to the faculty meeting that week. I doubt that many faculties exist which are strong enough to sustain such a suggestion.

Some individuals at Beta have said that Beta is, or symbolizes, an improved educational experience. Quite a few such phrases are thrown around the community. I believe we need to define such terms. We obviously function with definitions, and I would much rather be in the position of one who defines as opposed to one who is defined. My point is that if calls for support are to be heeded, we must communicate the definitions under which we function. By definition I mean setting a reasonable, realistic, and functional goal and then proposing means and direction to arrive at this goal. The lack of definition, communication, and support stands out all the more conspicuously at Beta, since we are ideally (relatively) suited to freely provide those essential features of community life. Share, not impose! I need not approve or agree with the goal of another staff member, but knowing his goal allows me to function, if I so choose, in a supportive manner toward him. Here I do most emphatically mean to imply that communication, meaningful and nonthreatening, is a *sine qua non*, and is missing in the extreme.

Again let me pose an analogy. Let us take two staff members, A and B, and choose two locations, say City Hall and 30th Street Station. In this analogy I am defining support to be the answer yes or no. A is traveling east on Market Street toward City Hall. He approaches B and asks if he (A) is going in the correct direction. Already the bind has been established. B then asks, "Where do you wish to go?" A responds that such a question and its answer are irrelevant and none of B's business.

The point is, to be supportive, to answer yes or no, B must know where A wants to go. If A wants to go to City Hall, then B responds, "Yes"; if A wants to go to 30th Street Station, B then responds, "No." But the reality of the situation is such that B does not know where A wants to go and A refuses to tell him; consequently, well meaning though he may be, B is curtailed from giving the very support to A that A is requesting. I am aware of the weakness in the analogy, namely, that B must know where the two points of destination are in relation to the point where he confronts A. Nevertheless, the point should be apparent at this juncture.

This is a game, assuredly. But I define *game* as a behavioral sequence defined by roles, rules, rituals, goals, strategies, values, language, characteristic space-time locations, and characteristic patterns of movement.

As such, the question is not whether one will or will not play the game; rather, it seems that the question is whether or not I will allow the game to play me. At Beta, because no one sees the need to inform anyone else of his goal, one is put in the position of not being able to support the person making the request for support. Consequently, there is a lot of talk about support and little, if any, support given. What little I have witnessed has been when the levels of frustration rise to such a peak that anxiety and guilt then take over and force support. My value judgment regarding this situation is that absolutely speaking it is "bad"; relatively speaking it is "good" in that at least this staff, the fifth in my experience, is talking about support and trying to address themselves sincerely to the problem.

This is a salient feature of the program in that problems are dealt with and solutions attempted. This seems to be a far cry from sweeping things under the rug.

Further, the race issue is also a factor. Most of the time white staff members relinquish the responsibility of talking to black students because the white staff members feel that because they lack similar experiences and background only black staff members are able to deal with black students.

In summary, the staff does not communicate functionally enough to allow the resources and talents of various staff members to be shared sufficiently to be of benefit to the entire community. Most of the time staff meetings are marked by an attitude of "let's meet to decide when we can get together to meet to decide what we can do and set another meeting to meet to decide when we can meet to further decide, *ad nauseam.*"

The purpose of education has traditionally been to develop people who will support the existing societal values. Parkway can develop a definition of the purpose of education which will develop people who will question the existing values. Community Beta is well aware that, as R. D. Laing has stated, "Social adaptation to a dysfunctional society may be very dangerous."

Beta is well aware that learning is not to occur essentially for 1970 but for 1980–1990, not to mention the year 2000! Changes in our attitudes toward the family institution, as well as advances in transportation, communication, medicine, and so on, have all contributed to our past, present, and future concepts of community. That in itself is an overwhelming concept. To be so audacious as to attempt to create not just a community, not just a learning environment, but a community of learners would seem enough to justify not only the existence but the perpetuation of the concept of the Parkway Program. It can be done *today,* not out of need but out of desire.

Reality is as one perceives it — no more, no less. Objectivity is nothing more than subjectivity to the nth power!

17

From a Unit Head–Tina Craig

THE ADMINISTRATOR AS LEARNER

"I don't think it's your decision to make."

"I know you were probably rushed, but next time I think you should consult us."

"We really can't *make* people do anything they don't want to do; we are absolutely powerless in that sense."

The above comments were made, respectively, by a full-time faculty member at a staff meeting; a university intern at a staff development session; and the program's director at our cabinet meeting. These remarks pointedly illustrate that in the Parkway Program the administrator (unit head) should not and does not make unilateral decisions. It can be plainly seen that a person who has learned to push a project, program, or idea by using railroading or bulldozing techniques will not be successful in this community where the decision-making process is a shared responsibility.

In a community of learning, what does it profit the teacher, the student, the unit head, or even the director if only one segment of the community is expected to do all the learning? Where is the growth and self-discovery for each member if it is decided beforehand that the student knows nothing and the teacher and administrator know it all? The student, teacher, and administrator are all losers if this attitude prevails. Unfortunately, in many educational institutions it does.

For me, the continuing, exciting aspect of the Parkway Program has been the variety of learning experiences. These have been as numerous as the 150 members (black, white, Puerto Rican) who make up our community. Daily, we have been in a constant state of teaching each other about our life styles, our interests, and our skills, as well as English, social studies, mathematics, science, foreign languages, art, and music.

Other than possessing the good listener quality, the ability to be flexible, and the belief in freedom for everyone, the administrator must have the willingness to unlearn what has been previously learned: To unlearn the experiences related to the bachelor's and master's degrees and ten years of teaching in a formal structure. This obviously does not mean to forget how to balance the petty cash account or efficiently organize work or coordinate activities, but it does mean to unlearn the accepted concept of authority and power and have the courage to reject it. This is difficult to do. Where in the world does one find an individual, group, institution, or nation willing to forfeit or even share its power! Usually, the hierarchy of power has been prearranged by those in power so that those who were not in on the original planning can never get in. Recall the traditional set-up:

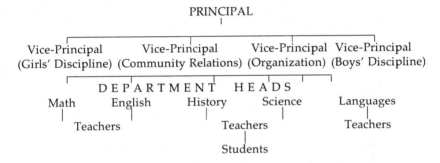

PRINCIPAL

| Vice-Principal | Vice-Principal | Vice-Principal | Vice-Principal |
| (Girls' Discipline) | (Community Relations) | (Organization) | (Boys' Discipline) |

DEPARTMENT HEADS

Math   English   History   Science   Languages

Teachers   Teachers   Teachers

Students

The chart suggests comfort and security; it helps each person know where to go for answers. But since the top is where the power is, then the student is way out of touch with the source. And isn't he what the whole business of education is about?

What about power in the Parkway Program? Who has it? Everyone and at different times. I offer some instances to illustrate:

1. A course is offered in the catalog; no one signs up for it; the course is cancelled (students)
2. The closing of the community house during certain hours (faculty)
3. Decision to leave present community house and find a new one (total community)
4. Courses to take (students)
5. Courses to teach—when and where (faculty)
6. Handling and disbursement of petty cash (unit head)

7. Control over who sees and what goes into students' records (students)
8. Filling of faculty positions (students, staff, unit head)
9. Compilation and organization of course catalog (students, staff, and unit head)

It becomes increasingly difficult to watch and wait for decisions to be made by students, staff, and/or the total community. But it is absolutely necessary to do just that. Sometimes the process drags on and on; frustration sets in; tempers flare. It can be an agonizing experience. I've tried to be guided by the fact that decision-making is difficult only because most people have had little practice in making meaningful and significant decisions. But what a learning experience when the process is completed! The beauty of it all is that each time it gets easier and better. Hence, the unit head serves as a coordinator to translate the decision into action. Now the skills of organization—shortcuts, contacts, methods—can be activated and the program can advance. It just makes good sense that the power for making all the decisions for all the community does not rest all of the time with one person or one group. This distribution of power gives everyone a stake in the development and responsibility of the community and at the same time (and this is the rewarding aspect) it allows time to create innovative projects and hatch fresh ideas.

When decisions are made in the Parkway Program that are contrary to one's experience, training, education, principals, philosophy, and all else that is held sacred, what happens then? A mini-death, a deep breath, and a mustering up of strength to gently persuade, convince, instruct, and hope that through these efforts the decision will be reversed. It is at these times that the structure and philosophy of the program are tested.

There was such a test in one of the units. A group of students decided to form a tutorial group outside of the given tutorial structure (two staff members and fifteen students randomly selected). This decision was based on their desire to be with each other because they had common interests, liked each other, and didn't like their given tutorials. The basic structure of the Parkway Program was being undermined; no real learning was taking place; all of the students were of the same racial group. They said they were not going back to their original tutorial. What was done? The group was not recognized as a legitimate tutorial; they were reminded frequently that their actions were undermining the structure of the program and that they were not learning about people who were different from themselves. Beyond that point we could not go. An authority in the traditional system would have forced them back into the organized set-up. (How dare they step outside of the existing structure?) But what would have been learned? Perhaps this: we have no power; therefore, no commitment. Results: the total structure crumbled, or worse still, the haunting words: you all have lied who told us freedom is ours. We felt the price was too high, so we waited. One day as this "bandit tutorial" was meeting on the steps, I overheard, "This isn't working!" It's painful to wait, but if we have the patience . . .

Much has been learned from the students, parents, and staff. One of the most satisfying experiences was a demonstration of the fact (or should I say a confirmation of a long-held belief) that when students have power, they do not abuse it. For example, after the community had decided to suspend a student for unacceptable behavior, it rejected a proposal to expel him if he "got into any more trouble." Another student's comment was, "Let's handle each situation and case separately and not get caught up in making a lot of rules for the future."

I recall a student's request to transfer out of her tutorial because she was in the minority and didn't care for the other students. She said that they had little in common and she wanted out. I suggested that she stay and accept it as a learning experience. At the same time I assured her that at the end of the quarter she could put her name in a box to be drawn for a different tutorial. Because she trusted and accepted the structure of the program, she was willing to wait. At town meeting, when a change of the tutorial structure was proposed, she was one of the most vocal proponents: "If you don't like your tutorial now, you have the freedom to change at the end of the quarter. But we certainly should not scrap the tutorials."

Even parents (often described as the most conservative group in society) will embrace an idea as radical as "freedom for children" if they can see the benefits and results. Parents have been responding:

> All I know is that my son has never enjoyed or appreciated going to school until he started Parkway. He is having trouble with algebra/math, but other than that he seems pretty content. He had a slow start in tutorial, but once he got used to it, he enjoyed it.

> I am looking for the progress that he has made, not how good or bad he is doing. Let me say how happy and enthusiastic I am about the Parkway Program. I wouldn't have him anywhere else, even if there were no progress reports whatsoever.

> Of course my evaluation of Parkway Program must be based on "L's" experiences only. Her outlook on everything from humor to her own future has broadened beyond my most optimistic hopes. I thoroughly approve and value your evaluation system.

I have noticed "W" is speaking more clearly and expresses himself more thoroughly.

Do they understand that while independence is wonderful, self-discipline must go with it?

From the staff I have learned how to work with teachers as a group who have as a task the building of a community, and at the same time to recognize the freedom of the individual teacher to do what he wants. I have tried to maintain a balance between the two. I remember the suggestion that the agenda for staff meetings be a compilation of every-one's ideas. So it was arranged that items for the agenda should be placed in my cinder block mailbox by 1 P.M. the day before the meeting. It was the feeling of the staff that we were not getting to the depths of what was on the minds of people because the "action" didn't really begin until we arrived at the agenda item called "other." By then, there remained only a half hour of the meeting. After this suggestion was heeded, we seemed to get to the "action" much sooner. Thus, the agenda became *ours* instead of *mine*.

I have also learned how to listen better, and when I listened I heard these comments from staff:

> We are not in a dream world. Students are constantly remind-ing us of this fact. They come to Parkway from near prisons; they come from the city and its racism, its poverty, its wars. They come into Parkway and they are not "free." Neither are we, for we've been even longer in this prison. . . . Most of our work needs to be in helping students grow out of the prison mentality into the responsible use of freedom which is naturally theirs.

> For me, Parkway is a place where I am free to define my role, exercise both freedom and responsibility, decide what to do in my classes, how to conduct them and how to deal with my failures. I have a great deal of respect for everyone else who is engaged in this perilous enterprise. I firmly believe it is the only way to get close to learning, for students and staff.

> My authority is determined by my relationships with people, by the consistency and lack thereof between what I say and what I do. I want no other authority — especially not one based on age, position, salary, etc. I want to exercise the authority which is due any individual member of the com-munity, no more and no less.

> We act as free and responsible people, with a will to cooperate and support each other whenever possible. In cases where

that is not possible, I can see no reason for hard feelings. As for tradition, let's go back to Plato, Aristotle, Zen Masters, and other wise men whose aim was to develop a free and independent man in a free and independent society.

I have learned to respect the various abilities of the staff members (everyone on the staff is under 30); I am aware that any one of them could do my job. Since we have adopted two-year rotating systems for the position of unit head, many will have the opportunity.

When I took on this job, there was no job description for unit head of the Parkway Program. There was no precedent, no guidelines, just a sentence: Be responsible for the day-to-day operation of the unit. So the days and weeks reflected the tenor of the times. Below is a synoptic account of a week's schedule:

MONDAY

Notices in teachers' mailboxes

Conference with staff member (black-white student relationships)

Meeting with university interns' coordinator (evaluation of performance)

Visitors from a suburban school system

Conference with university intern (re: position paper)

Writing checks for petty-cash disbursement

TUESDAY

Distribution of tokens for intercity transportation

Talk with staff member about a possible course offering: "On a Farm"

Telephone conversation with suspended student

Checked completed EH-14 reports

Developed agenda for staff meeting

Met with tutorial group #1

WEDNESDAY

Staff meeting

Writing checks for petty-cash disbursement

Telephone conversation with parent about her son's achievement

Extended invitation to representatives from participating institutions

Checked on cabinet meeting with director and unit heads

THURSDAY

Discussed day's activity with staff members regarding strike for peace

Dictated letter to students regarding courses for September

Met with visitors from Baltimore, Maryland

Met with students regarding strike for peace plans and the City Council meeting

Checked on next day's plans with Parkway Program's information officer

Conference with two people volunteering tutorial services

Conference with student who had been in Europe since March

Reviewed copy of community newspaper

Made appointment for student for psychological testing at her doctor's request

FRIDAY

Emergency town meeting

Staff development session

Buffet luncheon meeting with five U.S. senatorial representatives, eight students, and representatives from participating institutions

Completed petty cash account report

Completed token report

From what has been described, it becomes apparent that the administrator as learner must don new clothes. They should be loose, with a lot of room for growth. They must be changed constantly to emphasize the need to keep up with and ahead of the times. They ought not to be too comfortable.

Personally, I have found the role (*role* and not *position*) a challenging and stimulating one, mainly because the staff and students were not Summerhill graduates or gestalt theorists or Piaget's prodigies but just ordinary people in love with a beautiful idea and working on it every day to make it a reality.

18
From a Parent–Anne McNulty

Our daughter Claudia has just graduated from Parkway Program. She is, like her mother, no scholar. She is bright, pretty, talented, and enterprising, but does not take much interest in the purely academic. Her first high school experience was in a huge, highly respected academic school for girls where she found herself lost in anonymity and unhappy with the situation. There are several ways to escape from anonymity in such surroundings. The most acceptable, of course, is to become a straight A student. Another is to look bizarre, and yet another is to cut classes, ask questions (horrors!) when one *is* in class, and play hooky or *Le Malade Imaginaire*. Our daughter chose cuts, questions, hooky, and hypochondria; and in doing so changed from a cheerful, confident youngster to an unhappy, guilt-ridden, inadequate one. After a year of misery she withdrew from that school and entered a small tutorial school—so small that her social contacts were severely limited and subjects other than the required academic ones were nonexistent. This was hardly a solution to her plight, but our financial circumstances did not permit us to enroll her in one of the larger, perhaps more satisfactory, private schools, and the public school system offered no promising alternative other than Parkway Program. Claudia had become acquainted with Parkway and enamored of it by the simple expedient of sitting in on some classes with friends of hers who were duly enrolled Parkway students. There seemed pitifully little chance that she might get in, but she applied along with about ten thousand other hopefuls. It was her avowed intention, if not accepted, to drop out of school, study independently, and take the high school equivalency test when she reached eighteen. Happily for all of us, she was among the 140 lucky ones chosen for the new unit.

Several weeks before the beginning of the fall term the 140 chosen ones and their parents attended an orientation meeting. Most of us first met John Bremer at that time. He explained the concept of Parkway, introduced the faculty who would staff the new unit, answered excited questions from the kids and apprehensive ones from the parents, urged parents to join any courses that intrigued them, and expressed the hope that some parents might feel inclined to *give* courses. Many members of the faculty were young and hirsute or young and mini-skirted, and as the groups began to mingle at the close of the meeting, it became increasingly difficult to distinguish the younger members of the faculty from the older students. To make matters still more confusing, everyone was to be on first-name basis—even John Bremer is John to the kids. This would surely be no Harper Valley PTA!

As the product of a rather unusual experimental school, I was perhaps less concerned about the freedom of decision and action that the kids would have than were many of the parents, and more convinced from the outset that the Parkway idea was a sound, workable one. Even so, it took some adjusting to become a Parkway parent. The first two weeks of school seemed to consist largely of simply meeting and wandering around town—a new experience for some of the kids, who, though Philadelphians, had seldom left their own particular sections of the city. Here, the center-city and inner-city children were the guides and mentors, explaining the intricacies of the public transit system to the more sheltered suburbanites and helping them to find obscure places. The so-called advantaged kids took the lead in introducing others to the museums, galleries, theaters, and such.

Almost immediately these kids, from all kinds of different backgrounds, began to perceive each others' strengths and weaknesses, and, in many cases, old misconceptions began to break down.

In due time a catalog of course offerings was issued and the students, with advice from their parents and tutorial leaders, chose the courses which they thought would most interest and benefit them. There were days when Claudia seemed to have an inordinate amount of free time, but on other days she had classes from nine to five, and after dinner at home, left again for class in painting or one in Eastern religions. In all, it evened out to more class time than in her previous schools and less homework time, but it took some getting used to. Occasionally there was a weekend junket. One I particularly remember was a trip to a Tibetan lamasery in Freehold, New Jersey. I wonder how many people even know that there is a Tibetan lamasery in this part of the world.

Probably the most immediately apparent change in Claudia was the improvement in her health. During the three years prior to Parkway, Claudia had lost a tremendous amount of time from school with either real or imagined ailments. It seemed doubtful that she had suddenly developed some miraculous immunity to disease, so we were forced to conclude that she no longer needed the defense of ill health to protect her from an odious situation. Another obvious change was the absence of the many agonizing homework sessions in which we had all frequently been involved. Often, when Claudia hadn't caught on to the day's math lesson or was unable to conjugate the past imperfect of some irregular French verb, we'd been called upon for help. For the most part, if we'd ever known the answers we'd long since forgotten them, so homework was pretty grim for the whole family.

At Parkway, students are encouraged to ask questions when they don't understand, and help is freely given by teachers, interns, and other students. What tests there are are not punitive, as so often seems the case, but rather are guides to the students and faculty. As we became accustomed to the somewhat unorthodox schedules, a kind of serenity, which we hadn't known since the good old pre-high school days, began to return to the household.

Early in Claudia's Parkway career she had been nervous, almost to the point of tears, when called upon to conduct a town meeting. Toward the end of May, incensed by the killing of black college students in Georgia and Mississippi and the ever-increasing number of black killings here in Philadelphia, Claudia *called* a town meeting to organize a march to demonstrate concern about these dreadful events. Not only had she grown enormously in her awareness of human problems in the course of her Parkway year but her self-assurance had returned to the degree that she could and did organize and stage the march.

We don't know if Claudia is an A, B, C, or D student now, but she's a pass student and that's all we need to know. There is no censure where there is no grade. There is incentive to learn but no unhealthy competition for top spot in class. Claudia is taking a drama course at Penn this summer and will enter the Pennsylvania Academy of Fine Arts this fall. If she finds that her talent is important enough for her to hope for success as a fine artist, she will probably continue in the art field. If not, she will think about another career and college next year. This year she wants to develop in her own way and get her own priorities in order. She's also self-confident enough now to be trying to figure out a way to finance her own small apartment in town. She asked the other night if we would give her a subscription to the *New York Times* as a house present if her plans work out—an unexpected request from a turned-off kid. During the Parkway year we've had the pleasure of watching her revert to the delightful person she'd been before the stultifying high school experience had begun its destructive processes on her personality. We are grateful that there was a Parkway Program to save her.

Students who are high achievers, academically, are probably fairly happy in the traditional system because they fit the existing molds. I think it is fair to say that fewer of *them* feel sufficiently dissatisfied in their school situations to apply for admission to Parkway than do the less academically motivated ones. Those who did very well in their conventional schools but nevertheless turned to Parkway as a new experience continue to do very well and are offered far more scope for their studies than is generally available in other schools. Parkway, however, tailors the curriculum to the student and not the student to the curriculum, so those kids whose interests, talents, and abilities lie in other areas are not robbed of their self-esteem because they don't fit the academic mold. Instead, they are encouraged to develop the interests and aptitudes they have and are given enormous opportunity to develop new interests. Their opinions and decisions are considered every bit as valid as the opinions and decisions of the "academicians," and all share equally in the governing of their communities. Parkway is the only totally integrated (racially, socially, economically, intellectually) school situation that I know of, although others probably exist. There the kids are learning to relate to each other as individuals rather than as members of a race or class. Their respect, affection, and, sometimes, dislike are bestowed on persons, not groups. Recognizing the positive values of each individual and helping to develop them are, in my opinion, more important than the total absorption most educators seem to have with academic excellence—which is not a requisite to a healthy, happy, productive and rewarding life. Too many of today's schools seem to me to place most of their emphasis on facts in books and little on living, learning experiences.

About six weeks before the end of the spring term, city budgetary problems forced the withdrawal of funds from many of the public summer schools and Parkway was one of the schools so affected. Because Parkway was conceived as a year-round learning experience (summer term, however, being optional with the student), it seemed more than ordinarily distressing for its summer session to be eliminated. After numerous discussions with disappointed kids, some of the teachers and parents determined to make summer school available if at all possible. I had recently left my job (my paying job, that is) and had a lot of free time at my disposal, so when asked to do some fund-raising for a Parkway summer program I had no ready excuse for begging off. In the course of fund-raising I have, so far, had telephone conversations with about two hundred and fifty parents. These conversations have been fascinating, if not inspiring, as, one after the other, parents have related the changes, often dramatic, that have occurred in their children as the result of their Parkway association.

For the past week I have been trying to decide which of these conversations to report in detail, but there is such a wealth of material that I scarcely know how to present it. Perhaps the most memorable story was of a lad who had dropped out of, or been dropped from, four other high schools for a variety of reasons, including the length of his hair and his discomforting insistence on thinking independently and asking questions, and whose highest grade in any of those schools had been a C. He had been using drugs and was out of touch with his family and reality. He entered Parkway last fall, not only quit using drugs but began to hold antidrug seminars, bloomed academically, graduated in June, and was accepted by all three colleges to which he'd applied. Another parent—one I roused, unknowingly, from a sick bed—was so enthusiastic about her son's progress that she not only forgave me instantly but promised and produced help, both financial and otherwise. Her son had done well at his previous school but was bored and mechanical. She described his Parkway experience as "a coming alive—seeing your child as you'd always hoped to see him." He stayed voluntarily until five every day to work with the elementary school kids who were, for a time, part of his community. He sat in on actual court cases as part of one course, wrote trial briefs, and participated in the Nova games competition in New Orleans—all this in addition to a normally heavy course load. One mother reported that teachers had always said her son was retarded and should set his sights on simple vocational training. At Parkway he'd developed an interest in photography and in pursuing it had found that he was not "dumb." His advancement has been so remarkable that he now looks forward to going to college. Yet another student who forced herself to school each day because she felt each day she got through was "one less day I have to study math" is staying an extra term at Parkway, although she already has enough credits to graduate, so that she can take a course in calculus!

My daughter was not the only one whose health improved miraculously, and repeatedly I was told of kids who had grown in poise, confidence, and tolerance. There were a handful of people who expressed total disenchantment with Parkway; and some valid criticisms were offered and concerns expressed, but by and large everyone felt that the program was succeeding far beyond their expectations. Many of these parents had, at the outset, had doubts and reservations about this strange experiment in education for which their children had opted. Now, full of faith and enthusiasm, they were offering financial help for a public school program, which in many cases their own children would not be attending (due to graduation, summer jobs, or vacation plans), because they thought it important to make it available to the kids who *did* need or want it! When people offer economic encouragement under circumstances of this sort it seems ample proof that they are convinced that the plan is working—and working well. As this is written the fund-raising continues and I've no doubt that we will reach our goal. We have gained support not only from the Parkway parents but also from the parents of disappointed would-be Parkway students, as well as from individuals, businesses, and foundations who see this program as a practical and exciting new kind of educational experience and who hope that their show of faith will be instrumental in helping the Parkway Program to survive and to expand. The one truly imposing observation that keeps coming through is that the kids have become *happy*. As one parent put it: "Most kids go to school because they *have* to. Parkway kids go because they *want* to."

Fund-raising aside, these conversations with parents have been valuable in demonstrating what Parkway is doing right from the parents' point of view and also in pointing up some areas of concern which deserve attention. Parkway has problems. So do all schools. Parkway probably has fewer than most. More important, Parkway recognizes its mistakes and throws them out. It doesn't cling to them, cherish them, and perfect them. There's a way to do, but it's a wonderful, promising way!

Parkway's magic has liberated me as well as my daughter. I became involved as *me* (not as a parent) only about a week before Claudia's graduation, so there may well be many parents better equipped than I to write about the program, but few, probably, who feel any more committed to its principles or any more enthusiastic about what it can offer to the students and the community. While my husband's academic credentials are suitably impressive, mine are not, so I felt that I had nothing of worth to contribute to any kind of educational organization—hence my noninvolvement with a plan which I had believed from the start to offer a very sound solution to many of the problems of public urban education. Although I have managed, in my adult life, to cope (with reasonable success) as a wife and mother and have held several interesting and demanding jobs, I have always labored under a feeling of inadequacy because I have not a single degree with which to embellish my name. My recent, almost total, immersion in Parkway Program has given me a new sense of worth and has literally changed my life. I work much of the day and long into the night on Parkway affairs, do a minimum of housework, and fall into bed at 2 or 3 A.M. Then, often as not, I lie awake thinking up new angles and wild schemes or composing letters. Sometimes, as now, I get up again, come downstairs, and start writing the words that have been running around in my head. I've seen more sunrises in the past three weeks than I have in the last twenty years. I've even had wild notions of teaching things at Parkway and going back to college. (If I could get hold of an old-hand press and a few fonts of type I could teach the rudiments of printing . . . if I could talk Singer out of a couple of old sewing machines I could offer a class in basic sewing . . . hey, how about a class in beginning French?) Well, I'll probably manage to beat these ideas down — at least for a while — because with a daughter in art school and a son home (I hope) from Vietnam and back in college (another hope) I may not have time to work so hard at my own fulfillment, but even if my association with Parkway ends this summer, it will have left its mark on me. If only brief exposure to such deeply caring people can stir up a 45-year-old dropout, imagine what it can do for the kids for whom it's primarily intended!

As a final thought, it occurs to me that if there had been a Parkway Program available for our son a few years ago he might not now be in Vietnam.

19

From a Journalist–Nancy Love

Philadelphia Magazine

HIGH SCHOOL 2 GROOVING AT PARKWAY

It does not seem possible that this is a school. Here are these 15 or so kids sitting around on the floor of an elegantly appointed conference room in the IVB building arguing about the definition of hypnosis, and another group of eight sprawled on mattresses in a loft on Naudain Street completely absorbed in listening to rock music, and in a bare basement room of the First Presbyterian Church on Walnut Street a teacher is giving six students seated around a tippy old table mimeographed pages from an archaic, irrelevant American history textbook that illustrate why he doesn't use a textbook. It might not seem possible that this is a school. And it isn't—in the traditional sense.

It's the Parkway Program. It's a program that has taken 500 high school students who were fed up, bored, about to drop out, or otherwise not getting along in their own school, and put them into a learning situation where they willingly attend classes from 9 straight through to 5 and even on Saturday mornings if necessary, where there are no problems of drugs, gangs, race, dropping out, violence. The only problems seem to be trying to find the best and most exciting way for each student and teacher to learn—and to help each other to learn.

In a city where, from time to time, small-scale experiments have made little ripples in a generally stagnant school system, the Parkway Program is the biggest splash of the century. As a matter of fact, it might be one of the most innovative programs in the country. Last year *Life* said it was "probably the most radical of all current high school experiments." In March, *Time* called it "the most interesting high school in the U.S. today."

[258]

Every week visiting educators pour in from all over the country to probe and be shocked. Chicago has launched what is billed as a similar program, and other cities are nervously flirting with the possibility.

This program is showing that within the public education framework there is an alternative to the old system that turns off more and more kids and teachers every year, and keeps flashing danger signals that say, "Look, the learning system has broken down."

At first it is very difficult to comprehend how it all works, why this program succeeds when others don't. There are the obvious dramatic externals, the whole mystique of a school without walls; a school that uses the resources of the city—its museums, businesses, institutions, and their staffs—to help students to relate to the real world, to *live* in the real world out there.

As far as school administrators are concerned, a school which relieves crowded classrooms and at the same time saves money for the school district has irresistible magic. Because the Parkway Program relies heavily on the use of space and talent donated by other institutions, there are no new school buildings or equipment to pay for and not as many salaries as would be indicated by the staggering variety of courses offered. Even though there are no more than 15 kids in a class, and usually less, the per capita student cost is the same as for the traditional high schools, which pack at least twice as many kids in a class.

Another big asset of the program is director John Bremer, a plump, charismatic Englishman who combines the best qualities of an accomplished showman and a dedicated philosopher.

But what has captured the fancy of the press and public in most cases is only the superficial glamorous trappings of the Parkway Program: "Classrooms without walls," relating to life in the city, saving money.

The real heart of John Bremer's Parkway Program is much more radical and elusive. His alternative is not merely to add some new courses and field trips and reduce the size of classes. At the core of his plan is the destruction of the old order and the building of a new one where administration, teachers, and students are equally involved in the mutual job of learning.

He is promoting nothing less than a complete revolution. If they get the message, the Old Order must find it very threatening. Whether or not the people responsible for perpetuating the Philadelphia system intact fully understand the implications, John Bremer is not popular with everyone at the board of education. It would only stand to reason that a flamboyant figure who excels in grabbing headlines would throw a few noses out of joint, even if he weren't trying to destroy their empire. At present, in spite of all his national publicity, Bremer needs the ruling Establishment more than it needs him. In a city in such a delicate financial condition and with such a lack of commitment to improving the quality of education by any but the most cautious and ponderous means, the foothold of any experimental program is tenuous at best. The wrath of the Establishment when it is crossed can be swift and lethal, as it showed when it scuttled Bremer's new Paxson elementary school unit a few months ago.

Last month, when Bremer asked to resign as director of the program but to stay on in a consulting capacity, it threw the future of Parkway into more confusion and uncertainty. No one really knows for sure how it will fare.

The kids ask, "Why should education be a torture?" It is hard for adults to think up an answer for that.

They talk about the school they used to go to. It doesn't matter which one it was: "I didn't want to go. The things that they told us to do were so utterly ridiculous. You just sat there like a zombie, you know, while they put information into your brain that you didn't really want."

There is a lot of emphasis on talking and listening at Parkway — on verbal communication, conversation. Everyone communicates like crazy. And questions and argues. It's one confrontation after another.

Andy Appelbaum came to Parkway in September from Olney. He was in the 11th grade. "I don't know whether I'd ever have gotten out of the 11th grade if I had stayed there." Now he knows he'll go to college — maybe not right out of high school, but eventually. He's tall and powerfully built, wears his hair shoulder length and a hoop earring through one ear. He would make the principals of most schools very uptight just by his appearance. But he also has the inquisitiveness and openness that is appreciated in this environment, though not most others. "If you just *tried* asking questions at Olney!"

When pressed for more details about his schooling before he came to Parkway, Andy does a good job of expressing the Bremer educational philosophy as it relates to his own experiences.

> Every Philadelphia school is horrible. It's the way they teach. The relationships are awful — teacher to student, teacher to administration, student to student. [John Bremer says: "The social relationships must change; the hierarchy must be abolished."]
>
> The kids are bad with each other. Here it's easier with the kids, easier to get to know them. There are still rivalries and jealousies, but not as much competition here. ["Competition

produces anxiety, keeps the students apart."] There aren't any grades here, just pass or fail and an evaluation. You're much more relaxed with the teachers. They have more time for you. They don't put up barriers. They want to learn from students.

I don't really understand why but I feel I'm more of an individual here. But not as much as I'd like to be, but everyone here is working on it.

There's a lot of goofing off here. But they work with you and find out what's bugging you. At other schools they pretend they care but they don't. They just say, "You're a smart boy. Get wise." They don't get into what's really bugging you.

There's so much bullshit before you learn in other schools: there's lateness, suspension for fighting, suspension for smoking. You know that sooner or later they're going to get you. So why go? You turn it off. You get yelled at at home. You don't have to go to school for that.

I'm a much happier all-around human being since I've been here.

The kids have this fear that something will happen to the Parkway Program and that they will have to go back to their old schools. At a recent town meeting (held weekly so students and teachers can get together to discuss what is on their minds), the talk turned to drugs. One girl said she didn't think there was a hard-drug problem at Parkway and that if people wanted to blow grass she didn't see anything wrong with that.

Another girl got up and, in a display of school spirit that long ago disappeared in virtually every other school in the city, said, "If you come to school with dope and you're caught, it's bad for the school. People at the board of education are just waiting to find us doing something they can criticize."

School spirit or no school spirit, in the world of education where politics rather than merit often decides issues, it is always possible that something could happen to sink the Parkway Program.

Parkway has other problems, too. By its very nature it is an evolving project, always developing new approaches and outlooks because change and problem-solving are part of the learning that both staff and students have to go through together. But it's painful. People keep wanting John Bremer to come in and solve their problems. He knows this can't become a one-man operation. That would be failure. If it's to work, it must be able to function as well without him as with him.

He has always known he woundn't stay forever. And he knew that Parkway must also have the faith and confidence of the community it operates in.

The graduation was sort of the Parkway Program in microcosm. It was somewhere between a Hollywood production and a Quaker meeting. No one was bored. Everyone learned something. It was held in mid-February for the handful of students who had graduated *last* June. (There will be a graduation for the first full class later this month.) The only rational explanation for a ceremony celebrating an event that far in the past seemed to be that it was the first anniversary of the program and this seemed like a good way to get some mileage out of it.

The television stations and newspapers were delighted to buy the event on any terms. The art museum was awash with floodlights and cameras. VIP's, parents, board of education types — and, of course, the scruffy kids themselves, unself-consciously sprawling all over the main staircase in the great hall, much to the consternation of the guards, who looked as though they expected them to heave the statues off the steps any minute. The school superintendent was not there.

John Bremer, looking boyish and jolly, and for all the world like some British film comedian whose name you can't remember, opened the exercises by saying, "I don't get a chance to make public statements anymore, so I'm going to make some remarks." Everyone seemed to understand what *that* meant, that since the Paxson elementary unit's closing, he has been more or less in the board of education's doghouse.

Then Bremer said he wanted to give credit for the Parkway conception to Cliff Brenner. Brenner was in the board of education's development office and was wrestling with the nightmare of overcrowding in the city schools when the idea came to him that the museums and other institutions along the Parkway — the Academy of Natural Sciences, the art museum, the Franklin Institute, the Free Library — would be a perfect environment for certain kinds of learning. It would also be good for the institutions: playing host to more school-children would add some life during usually inactive museum hours and provide a legitimate claim on the public for financial support in return for doing their part in helping education. He came up with the idea of a new high school that would use all these buildings as classrooms. It couldn't be worse than the existing system and it could be a heck of a lot better.

It was an instant success.

Cliff Brenner was at the graduation and he is very proud of the program that started with 150 kids a year ago and now numbers 500. He is pleased that there were 10,000 applicants for the 350 places to be filled in the fall lottery and that 500 teachers applied for the 18 faculty openings. The students come from all over the city and suburbs, have the widest imaginable range of IQ's and interests, and are equally divided between black and white.

In his opening remarks, John Bremer recapitulated some of Parkway's history: the Ford Foundation grant of $100,000 that got the project launched, his hopes for another grant for next year to help with expansion. Then he went into some of his pet theories about structure, and order and disorder. Everyone accuses the Parkway Program of having no structure. Bremer says, "We are not unstructured. We just have a *different* structure." And that is why there is so much confusion about what he is doing. He is really in favor of order, but he is also in favor of enough disorder to allow students to grow, to really learn how to order events themselves. It isn't easy to surrender control or to be reconciled to the inevitable messiness of it all.

Then Bremer began giving out diplomas to the eight graduates who marched to a different drummer at Parkway last year. They looked the part: one in a white suit, pink shirt, and flowing hair; one in a sweater and well-trimmed hair; girls in micro-minis. There was a pervasive family feeling as each student stepped up. The girls stopped to kiss Bremer and the faculty seated on the platform. By the time the last graduate passed by, even the guest of honor, staid U.S. Commissioner of Education James Allen, who had come all the way from Washington for the occasion, was into the mood and solicited and received a kiss to a burst of delighted applause. It was a mini-encounter Parkway style.

After Commissioner Allen's speech, Bremer pulled off another radical play—still very much in the spirit of Parkway. He asked for testimonials from parents, faculty, students—anyone who cared to share a thought. (After all, one of the tenets of the faith is that *all* are responsible for furthering the learning of the group.)

A mother got up and thanked the school for bringing her son out of his shell. "You saved his life."

A teacher reported how he'd been turned on by the program. He said, "No one thinks of *teachers* who drop out of the system—but they do, either literally or figuratively, just like students." Then one of the kids on the steps stood up and said, "I just want to say that Parkway is a wonderful loving thing. Everyone loves each other."

Andy Appelbaum is a drummer. He likes performing and composing. He really digs the music class he takes with Jim Keene at Jim's apartment on Naudain Street. He and the other seven in the class climb up to Jim's third-floor loft twice a week for two hours. It is everyone's fantasy of an artist's studio: skylight, empty wine bottles, dirty glasses, three mattresses on the floor for furniture, a turntable and tuner, and rows of record albums leaning against one long wall.

Jim Keene puts a rock record on the turntable. He is a very serious, cultivated young man who studied music at Haverford College. With his Prince Valiant hair, jeans, and boots, though, he looks like an older version of the kids lolling on his floor and mattresses. He bums cigarettes from them; he's even picked up their way of speaking. He doesn't put down their music. In fact, he knows more about its nuances, history, and artists than they do.

The theme of the day is Crosby, Stills, Nash, and Young and the intricacies of the progressive rock and folk-rock idiom. He works in some early Charles Ives which the class listens to with as much attention as the rock and then switches back to rock that has an obvious relation to the classical music he has just played, although he doesn't announce it. He does the same thing with Bach, juxtaposing a record of Julian Bream playing guitar music by "some obscure cat named J. S. Bach" with an Arthur Lee folk rock cut that has the same baroque sound. Again, he makes no verbal connection.

Jim Keene explains later that he has mentioned classical-pop connections at other times and would prefer to let the kids make their own hookups.

"To me, listening is what's important. If you sit kids down somewhere in a nonthreatening atmosphere where they can listen to music three or four hours a week in a situation where the music comes across, their desire to listen to music generally will increase. I find that a lot of kids who refused to listen to classical music before will begin to listen to it."

Andy Appelbaum's next class on Tuesdays is at 6th and Buttonwood, at Paxson, the old school that housed Bremer's short-lived elementary program. Andy folds himself into someone's dented convertible along with some of the other kids and Keene for the ride to Paxson where his tutorial group is supposed to be meeting.

The tutorial is the only compulsory element in the program's curriculum. Oh, of course, all students must meet state requirements for physical education, English, social studies, and the like, but they can select how they want to get the credits from a fantastically varied curriculum. For instance, you can get English credits by taking a Shakespeare course, or one in creative writing or magazine writing, or one of maybe twenty other choices. A course in Marxism and socialism would be good for credit in social studies. The courses are taught by faculty, interns, students from the school or from neighboring colleges, and community resource people.

But the tutorial group is the basic unit—a compulsory hour four times a week—and its function is to provide an opportunity for counseling and to make sure students have mastered basic skills in language and math. One teacher and one intern meet with 15 students, and it's up to them to work out their own way of reaching these goals. Most classes are conducted this way, but the difference is that tutorial is compulsory.

Andy's tutorial group is in trouble. Some of the students have decided to oust the teacher and to take charge themselves. The teacher is sick this particular day, though, and Andy's tutorial joins another one which is screening a film about the young Great Society. At the town meeting that week a rebel group of students announces it is starting its own tutorial also. Tutorials have come upon hard times.

The teachers and students search painfully for ways to relate. Some make visits to each others' houses. Some spend the time tutoring, others playing games. Dan Shapiro, an educator who taught a tutorial group last year, said he had trouble getting kids to attend at first. "I started telling them I missed them when I'd see them after they'd cut my class. Then, believe it or not, they'd show up. They just wanted to know that I cared. I hit on asking them to fill out sheets that showed which classes they'd been going to and which they hadn't. Some kids don't know how to handle freedom." At Parkway students don't *have* to go to classes, but they don't get credit if a teacher doesn't think they've gotten enough out of the course.

"It was funny how that helped give me some idea of what they needed, what kind of counseling to do. A pattern would show up, like a kid not going to a math class. If I asked why, I'd find out there was something they didn't understand or maybe a relationship with a teacher that needed straightening out. Then they'd start going to the class again, and they'd make a point of bringing it to my attention. 'See, Dan, I'm going to math again.' "

How do you handle freedom, authority, responsibility? Not just the abstraction or mock situations like imitation U.N.'s or pretend self-government, but the real thing. That's what learning is all about—for teachers and students both.

John Bremer is the first to admit that parts of the program are not working smoothly, but in his Olympian view there is nothing wrong with that. "Tutorial is really a course in authority. Some teachers and students have mastered it; others are still struggling with it. On a second level, it's learning to do a common task with a group of people you didn't choose to be with. On a third level, it's a basic social unit. It's a kind of home whether you want it or like it or not."

You have to remember that the school is made up of teachers who've never had this kind of experience before and of young people who've been brainwashed by the other system for as much as eleven years. You suddenly give them freedom for the first time in their lives. Some adjust in a few weeks; some are still adjusting.

[265]

The management-group concept is still developing, too, but without quite as much stress. In addition to regular courses of study and tutorial groups, students are expected to help run the Parkway Program itself. Kids running their own school!

The public relations management group helps show visitors around; curriculum management helps to evolve courses of study and write the catalogs. But it's hard to predict what groups will do. For instance, a facilities management group came to Bremer with a request for money to buy paint to cover over a hallway where visitors from another school had left their names. Bremer steered them to the fund-raising management group. The next thing he knew, there was a cake sale out on the corner of 18th and Market. The kids raised $60.

The fund-raising management group immediately opened its own checking account, paid for the paint for facilities management, and ended up with money left over. So, troubled by the increase in card-playing and gambling, they went to the recreation management group and asked if they wanted to buy some games. Recreation management bought a dozen chess sets. Bremer says it with amazement: "I don't know why a dozen chess sets, but that's what they bought."

After his tutorial and lunch at a nearby diner, Andy Appelbaum's day is still only half over. He and the other kids don't seem to mind the hours they put in getting from one part of the city to another and sitting in classes for two hours instead of the usual 45 minutes.

They really get wound up about a lot of their imaginative classes and teachers, "who are hip people, who really understand other people." Cinematography is one of Andy's favorites. The class just made a commercial for a fictitious product that will grow hair on your chest. Andy wrote the music. Predictably, film-making along with photography, psychology, and black literature are the most popular courses.

Andy decides to sit in on Bernie Ivens' elementary math functions class because he has a free period. The class is held in the library where *Saturday Reviews* and Herman Hesse paperbacks are strewn about on desks and the floor. The wall clock is about 45 minutes slow. None of the clocks in the Paxson School agree on the time, but no one seems to care because nothing really works on time anyhow. With kids moving all over the city, it would be a miracle if they all converged on a classroom at the same moment, so everyone is relaxed about lateness. You get the feeling that other things are more important.

Andy thinks Bernie is a beautiful person. Bernie, bearded and in jeans, presents a new formula—a distance formula—to the class after he goes over the homework with them. He takes them a step at a time, making sure they are with him at every step, with the precision and logic of a teaching machine, but with such grace and good humor that he brings applause from the class when he finishes.

Bernie Ivens taught at West Philly High for eight years before he came into the program. He liked it there, he says,

> but the Parkway philosophy was consistent with my own — that students and teachers can work cooperatively with the administration, can really all work together on the same level. I thought maybe it was a fake. But I took a gamble. I found out it's for real. It's like a joy.
>
> I'm sure uptight teachers wouldn't be here. It's not like a jailhouse where you have to be the keeper for 30 or 35 kids. Everyone is trying to help each other out.
>
> I wonder whether I'd be able to function in another school situation now with bells and 35-minute periods and trivia — all the unimportant things that become important. When you have all those kids in a class, checking homework is impossible, getting to know them is ridiculous. Here you know the kids well. They think nothing of calling up and coming over to see you. I don't see how it's possible for them *not* to learn. In my classes at Parkway I'm covering more material and covering it faster.

Andy's next class is in physical science at the Franklin Institute. He takes a bus and then walks to the library first to get a book. The class is taught by Mitch Struble, who is on the Institute's regular teaching staff. Mitch is 23 and he has long luxuriant sideburns growing over his jowls, but he is wearing a coat and tie — an unusual way for a teacher in the Parkway Program to dress. But Mitch is really more Franklin Institute than Parkway.

As a class experiment gets underway to illustrate Boyle's law by measuring the volume of air in a tube displaced by the weight of bricks, it's obvious that he is a little uneasy with these kids. There is the tiniest edge of tension as they start dropping bricks to be disruptive. It grows as they begin to complain loudly about repeating each step of the experiment three times. "Three times!" "You're a mad scientist, Mitch!"

"Scientific experiments always have to be done three times," Struble replies primly.

That only brings a derisive hoot and more complaints. They have a way of questioning everything, of trying to guess the results before they start — of really refusing to play the game of "experiment" by the rules.

Mitch Struble doesn't really know what to make of these kids. "Their outlook on everything is different from that of the kids I usually teach," he says. For one thing, he usually teaches youngsters who are seriously science-oriented. "These kids aren't intending to go on with science. They aren't necessarily ready to work. They have an attitude of, 'I dare you to teach me anything.' "

It could easily be disruptive to someone in the traditional system to encounter these creatures from—well, from a different system, almost from outer space. The guts of Bremer's program, the Parkway's program, remember, is not just the "classroom without walls" concept and those other frills, it's a whole new system of social organization.

Teachers don't necessarily take to it all at once even if they are part of the faculty. All the formlessness, the confrontations, the casualness. . . . Lisa Strick says that after her first week at Parkway with all the unaccustomed chaos and confusion, she was ready to climb the walls. "I said to John Bremer, 'Is it always like this here?' I'll never forget what he said to me: 'Education is not a neat process. When you try to make it neat, it's not education.' "

Lisa Strick, a young mini-skirted blonde, is the program's informations officer and also teaches communications. As a teacher she had a rough time of trial and error until she found a way to steer between anarchy and too much organization.

> I found that two things are fatal: saying to kids, "You are all going to shut up and do what I tell you," and, "What do you want to do?" There are as many approaches as there are teachers.
>
> My students and I have a pact of mutual respect and mutual learning. I know more about the tools than they do, but they know what they want to do with them. They must cope with *their* society and they know ten times more about that than you do. If I just try to stick to my bag and be what I am—a white, middle class liberal—I'm all right. If I try to phony it up they spot it right away.

Parkway is difficult for some parents, too. All have given their approval for their children to go there, of course, but the reality of the program is something else again.

A girl named Marlene, with curly blonde hair, talked about how her parents couldn't understand what was going on. "They don't see how you can learn like this. Everything's so free. It upsets them that I have no homework except math. The classes are so long, you do most of the work in class except reading. But I like reading and I always read all the time, anyhow. To them, if you like it it's not the same as *homework.*"

Parkway is not for all students, either. Some have come, looked, and returned to their former schools. In the process they have probably learned a great deal about themselves—in the Bremer sense of learning.

Among those who stay, all is not sweetness and light all the time. Take race relations. Everyone seems to be vaguely dissatisfied with those. Relations between the races seem to be all right on the surface. Some of the kids complain that they work together all right, but that socially they break into white and black cliques. The head of one unit, Anita Hackney, thinks the kids who are bolting to form their own tutorial are white, suburban kids who are unwilling to try to get along with people whose backgrounds and concerns are different.

Donna Chavers and her friends didn't put it quite that way. Donna is a senior with a natural hairdo and a sweetly direct way of expressing herself. She thinks that blacks and whites relate better here than they did in the schools they came from, but that in general things aren't as close as they were when she first came at the beginning of the program.

There is nostalgia in her voice as she talks about how the Parkway Program "used to be on the right track. It's off now. We expanded too fast. Last year it was chaotic but tight. Nothing is happening in tutorials now. People aren't coming. We had a really good group last year. We all felt close to each other, but they had a lottery to pick new groups. That really turned everyone off."

Not that Donna is disillusioned about the whole program. She had been doing terribly at Overbrook before she came here and her outlook for being admitted to a good college was pretty dim. Now she thinks she has a good prospect of getting into Radcliffe or Antioch or one of the other top colleges she has applied to.

But she liked it better in the old days when John Bremer was into everything himself. She and some of the other students have the feeling that John has deserted them. "He used to come to town meetings, but he doesn't anymore. When we go in to talk to him he says, 'Go to your unit head.'"

What Donna doesn't understand is that John Bremer has to withdraw this way. If the program is to succeed, it has to be able to work without him. One of the points that he makes very clear is that not only is it the task of the educator to create a matrix which will support everyone who wants to be in it but that he must prevent anyone from capturing it. That means him, too.

And John Bremer wants the program to succeed and to expand so that literally everyone who wants to will be able to be in it—all those kids who lost in the lottery, all those kids who try to buy their way in, who hang around Parkway after their own school hours. He wants room for all the kids who want to come to a school without anxieties, so they can learn.

It took an extraordinary man to carry off what has already been accomplished. Expanding might require a *superman*. Bremer's next move was going to be an attempt to put the Parkway Program into practice on the elementary school level. He had an elementary group for a while occupying the Paxson School along with a high school unit. "Separating younger and older grades is artificial. The older children could help and be helped by the younger ones."

It was the middle of last August when Bremer got the go-ahead to use Paxson. According to him, it was too late to run a lottery to select students. "I thought if we didn't get started then we'd never be in the elementary business with the budget cuts coming."

He needed children desperately. There were none in the immediate area because the Paxson School is in the midst of a redevelopment site and all the houses have been condemned or leveled. This is the one school district in the city where schools are not overcrowded. Bremer found his children in Germantown. A group of parents had been in touch with him and with the school superintendent about doing something along the Parkway lines for their younger kids. They were the nucleus of his elementary unit. He also recruited some from as close as twelve blocks away.

All hell broke loose when word went out that the kids got in through pull rather than a lottery. Bremer says the unit was sabotaged. The school superintendent would prefer to let the whole issue die, but he hoped, like Bremer, to be able to start it up again. With a change in Bremer's status, who knows?

The superintendent feels the need for community and board of education commitment to sustain the Parkway Program. "There are people in the system who don't want it and think it's a waste of money. They say, 'Why are you spending money on this?' " As far as he is concerned personally, though, "I think absolutely it's worth the money. We must commit ourselves to developing alternatives within the system."

He seems sincere in that belief and to think that Parkway is "within the system." The superintendent has gotten a little fleshier and a little more wary in the two-and-a-half years since he came in as a fair-haired boy to straighten out the mess in the Philadelphia schools. You don't get clobbered by the system all the time without developing some protection.

In answer to the question of what he thinks of the Parkway Program, he says, "It's the most dramatic departure we've had in content and structure." When pressed to express an opinion of its success, he hedges by saying, "I have no evaluation at this point. It's much too early."

Maybe he wasn't hedging. After all, there's no data yet, and educators must have data to make evaluations. They don't even know how to get the data. All anyone knows at this point is that the first handful of graduates got into the colleges of their choice. When asked how kids with reading and math problems do in the program, Bremer can answer only in terms of his own philosophy:

> I'm not involved in reaching preset goals. We can only help students find starting places. In traditional schools students have impossible goals to reach so they give up. If he finds his own starting point, a student will go wherever he has to go on his own terms. Our stress is on listening and speaking as well as reading and writing. If the kids do that, you can't stop them from reading and writing, unless—he smiles impishly—unless you have a *method.*

And so John Bremer goes on plotting not only the expansion of his Parkway Program as an alternative to traditional public education but ultimately the destruction of the entire old order. He sits there looking plump and jolly and so much the British gentleman that it's hard to believe he is out to topple the whole hierarchy.

But maybe he'll never get the chance here, now that his status is changing.

> John Bremer has issued his manifesto that the old order must go: The days of the school system as a triangle, with the superintendent at the apex, have gone. The new geometrical figure is a circle with the work task—learning—at the center and with the total community on the circumference. For all of us—student or superintendent, principal or parent, taxpayer or teacher—are equidistant from that work task, and nobody can claim priority.

It would be a tragic waste if the Parkway theory could not get its ultimate test in Philadelphia.

Appendix

The Parkway Program Brochure

Fourth Edition, January 1970

By John Bremer

This booklet is an introduction to the Parkway Program and some of
the thinking that has gone into what one student applicant called
"the school for kids." It is not a final statement but reflects the
Program as it is operating at the present time. The final test of any
educational program is the response of the students. You are, therefore, welcome to visit and see what goes on, you are encouraged to
discuss the program with students, faculty and parents, and to decide
on the basis of the evidence whether this is a viable alternative in
public education. Suggestions and offers of help will be gratefully
received by us at

> The Parkway Program
> 1801 Market Street
> Philadelphia, Pennsylvania 19103
> Telephone: (215) 448-3761

Contents

[275]

I. SOME THOUGHTS ON EDUCATION

America has never had an educational system worthy of itself.
After pioneering a continent, developing new forms of social and
political organization, absorbing countless immigrants and bringing
technology into a close relationship with human life, it is nevertheless true that Americans have adopted principles and practices of
education belonging to another age and imported from another society.
The Parkway Program tries to provide a mode of education in keeping
with the major traditions of American life.

From an examination of our high schools, who would ever suppose
that bold and adventurous exploration was a major part of the American
heritage? Who would realize that American society has given new
meaning to self-reliance and individualism; that communities, founded
for survival, have made internal cooperation a way of life and yet
have been able to incorporate the rich and varied customs brought by
those seeking new homes? Who would ever conclude that American
society has been compelled to test its knowledge against the realities
of the world? Why is the American high school so out of touch with
American life? Why is the American high school so out of touch with
Life? It is because the boundaries of education are no longer correctly drawn.

Our schools imagine that students learn best in a special building
separated from the larger community. This has created a refuge in
which students and teachers do not need to explore but only to accept.
Within this separated refuge, students are expected to learn in so-
called homogeneous groups known as classes, and within these
classes students are isolated, separated from each other by the seat-
ing arrangement and by the competition for approval. It is seldom that
they are allowed to cooperate in a systematic, friendly manner. Finally, within these "boxes," the school houses and the classrooms,
life is self-reflecting, with no relation to anything outside of itself,
and so it becomes a fantasy, it becomes unreal. The students' learning is evaluated within the "boxes," and it is never tested against
the realities of life. It is a common feeling (particularly on the part
of students) that what is learned in school is learned only for the
purposes of the school. This is the well-known irrelevance of
education.

In more concrete terms, when we look at a student program, is
there any connection between what the students are learning and the
exploration of physical space? Are our students capable of becoming
astronauts? or even aware of what that would mean? Whatever awareness they have is due to television and not to the schools. But television itself and the other means of communication (including the art
of private conversation), the exploration of new ways of crossing

social space, as it were, are almost totally ignored. Television viewing is now a basic skill, but the schools are still trying to catch up with the invention of printing. It is well known that personal anxiety is increasing, largely, in my opinion, because of the inability of the educational system to help people understand themselves and their environment. What are schools doing to assist us in the exploration of inner space, of ourselves? Virtually nothing.

With the advances of knowledge, it is clear that we depend more and more upon the ability of men to cooperate in teams--witness space exploration, urban renewal, scientific research, and the new medicine--and yet our schools continue to separate students, to make them compete with each other and do not help them to learn the cooperative ways of behavior upon which our future rests. The balance between cooperation and competition in our schools needs to be readjusted to conform to the realities of modern life. Above all, we should realize that studies will show themselves in behavior, whether we like it or not; our students are generally dissatisfied because their studies, and therefore their actions, are uncoordinated with the real world. This increases their anxiety and makes it very difficult for them to make a constructive contribution to society. The responsibility does not rest primarily with the students; it rests with the educators.

As I said, it is the boundary conditions that are all wrong. It is the division between inside and outside, between insiders and outsiders. We pretend that students learn inside the school, and not outside in the community. The written American language is inside the curriculum, the spoken language is outside. Teachers and administrators are included in the group of educators; parents, employers, businessmen, ministers are excluded. And so on. The boundaries are no longer useful to us. In fact, because they are wrongly drawn they cause us insoluble problems. It is not possible to improve the high school; it has reached the end of its development. We now need a new kind of educational institution.

The year around Parkway Program sets up new boundaries, and provides a new framework in which the energy of all of us can be used in learning, and not in maintaining an obsolete, inefficient system. There is no school house, there is no separate building; school is not a place but an activity, a process. We are, indeed, a school without walls. Where do the students learn? In the city. Where in the city? Anywhere and everywhere. If students are to learn about television, they cannot do this apart from the studios and locations in which television is produced. So we use television studios and we use radio stations, and we use the museums, social service organizations, and we use the business community. The Philadelphia City government departments assist us--the Police Department, and the District Attorney's office to name only two. Parents help us.

[278]

A large number of people help us and we are very grateful. Everyone has a stake in education, everyone has a right and a duty to be involved, to participate. The community helps us in a great variety of ways; by providing us with meeting space, with resources, with instructors, even with total programs. And without the community's help we cannot do our job.

The great variety of ways in which the community helps us is a reflection of the tremendous variety of the community itself. The complexity of social life today is immeasurably greater than that of social life in 1900 or even in 1940. Education must respond to this complexity, this heterogeneity; must accept it and put it to educational use. It used to be that the ideal teaching situation was thought to be a teacher (who knew what was to be learned by the student) telling a homogeneous group (as similar as possible in age, background and presumed ability) what they ought to know, with emphasis on that aspect of knowing which we call remembering. All that has changed. The standards by which these homogeneous groups were formed are no longer useful or relevant; the teacher does not know, cannot know in many cases, what the students should be learning; and you cannot memorize the future.

In the Parkway Program it is true we teach some conventional subjects, but the study groups are mostly small, under ten students, and the old ways of classroom teaching just do not make any sense. So students and faculty are re-defining what we mean by teaching and learning. Our faculty members teach, but when they do it is not in a classroom; it is in the city, in an office building, in City Hall, in the street, depending on what they are teaching. The city is our campus.

The city is also our curriculum because there is nothing to learn about but the city. If education isn't useful in life, it is difficult to know why we would bother with it, so all of our work must in some way help the student become a better, more active citizen. Students are offered a wide variety of courses and they are asked to choose out of close to a hundred offerings those studies that seem interesting and significant to them. We find that they schedule themselves for programs well beyond the normal school hours (and also over weekends) to take courses ranging from Law Enforcement to Modern Dance, from Film Making to Computers, and from Philosophy to Model Clipper Ships. If we do not offer what they want, they know they can ask, and together we try to provide what they want.

Most educational programs treat learning like a journey to some distant destination and students are graded in terms of how far they get along the road. If you go all the way you get an A. The Parkway Program is set up differently. It views the educational problem as being one of finding a starting point for learning. Many students in ordinary schools never get started, but if they ever were to get started their journeys would far exceed the expectations of their teachers. We have great faith in our students, and they do not disappoint us, even though we have a credit or no-credit system. The only grade given is pass.

Every student and faculty member belongs to what we call a tutorial group consisting of about fifteen students, a faculty member, and a university intern. The group has three functions. First, to act as a support group in which counseling can take place. Second, it is the group in which the basic skills of language and mathematics are dealt with. Third, it is the unit in which the program and the student's performance is evaluated, and evaluation is seen as part of the educational process and not something separated from it.

Within the four years of the Parkway Program every student always has a choice available to him. Similarly, no student is ever assigned to the program, they always volunteer and if we have more applicants than places, as seems the usual situation (we had nearly 10,000 in June 1969), we publicly draw names from a hat. Every student in the city in grades nine through twelve is eligible without regard to his academic or behavioral record. In addition, we allocate equal numbers of places to the eight school districts within the City of Philadelphia, so that our student body, like our faculty, is properly integrated. We also have many students from ten or more suburban systems mostly on an exchange basis, and the demand for our program among suburban students is getting to be as great as that among city students.

Our students have to learn to be responsible for their own education, to make choices and to face the consequences of those choices. It is difficult, and many people at the beginning thought that it would not work, but it is working and the demand is so great that we shall expand rapidly. It is our intention to set up a series of units of about 150 students, ten faculty members, and ten university interns, in various parts of the city, because this unit enables the students to have a human relationship with each other and with the faculty. The educational community should really be small enough so that everyone can know everyone else. It is also true that above that number the group can no longer control itself. Although our community unit should not exceed 150, there is no reason why we could not set up 100 such units in Philadelphia. In the first place, we do not require large capital expenditure and school buildings, and in the second place, our operating costs are approximately the same as those in an ordinary school. What could be more practical?

Appendix

II. STUDENT RECRUITMENT AND SELECTION

The Original Letter Sent to All City High Schools Students
January 1969
The School District of Philadelphia
Board of Education
Phone: 448-3761

From: John Bremer, Director
The Parkway Program
1801 Market Street
Philadelphia, Pennsylvania 19103

The Parkway Program is like a high school.

In some ways.
It offers a four-year full-time program; it gives a diploma; it satisfies state requirements.

And in some ways, it isn't.
The Parkway Program will not be a school with classrooms or bells. The organizations around the Benjamin Franklin Parkway will provide laboratories, libraries, and meeting space. Although participation will only be required for the length of the normal school year, study and work programs will be available year-round. Students and faculty will form small groups for discussion, study, counseling, and self-evaluation. Learning situations will vary from films, jobs, and lectures to special projects.

The Parkway Program is a chance for you, the student, to build your own education. You will use the Parkway, the seminar and tutorial groups to design your learning program. The institutions around the Parkway will give special offerings; the teachers will have special skills and interests. You can work, get job training, take courses, do independent study, work on research projects. You can work on these by yourself, with fellow students, with faculty, and with individuals from the institutions. Vocational? College Preparatory? Do you want to study city government, be a reporter for a newspaper, improve your ability to read and write, get secretarial training, study electronics at the Franklin Institute or art with the Philadelphia Art Museum?

[281]

This Program is a chance for you to expand your education in as many ways as you--and the Parkway--can create.

ADMISSIONS

Any Philadelphia public school student (in grades 9-12) can join the Parkway Program. The requirements are simple: the willingness of the student and a parent's signature. If there are more applicants than places, names will be publicly drawn from a hat, with provision made for equal distribution among the city school districts. The program is not designed for any special group of students. It doesn't matter what your subject grades are, whether you're in "modified" or "star," or what your grade in behavior is. The deadline for applications is 29 January 1969. The program will begin on 17 February 1969.

. . . .

PLEASE PRINT

I would like to join the Parkway Program.

Name_____ Present School_____

Address_____ Grade_____

_____

_____   _____

Signature of Student   Signature of Parent

MAIL TO: Admissions, The Parkway Program, 1801 Market Street, Philadelphia, Pa. 19103

Director's Statement at the First Student Drawing, Friday,
31 January 1969

I do not know of any other educational program that admits its
students by lot, by chance, and it is, perhaps, worth saying a little
about why this has been thought the best method for the Parkway
Program.

First, we are a public educational program and the best of what
we have to offer is freely available to any public school student.
We are not the private preserve of any racial, social, economic or
professional group, and, if we were, it would be impossible for us
to be an educational program at all simply because the students
would then be instruments of somebody else's purposes, that is, of
the purposes of that special group. But in education, the student is
always the end, never a means.

Second, if we were not willing to admit any and every student
we would have to set what are called admissions standards. In my
opinion, admissions standards are a method of discrimination, not,
as is often pretended, on the basis of scientifically established
criteria, but on the basis of social criteria. To use them would be
to destroy the community in which alone education can take place.

Third, the prime object of all study is life--what we learn must
always, in some way, be useful to us in life. Now our lives are
urban lives-- not rural lives, not suburban lives but urban lives.
The city is life, it is where the action is. But Philadelphia is a city,
is one city, only insofar as it belongs to all of us and it cannot ever
belong to all of us if it provides the curriculum for an elite, for some
select group.

Fourth, by adopting our method, all students, whether admitted
now or not, learn the most fundamental of lessons that we can relate
to one another on the basis of love and honesty. It is, perhaps,
small comfort for those not now admitted, but such students are
better off than if they had been admitted by dishonest, discriminatory
or corrupt means. And if we had been dishonest and admitted them,
what would our love now be worth?

You may find these four reasons persuasive, and yet still fear
for our success. I thank you for your charity and concern. But if we
accept any student, without judging him, if we introduce him to a
community of learning, and to a richer life in the world, and preserve
our own integrity, how can we fail?

The Parkway Program Brochure

Director's Statement at Second Student Drawing, Friday,
13 June 1969

The whole city of Philadelphia is our campus. And Philadelphia is our curriculum. We study the city in the city. Our lives are inseparable from the city, just as the city is essentially its citizens; all of its citizens.

This means that education and politics are inseparable activities and that every political act is an educational act and that every educational act is a political act. We should not want it any other way, for if politics is concerned with power, education is concerned with love, and one without the other is corrupting. Power without love produces tyranny, love without power produces anarchy. Starting from different points of view, educators and politicians alike have to reconcile, to bring into harmony these two forces, and the future of all of us depends on the accomplishment of this difficult task.

In the Parkway Program we have tried, in a modest and simple way to do this, and I personally have tried to care for our community without letting people do simply as they like and to be responsible for it without controlling it. Others can report better than I the degree of my success.

It is harder to care for people we seldom see than to love those we meet with daily: it is harder to regard charitably those whose actions affect us if we seldom, if ever, have a chance to discover their purposes. But in the Parkway Program we seek to understand not to judge, to support not to criticize, and we owe our thanks to many people.

The purpose of this meeting on the Plaza named after John Fitzgerald Kennedy, is to select by lottery the next group of students for the Parkway Program.... Even as we have new units, we shall still be the Parkway Program and together we may yet reconcile love and power.

III. ORGANIZATION AND ADMINISTRATION

The Parkway Project is a venture in public education and whatever program it offers should be available to the public at large. For this reason, the only criterion for admission is the expressed interest of the prospective student and his or her parents. Admission is made on a random basis, with the only proviso that approximately equal numbers be admitted from each of the school districts to ensure that the student population is representative of the City population. There are nearly 500 students from Philadelphia city schools, about 20 students from suburban systems (most of them on an exchange basis) and 4 students from parochial schools. The city students are, racially, about 60% black and 40% white.

At the present time 500 students, 30 faculty, and 30 university city interns constitute the Parkway community. The group is divided into three units small enough to make possible creative experimentation in the teaching-learning process. The lower than average faculty-student ratio of 16 to 1 is necessary in order to give faculty time to develop new skills for a new kind of teaching and for planning. In the long run, the faculty-student ratio will compare with that of the city's high schools as a whole, that is about 20 to 1. Students are in all four of the normal high school grades, making possible a carry-over in the student body from this year to next that will greatly facilitate expansion of the program.

The Parkway Program is currently organized into the following components: (It should be emphasized that while the structures described here have been found to be viable in many ways, their effectiveness is open to constant evaluation, and they, like the Parkway concept in its entirety, are subject to revision and evolution.)

1. The 150 or so students of each unit are randomly divided into 10 groups of about 15 called Tutorial Groups.
2. Each full-time faculty member is paired with a university intern, and each pair is assigned, jointly, to a tutorial group.
3. Each student chooses, within the context of state subject distribution requirements, one or more programs offered by the Parkway participating institutions, as well as courses taught by Parkway faculty members.
4. Each student may choose to participate in a Management Group responsible for one aspect of the program's day-to-day operation.
5. Each student, then, participates in:
   a. A tutorial group with one faculty member, one university intern, and 15 other students.
   b. A program of study including at least one course offered

by a participating institution and additional courses offered by Parkway faculty members.

   c. A management group consisting of other students and faculty who assume responsibility for one aspect of the program's functioning.

   d. The Town Meeting.

6. The function of the Tutorial Group is twofold:

   a. It is the unit within which personal encouragement, support, and counseling is given, and it is the unit in which continuous assessment of the Program as a whole is carried out.

   b. It is the unit responsible for the acquisition of those basic skills in language and mathematics required by the students in their work in the Parkway participating institutions and by the requirements of life in our society. Each group will, of course, go about performing its functions in the ways seen by students and staff alike as being most successful. The various groups have experimented with a variety of experiences and activities ranging from formal tutoring sessions in mathematics and English to individual faculty-student conferences to free-for-all discussions, recreational gatherings, and field trips.

7. The functions of the Management Groups are:

   a. To perform the functions and provide the services necessary for the Parkway's successful operation.

   b. To involve students in a meaningful way in determining the nature of the program.

   c. To help students develop the skills of management which are the source of power in the community. Management groups have formed around the following problem areas: self-government, public relations, office management, athletics, facilities, fund raising, extracurricular activities, the printing of a Parkway newspaper, and, in conjunction with professors from Temple University, attempting a scientific analysis of the effects of the Parkway Program on its students.

8. The Academic Curriculum consists of:

   a. Institutional offerings--programs of study offered by participating Parkway institutions and taught by staff members of those institutions.

   b. Basic skills offerings--math and language arts courses taught by Parkway faculty which provide both remedial and advanced level work for students who need or desire it.

   c. Elective offerings--classes in the humanities, physical sciences and social studies taught by the Parkway faculty.

9. The Town Meeting is an opportunity for the whole community to discuss common problems and to find common solutions. They occur frequently--usually once a week.

10. In addition to the three types of study listed above, each student is encouraged to participate in a program of individual study in an area of his own interest. This may be done in collaboration with one or two other students.

11. Students are encouraged to participate in work programs of the Parkway institutions as an extra non-required component. This can lead to vacation jobs or to career possibilities. In addition, and not of least importance, will be the opportunity of community service in a variety of social agencies.

IV. A PARTIAL LIST OF COOPERATING AGENCIES

Academy of Natural Sciences
Addressograph-Multigraph Corp.
American Civil Liberties Union
American Friends Service
  Committee
Archdiocese of Philadelphia
Art Alliance
Atlantic Richfield
Catholic Youth Organization
Center City Magazine
City Hall
Commission on Human Relations
Convention and Tourist Bureau
Council for Professional
  Craftsmen
County Court
County Medical Association
Day Nursery for the Deaf
Delaware Valley Regional
  Planning Commission
Drama Guild
Fellowship Commission
Fidelity Mutual Life
  Insurance Company
Film Media Center
Franklin Institute
General Electric
Gratz College
Greater Philadelphia Chamber
  of Commerce
Greater Philadelphia Movement
Hahnemann Medical College
  and Hospital
Health and Welfare Council of
  Greater Philadelphia
  Metropolitan Area
Industrial Valley Bank Building
Insurance Company of North
  America
IBM
JCRC
Metropolitan Associates of
  Philadelphia

Moore College of Art
Municipal Services Building
NAACP
NYU Educational Network
Parochial Schools Administration
  Building
Peale House
Pearl Buck Foundation
Penn Center
Pennsylvania Academy of Fine Arts
First Pennsylvania Bank
Pennsylvania Railroad: Suburban
  Station
People for Human Rights
Perfect Copy Service, Inc.
Philadelphia 1976 Bicentennial
  Corporation
Philadelphia Board of Education
Philadelphia College of Art
Philadelphia Free Library
Philadelphia Museum of Art
Philadelphia Music Academy
Philadelphia National Bank
Philadelphia Zoo
Pocket Playhouse
Police Administration Building
Pomerantz Office Supplies
Print Club
Regional Film Library
Rodin Museum
Smith Kline and French
Society Hill Playhouse
Temple University
J. Reid Thomson, Architect
United Gas Improvement
University of Mass. School of
  Education
University of Pennsylvania
Urban Coalition
Urban League
John Wanamaker of Philadelphia
Weinstein Geriatrics Center
YMCA of Philadelphia

YWCA of Philadelphia
YMHA of Philadelphia
YWHA of Philadelphia
Philadelphia Community College
Comet Camera Repair Co.
Taurus Leather Co.
Joy Camp Co.
Center City Hospital
John F. Kennedy Vocational
    Center
Neupauer Conservatory
    of Music
Society to Protect Children
Center for the Whole Person
Resistance Print Shop
B. Bornstein and Sons
World Affairs Council
American Red Cross
Philadelphia Wireless
    Technical Institute
McCarrie School of Dentistry
1st Baptist Church
1st Presbyterian Church
Swedenborgian Church

Unitarian Church
Philadelphia Magnet School
    of Languages
WIP Radio
Philadelphia Credit Bureau
Spectrum Film Processing
Drexel Institute of Technology
United Health Services
Horizon House
Committee of Seventy
Philadelphia Gas Works
General Tire Co.
Evening and Sunday Bulletin
KYW
Philadelphia Daily News
Philadelphia Inquirer
Philadelphia Tribune
WCAU
WFIL
WIBG
WPEN
WUHY
WIBF
WKBS

Appendix

V. ORIGINAL ANALYTIC DESCRIPTION OF THE PARKWAY PROGRAM (AUGUST 1968)

The Philadelphia Board of Education, in cooperation with the cultural, scientific and business institutions along and around the Benjamin Franklin Parkway, has initiated a four-year educational program for students of high school age. The Parkway Program, as it is called, has starting points which differ from those of conventional high school education in at least two basic respects. In the first place, the Parkway Program does not have a schoolhouse, a building of its own--it is a school without walls; in the second place, the institutions and organizations along and near the Parkway constitute a learning laboratory of unlimited resource.

The adoption of these two starting points opens the way for a complete reformulation of what education means for the present-day urban student. There is little doubt that such a reformulation has far-reaching consequences for both the theory and practice of education since it indicates reformation in every aspect of the student's activity. The spatial and temporal boundaries of the educational process have been subjected to a thorough examination and have been radically altered; within these new limits, the social structure of the learning community has grown and the description and allocation of roles has been revised to conform to the Program's purpose as a learning community. In addition, the nature and function of subject matter has been redefined and brought into a new relationship to life so that the total learning community, the Parkway Program itself, has assumed a different role and status within the greater community of Philadelphia.

The spatial boundaries of the educational process in the Parkway Program are co-terminous with the life space of the student himself. Learning is not something that goes on only in special places called classrooms, or in special buildings called schools; rather, it is a quality of life appropriate to any and every phase of human existence, or, more strictly, it is human life, itself. The problem that the Parkway Program confronts has two aspects; first, how to help the student to live learningly within his present life space, and, second, how to expand this life space.

From the time of their application, students view the Parkway Program itself as a proper object of study, so that there is a continuing reflection on what is going on, as it is going on. Not only are there opportunities for continuous reflection and evaluation, but also for planning and execution by the total learning community; in short, the students as well as the faculty and cooperating institutions are responsibly involved in conceiving and carrying out the educational program. In this way, the educational program is itself a component

[291]

in the student's education, instead of being simply a precondition.

In addition, from the beginning, the parents of Parkway Program students have been cooperating in forming current educational programs, within the framework afforded by the Program, in planning with their sons and daughters further educational and career possibilities, and in pursuing their own educational purposes, partly through programs offered by the faculty and participating institutions. It is to be hoped that some sort of parents' association will offer help and support to the Program in a variety of ways, although the interest and involvement of the parents alone will be a material factor in the progress of students.

Responsibility for education planning carries with it the incentive to think more deeply about educational purposes. By sharing responsibility among students, parents and teachers, a continuing dialogue on education has developed which must have a beneficial effect on the people involved. Through this dialogue, students, particularly, have come to reflect on, to understand, and to control more effectively their own lives.

At the same time, the facilities of the institutions along and near the Parkway are available, to a greater or lesser extent, to the students in the Program. They choose their activities from offerings made by such scientific centers as the Franklin Institute, by such humanistic centers as the Museum of Art, by such business centers as the Insurance Company of North America, by such manufacturing centers as Smith, Kline and French, and such communications centers as KYW and the Philadelphia Bulletin and Inquirer. By choice and with encouragement and support, the student goes beyond the restrictions of his present life and, by furthering his experience, he will further his capacity to have an experience.

If learning is not confined within the spatial limits of schools and classrooms, then it is not confined within the conventional temporal limits either. The concepts of class period, school day, school week and school year all need serious modification and possible abandonment. The Parkway Program has abandoned them, for the most part, and it provides a year-round, full-time learning opportunity for anyone in the Program. The schedule of each student is determined by his learning requirements and not by the clock hours of administrative and organizational convenience.

By adopting these new spatial and temporal boundaries, determined by the view of education as a mode of life and by the learning needs of a particular student, school has ceased to be a building and has become a process, an activity, in which the student participates, or more properly, which is nothing other than the life of the community of learning. The fundamental teaching problem is how to help the student enter the process.

Since learning is a human activity--and, in a sense, the

characteristic human activity--it is intimately bound up with the human group. The problem of how to enter into the learning process, or to be a learner, can be restated in terms of group membership-- how to be a member of a learning community. It is for this reason that the social structure within the Parkway Program is of utmost importance. What are the characteristics of a community which has as its purpose the learning of its members? To frame the question in this way--and it is the appropriate way--indicates that the commu- nity is concerned with the learning of all, and not merely some, of its members. This acknowledges frankly the need of everyone for more learning--it is not something appropriate only for people cast in the role of "student"--and it makes easier the possibility of coop- eration, of partnership, of a true sharing in a common enterprise. This view is in strong contrast to the conventional view of education in which there are teachers and learners--that is, superiors and inferiors--and in which knowledge is treated as alien and self- subsisting to be imposed on the student from without by the exercise of authority. In the Parkway Program, energies are not tied up in maintaining the conventional social system of the school, which is under considerable tension from the conflict arising from declared inequality, and which has little or no relation to learning; students' energies are enlisted on behalf of their own education, individually and in formal and informal groups.

The appropriate model for the Parkway Program is the kind of working together seen in space exploration teams, or in medical teams engaged in transplant surgery. With differentiation of func- tion, there is an intricate pattern of interdependencies in such teams dictated by the complexity of the means necessary to achieve the end and by the variations in functional responsibility, generated as the situation changes. The activity of the Parkway Program is not essen- tially different. The hierarchical ordering of the roles in such teams is determined and re-determined as one stage of operation succeeds another, as crises and emergencies come and go. This has its coun- terpart in the Parkway Program but, in addition, the people change their roles as the learning needs require it. Members of the learning community are acquiring adaptability and flexibility as they respond to the potentialities of the Program, learning how to play new roles and, by so doing, achieving new satisfactions.

It has already been stated that by using the institutions along the Parkway, students extend their life space and increase their capacity for experience. This is a very real function but it is one which any area--urban or rural--could perform. The unique and specific importance of the Parkway institutions lies in the unparalleled wealth of material and human resources which they bring to a very small area of the city. Within a few short blocks there can be found some of the best museums and collections in the world, and the research work that is conducted along the Parkway is of civic, national and even international importance. To have easy and continuous access to the fine collections of paintings, sculpture, scientific instruments and books available along the Parkway would enhance any educational program. Beyond this, however, business, industrial and communications organizations--again of national and international reputation--have expressed interest in providing opportunities for students to study intensively with them, and to pursue work-study programs.

There are two further advantages for Parkway Program students. First, in addition to the material resources of these institutions, there is the possibility of intense and varied contact with the highly skilled professional personnel who are responsible for their continuing life; to have such people as, in a sense, faculty members, is to provide specialist teachers of the highest possible caliber. Second, as an optional and additional activity, there is the possibility of participating in the work of these institutions, and, particularly, in their research work; this is an opportunity for sharing in exciting, creative and original work denied even to most college students.

Finally, it must be remembered that the Benjamin Franklin Parkway begins at City Hall and that for many years the organization of Philadelphia's city government has been a model for the nation. Students in the Parkway Program will be able to study, at first hand, the administration of a city which is a recognized leader in urban renewal. It is not necessary to point out that the modern city government of Philadelphia is the outcome of a tradition as old as the Nation, itself with a wealth of historical resources available, almost on every street corner, even to the most casual student.

PARKWAY PROGRAM BIBLIOGRAPHY

NATIONAL PUBLICATIONS
American Education Publications:
"Know Your World": May 7, '69
"The American Teacher": Jan.'70
Changing Education: Spring '69
Education Digest: Sept. '69
Life: May 16, 1969
Media and Methods: Jan. '70
Nation's Schools: Sept. '69
Parent's Magazine: Sept. '69
Saturday Review: May 17, '69
Scholastic Teacher: Dec. '69
School Management: Dec. '69
Think (IBM): Nov/Dec. '69
Junior League Magazine: Sept.-
    Oct. '69
Time: Mar. 23, 1970
Atlantic Monthly: Aug. '70

LOCAL PUBLICATIONS
Annual Report of the City of
    Philadelphia: 1968-69
Center City Philadelphian: Apt.
    '69/Feb. '70
Delaware Valley Science and
    Engineering Newsletter:
    Nov/Dec. '69
DRPA Log: June '69
New Jersey Education Associa-
    tion Review: Sept. '69
Urban School Report (N.J.):
    Nov. 1, '69
Center City Philadelphian: Feb.'70
The Philadelphia Bulletin Magazine:
    Feb. 22, '70

INSTITUTIONAL PUBLICATIONS
Amalgamated News (Amalgamated
    Clothing Workers): May 2,'69
Franklin Institute News: Summer
    '69, Fall '69
Smith, Kline and French News:
    June 6, '69

NEWSPAPERS: The following
newspapers have published
articles on Parkway Program:
The Ambler Gazette
The Boston Globe
The Christian Science
    Monitor
The Distant Drummer
The London Evening News
The London Sun
The Los Angeles Times
The Philadelphia Bulletin
The Philadelphia Daily News
The Philadelphia Inquirer
The New York Times
The San Francisco Chronicle
The Toronto Daily Star
The Washington Star
The Times (London)
The Wall Street Journal
The Kansas City Star

FOREIGN PUBLICATIONS
Orbit (Toronto, Canada):
    Sept. '69

FILMS, VIDEOTAPE AND
TAPE RECORDINGS: The fol-
lowing have complete docu-
mentaries on the Program:
The Canadian Television
    Network
Educational Television
    Branch, Ontario Dept.
    of Education
NBC-TV
National Educational TV
New York University
U.S. Information Agency
WCAU-TV Philadelphia
WFIL-TV Philadelphia
WUHY Radio Philadelphia
KWY-TV Philadelphia